INTERNATIONAL CHRISTIAN
GRADUATE UNIV

Y0-BDK-042

Austin C. deBlois

Philadelphia

BOOKS BY EDGAR SHEFFIELD BRIGHTMAN

MORAL LAWS
THE FINDING OF GOD
THE PROBLEM OF GOD
A PHILOSOPHY OF IDEALS
AN INTRODUCTION TO PHILOSOPHY
RELIGIOUS VALUES
THE SOURCES OF THE HEXATEUCH

MORAL LAWS

EDGAR SHEFFIELD BRIGHTMAN

Borden Parker Bowne Professor of Philosophy
in Boston University

THE ABINGDON PRESS

NEW YORK   CINCINNATI   CHICAGO

BRIGHTMAN
MORAL LAWS

Copyright, 1933, by
EDGAR SHEFFIELD BRIGHTMAN

All rights reserved—no part of this book may be reproduced in any
form without permission in writing from the publisher

Printed in the United States of America

INTERNATIONAL CHRISTIAN
GRADUATE UNIVERSITY

BJ
1011
B 855
1933

21953

CONTENTS

CONTENTS

CONTENTS

PREFACE

MORAL LAWS has been written with the conviction that ethics is truly a science; not, indeed, a natural science or a merely descriptive one, but a normative science of ideal principles. While the method of presentation is new, the substance of this book is no novel discovery; it is an interpretation of the results of centuries of reflection by the wisest minds of the race. Truth is no modern convention, but the co-operative achievement of all who think. Little stress is laid, however, on some points which have been discussed often enough to very little profit, such as the problem of hedonism *versus* formalism. An attempt is made, rather, to discover the universal moral laws which rise above the quarrels about less important and less fruitful details.

The central idea of the book is that the moral life is a rational life. Goodness is not mere convention or *mores,* nor mere fulfillment of instinctive needs, but, rather, a control of our social behavior and our instinctive tendencies by rational laws. As a defense of reason, the book is not intended to be entertaining; it is intended to be clear, logical, and true to experience. The specific Moral Laws are offered as attempts to embody these qualities in an ethical theory. The success or failure of the attempts should be measured, not by the reader's agreement with what is said, but by the degree to which it leads the reader to think clearly, logically, and empirically about moral life.

Most of the book was written during the author's Sabbatical leave in Germany. This was done deliberately, in order that material not easily accessible in

9

America might be included and that the influence of conventional environment might be avoided. The author takes occasion here to express his gratitude to several German friends for their suggestions, particularly to Professor Arthur Liebert, of the University of Berlin, and also to a group of American students who offered helpful criticisms.

EDGAR SHEFFIELD BRIGHTMAN.

Newton Center, Massachusetts.

CHAPTER I

ETHICS AS A SCIENCE

1. WHAT ETHICS IS

THE science of ethics, like many other branches of knowledge, was founded by Aristotle. Under the influence of Aristotle, and his master, Plato, the field of knowledge in ancient times was divided into Physics, Dialectics, and Ethics. The names of these three divisions were made explicit in the older Academy (the school of philosophy which Plato founded) by followers of Xenocrates.[1] From the days of Aristotle to the present time ethics has been continuously studied.

The name "ethics" is derived from the Greek ἦθος, which means custom or habit, and in the plural, character. This suggests that ethics has to do with what is customarily done or approved, a suggestion that reappears in the word "morals," derived from the Latin *mores*. The terms "ethics" and "morals" are, however, ordinarily distinguished in modern usage. Ethics refers to the theory of the good life, while morals means the actual practice of it (successful or unsuccessful). This usage corresponds to the genius of the languages from which the words are derived. Greek is the language of philosophy and science; Latin is the language of administration and action. Thus it is doubly appropriate to speak of ethical theory and moral action; for "theory" is another Greek word and "action" another Latin one.

This etymology suggests that ethics is either a study

---

[1] Runze, EPE, 1-2. The abbreviations which are used throughout are explained in the bibliography at the end of the book.

of customs and habits or a study of character. Both of these suggestions are somewhat misleading. The study of customs falls chiefly under sociology; the study of habits is psychological, as readers of James know. Even to call ethics a study of character is not precise, because a psychoanalytic investigation of character is not ethics; and in Germany and elsewhere there is developing a new branch of science called character-ology, which is a description of character without ethical evaluation.[2] Yet it is true that ethics deals with customs, habits, and character, although by a method different from that of sociology, psychology, or characterology. What that method is we shall see later.

It is natural that the etymology should not furnish us with a precise guide, for ethics was named in its earliest days, before the investigations of later centuries had been carried out. It is, therefore, quite unreasonable to suppose, on account of etymology, that morality is merely a matter of custom and convention. The relation of our ideals of goodness to social customs is a matter for scientific investigation and cannot be perceived offhand by a glance at an etymological dictionary.

If we are, then, to find what ethics is, we must observe what it has become as a result of its long evolution through the centuries. Such observation shows us that ethics is not a mere formulation of socially approved customs, but that it attempts to determine what customs are good and what are bad. It is not merely a descriptive analysis of character, but undertakes to furnish some standard for distinguishing between a better

---

[2] In Germany, Utitz, and in America, Roback, have made important contributions to characterology. Bahnsen wrote *Beiträge zur Charakterologie* as long ago as 1867. The Austrian, Rudolf Allers, in *Das Werden der Sittlichen Person*, has written a valuable survey of results in the field, although sometimes colored by religious preconceptions.

character and a worse one. It aims to find what constitutes the best kind of life for individuals and for societies, and to show why that kind is regarded as the best.

A science that tries to determine standards of any kind is called a normative science (from the Latin *norma,* meaning "a rule"). Ethics, then, may be defined very simply as *the normative science of morals,* which means that it is the attempt to discover and justify reasonable standards of conduct.

A more complete definition would run as follows: *Ethics is the normative science of the principles (or laws) of the best types of human conduct.* Analysis of this definition shows that it contains several important assertions. Since ethics deals with human conduct, it is, like other sciences, based on actual experience. Since it aims at principles or laws, its goal resembles that of other sciences. The difference between ethics and most other sciences is brought out by the use of the words "normative" and "best types." The so-called descriptive sciences deal only with the actual and the necessary; ethics deals with the ideal and the possible. The descriptive sciences give us the facts; the normative sciences estimate the value of the facts. Finally, the word "normative" implies further that ethics deals with what ought to be, rather than merely stating the value of what is. It deals with obligation as well as with the good.

Thus our definition implies three basic concepts in ethics, namely, law (principles), value (the good), and obligation (ought, duty). This analysis is fundamental for the point of view of the present work. It should therefore be noted that the present analysis diverges from that of Schleiermacher, followed by Bowne,[3]

---

[3] Bowne, POE, 20.

which asserts that the three fundamental concepts are the good (or value), duty, and virtue (a dutiful and constant realization of the good). It seems clear that good and duty, or value and obligation, are essential to any ethical theory. Ethics must reveal what value (good) ought (duty) to be attained; it must explain the obligation to achieve the good. But the concept of virtue is not an additional theoretical principle; it is simply the practical application of theory, and so does not stand on a parity with value and obligation, in spite of the fact that ancient ethics—that of Plato and Aristotle in particular—started with a study of the virtues. On the other hand, the concept of law is absolutely essential to any science, a fact which Socrates discovered and first applied to the definition of moral principles. Without laws we have a miscellaneous collection of unrelated facts, but no science. It is one thing to feel value and obligation; it is another to define laws of good conduct. Kant and Schleiermacher identified duty with moral law. Yet a sense of duty may conflict with moral law.

Therefore the three foundation pillars of ethics are value, obligation, and law; and law is the most essential of the three, if ethics is to be a science. If we summarize these three in the formulæ: "I evaluate," "I ought," "I universalize," we bring out the basic fact that the foundations of ethics are actual personal experiences.

This definition and its implications will need explanation and proof, which will come in the course of our study. Meanwhile one particular point should be made clear. It may be asked why "morals" or "conduct" should be chosen as the field of a separate science. The term "conduct" (with which "morals" is synonymous) refers only to voluntary human behavior—behavior which occurs as a result of will (*i. e.,* choice). Is there sufficient difference between voluntary behavior on the one hand and involuntary and nonvoluntary on the other to warrant the former's being made the basis of a special science? The experience of the human race justifies a definitely affirmative answer to this question. One of the greatest problems of life—the greatest practical one—is the problem of control, both individual and social. How far and in what direction can and should the human being control his own life, individual and social? Ethics concerns itself with the normative aspects of this problem of control. The Stoics taught us to distinguish sharply between "the things that are in our power" and "the things that are not in our power." If the exercise of human power is an important problem, then ethics is important. "The historical world," says Treitschke in his essay on Luther, "is the world of the will, because not thought but action determines the fate of nations."[4] Moreover, "the best types of human conduct" in our definition does not refer to some distant Utopia or to some purely theoretical ideal. It refers to the best types of willing (choosing) that can be practiced by human beings constituted as we are. Ethics certainly sets up ideals, and very exacting ones; but it is not justified in setting up ideals that are irrelevant to actual life.[5] It deals, then, with practical problems of control.

2. Types of Ethical Theory

A very brief survey of the most important theories which have developed in the history of ethics may serve

---

[4] Treitschke, DL, 19. Translations here and elsewhere are by the present writer whenever sources in foreign languages are cited.

[5] For a discussion of the extent to which ideals lead beyond the actual, see Brightman, POI, Chap. III. On the relevancy of ideals to life, see Chap. X of *Moral Laws.*

at this point to render the nature of the science clearer. Four theories are selected here as most representative and most influential historically, namely, the theories of Aristotle, Epicurus, Christian Ethics, and Kant. Our interest in these theories just now is not so much for their own sake as for the sake of the type which they represent. Accordingly, we shall discuss the Aristotelian type, the Epicurean type, the Christian type, and the Kantian type.

The Aristotelian type of ethics holds that the good life is the life in which the powers of man come to their fullest and most harmonious and balanced development. Since this type of life brings satisfaction, the theory is often called eudæmonism (from the Greek εὐδαιμονία, "happiness"). From another point of view it is called perfectionism, since it requires the well-rounded development of all the powers of man. It may be said to be a cultural ideal. Aristotle's description of the virtues has been called the ideal of a Greek gentleman. There is much in common between the ethical thought of Aristotle and that of Confucius, whose picture of "the superior man" is the ideal of the Chinese gentleman.[6] Aristotle and Confucius both lay stress on the need of harmony between the inner life and the outer environment, and Aristotle even insists that wealth and health are both essential to the attainment of the moral ideal. Both Aristotle and Confucius were interested in the participation of the good man in the life of the state; Aristotle's *Politics* was Volume II of his *Ethics*. Both teach the doctrine of the mean. Confucius, however, emphasizes more than does Aristotle the virtue of good will, in his famous

---

[6] A comparison between Aristotle and Confucius has been admirably worked out in an unpublished Master's thesis (Boston University) by Miss Julia Syn (now Mrs. H. J. Lew).

negative version of the Golden Rule (which is substantially identical with Tobias 4:16 and with the teaching of the Rabbi Hillel) : "Whatsoever thou dost not wish to have done to thyself, do not do to others." The Aristotelian is historically the most influential system of theoretical ethics.[7] It became standardized in the Middle Ages as the backbone of the ethical theory of the great scholastic, Thomas Aquinas, who supplemented the basic Greek virtues by adding the Christian ones of faith, hope, and charity. The Aristotelian influence persisted also in Protestantism, as Melanchthon's accepted view, and remained dominant down to the time of Leibniz.[8] Both Spinoza and Hegel present perfectionism of a broadly Aristotelian type. The Aristotelian is the most widely advocated view in recent manuals of ethical theory: *e. g.*, Paulsen, Bowne, Seth, Everett, Mackenzie, Wright, Urban, etc. The social and active emphases of pragmatism place that philosophy also in the Aristotelian tradition, so far as ethics is concerned.

The second great type is the Epicurean, which is less complex and eclectic than is the Aristotelian. Epicurus teaches that pleasure is the supreme good and that the best life is the life embodying the maximum of pleasure. This theory is called hedonism (from the Greek ἡδονή, "pleasure"). While hedonism sounds very simple, it is not quite so simple as it sounds. Hence there are wide variations within this type. The earliest Greek hedonist, the Cyrenaic Aristippus (like the Chinese poet, Li Po), held that immediate physical pleasure was the most intense and most desirable, although he taught the need of control. Epicurus, however, found pleasures of the mind superior to pleasures of the

---

[7] *Cf.* Schleiermacher, *Werke*, I, 115.

[8] Trendelenburg, HP, 1.

body; but, unlike Aristotle, he took no pleasure in political life, and derived all interest in society (such as friendship) from, the pleasure which he himself found in it, and not from the giving or sharing of pleasure. The famous Rubaiyat of Omar Khayyam embody a Persian form of hedonism. Modern hedonism, on the other hand, doubtless under the influence of Christianity, is universal or altruistic and has adopted the name "utilitarianism." Men like Jeremy Bentham, John Stuart Mill, and Henry Sidgwick held that the aim of life is not the increase of my personal pleasure, but the increase of the total pleasure in the world, "the greatest good of the greatest number." Feuerbach, Karl Marx, and other socialistic writers are likewise social hedonists. But all hedonists, whatever their differences, agree that pleasure is the only good there is, so that pleasure is the criterion of value. They do not feel the need of any principle for the criticism or limitation of pleasure, except the principle of pleasure itself—the greatest pleasure, for the longest time, with the least amount of pain, and (as modern hedonists add) for the greatest number of people. This theory possesses undeniable attractions, and still has defenders among ethical theorists, e. g., Sharp, Drake, and Blake in America, and Schlick in Austria. Germans tend to regard it as the typical English philosophy, and as proof of the low ideals of the English nation. But this is one of the many cases of the narrow provincialism that makes progress difficult; for hedonism is not a low ideal to one who takes pleasure in noble things. Lucian called Epicurus a "holy man."[9] The chief theoretical difficulty with hedonism is not that it is a low ideal, but that pleasure is so relative and indefinite a criterion as to seem to many not to be a scientific guide to conduct,

---

[9] Lucian, *Alexander, the False Prophet*, 61. See Guyau, ME, 10.

and also that pleasure is an insufficient definition of value.

The third type of ethics is the Christian. While the teachings of Jesus and their later institutional development do not constitute a scientific ethical theory, they present a definite evaluation of life and have exerted an incalculable influence on history.[10] The two central principles of Christian ethics are love and sacrifice. The former principle, as we have seen, was also taught by Confucius, and, we may add, by Buddha ("hatred is not appeased by hatred, but by love"), and is a central teaching of the Bhagavad Gîtâ. It was an ideal of the prophet Hosea (Eighth Century B. C.) as well as of the Rabbi Hillel (First Century B. C.), and of the later Stoics. The teaching of love was no discovery or invention of Jesus; but he made it so central and so radical (love of enemies) and connected it so closely with the idea of a loving Heavenly Father that his teaching has been more influential in making humanity gentle and altruistic than any other single force in history. The maxims of the Sermon on the Mount have not been practiced; but they never die. In addition to love, we have mentioned sacrifice as a Christian principle. It lays emphasis on the need of self-denial and suffering in order to attain the true value of life. "Deny yourself. Take up your cross. Cut off your right hand." Ascetics in Christian and non-Christian religions have sometimes pushed this principle to the extreme of a certain delight in the keenest suffering, even when voluntarily imposed, for the sake of gaining eternal happiness. But even where the principle of sacrifice is not carried to ascetic extremes, it stands in marked contrast with the emphasis of Greek ethics, both Aristo-

---

[10] See Paulsen, SOE, 33-97, for a comparison of Greek and Christian ethics.

telian and Epicurean. Even a modern Epicurean like
Bentham was suspicious of it.[11] It is a consequence, in
part, of the more aggressive nature of Christian morality, which is prepared to undergo greater suffering for
the good and to envisage a longer delay of its full attainment (either in the individual or in society) than is
the Aristotelian or the Epicurean type. Nietzsche, the
most virulent modern critic of Christianity, with his
scorn of hedonism and his appeal for strength, is in this
respect nearer to Christian teaching than to Greek
thought. Schopenhauer, another great critic of Christianity, makes pity his fundamental ethical law, so that
he builds on the part of Christian ethics which Nietzsche
rejects. Christian ethics is, then, a synthesis of benevolence and severity; or, in terms of our foundation principles, of value with duty and law.[12]

The fourth type of ethical theory is the Kantian.
Immanuel Kant taught that morality is essentially a
matter of the will itself, not of the success of the will in
attaining its ends; and further that the goodness of a
will is to be judged, not by the ends for which it is
striving, as the Aristotelian and Epicurean types both
plainly held, but, rather, by its own self-consistency, or,
to refer to two of our three foundation principles, by
the extent to which it recognizes itself as *obligated* to
choose in accordance with universal *laws*. In so far as
Kant's system consists in laws which the will imposes
on itself, it is moral autonomy; in so far as it makes
goodness consist in the principles which the will obeys

---

[11] "Mischievous is the influence that connects morality with suffering." "Socrates's contempt of riches was . . . just as meritorious
as it would have been to have remained standing for a long time on
one leg." Bentham, DE, I, 34, 260.

[12] Saint Paul seems to have been somewhat aware of a dualistic
synthesis in Christianity, for he wrote, "Behold then the goodness
and severity of God" (Romans 11: 22).

as distinguished from the content of the ends realized, it is formalism; in so far as it dwells on the rigid universality of moral law, it is rigorism. Kant himself felt that his system was a scientific embodiment of Christian ethics and its universality and respect for personality to some extent justify him in this. A moralist of the Kantian type says, *Fiat justitia ruat coelum*—"Let justice be done, though the heavens fall." He proposes to be loyal to the principles which he believes are right, regardless of unpleasant or even disastrous consequences. The ancient Stoics, who emphasized the rational will in contrast with all externals, were of this type, as was the modern American, Josiah Royce, in his *Philosophy of Loyalty*. Even Nietzsche, who opposed Kant as vigorously as he opposed Christianity, is closely allied to the Kantian type of ethics, for both Nietzsche and Kant insisted on a strong and sincere assertion of the will as the heart of goodness. It has been widely held that Kant's system does not take sufficient account of the experience of value. The merits and defects of this type will be discussed in Chapter VI.

3. The Unsatisfactory State of Ethics

This brief survey of four main historical types of ethical theory may serve to illustrate at least two points, namely, that there are elements of truth in all of the great moral systems of the past, and that there has been a lack of clear-cut progress and of scientific systematization in ethical thought. One who reads very extensively in the literature of ethics is easily led to pessimism about the scientific character of the subject. Borden Parker Bowne has said that if by some chance all of the writings of the British moralists were to be burned, they would not be missed. If one were to modify this, one would be tempted to enlarge, rather than to narrow the scope of the bonfire. The question rises, Is there any ethical truth at all? Yet before committing oneself seriously to ethical skepticism on this basis, one should inquire what such skepticism involves. We must face the question, Is there known or knowable truth about what human conduct at its best may be and ought to be? If there is such truth, is it capable of scientific formulation?

To answer these questions in the negative is to give voice to a conviction of the meaninglessness of all ideals and of the aimlessness and worthlessness of human living. It is the ultimate despair. To call it despair, however, is not to refute it. The refutation of ethical skepticism must lie in the appeal to experience and to reason. The appeal to experience will determine whether we do actually experience values: Do I evaluate, do I feel obligation, do I think in universals? If these facts are there, they are the materials of a science of ethics. If I actually experience the value of at least some moments of life, I cannot logically deny all value to life, nor can I deny the possibility of some knowledge about that value. Further, the case against ethical skepticism rests, as has been stated, on the appeal to reason. If anyone casts ethics to one side as worthless, he must have reasons for doing so, or no reason. If he has no reason, he deserves no attention. If he has reasons, they must consist in some kind of knowledge and thought about the subject matter of ethics and such knowledge and thought would be at least the basis of some sort of science of ethics. We cannot escape the recognition that a theory of ethics is both possible and necessary.

Yet it must be admitted that the science of ethics is in a very unsatisfactory condition. As Gerhard Lehmann has said, we may well speak of a crisis in ethics at the present time.[13] We have plenty of practical application, without clear ideas of the principles that ought to be applied; plenty of discussion by persons who lack adequate training in the field but who are confident that their group conclusions will be intelligent despite the ignorance of each member of the group; plenty of statistical reports, without criteria for moral interpretation and evaluation of the facts; plenty of information about the *mores* of primitive man, but little light on the duties of civilized man; plenty of isolated studies about special problems of morality, united by no common laws and principles into a genuine science. This does not mean that there have been no significant contributions to ethics as a science. The great work of the four types of theory has not been in vain. Many insights into the problems of ethics have been achieved; but ethics falls short of the scientific character, not merely of mathematics and logic or physics and chemistry, but even of economics, which is now so hotly debated, and of psychology, which is itself far from a unified science. Only sociology, æsthetics, and philosophy of religion are in a state of uncertainty paralleling that of ethics. Yet precisely the fields in which confusion prevails are of the greatest importance for intelligent and satisfactory living.

There is, therefore, great need both for the more intensive study of ethics and for constructive work in building up a genuine science of the moral life. The present study is offered as a step in the development of such a science.

4. What a Science Is

If we propose to treat ethics as a science, we need to

---

[13] Gerhard Lehmann, "Rückkehr zur Ethik," in *Blätter für deutsche Philosophie*, 4(1930), 120-125, esp. 120.

have a clear idea of what science is. The dictionaries
will tell us that science is systematized knowledge,
which is true enough, but vague. There seem to be at
least three definite marks which all sciences have in
common. These are: that every science has a limited
field, employs methods of observation, and aims at the
formulation of laws. Let us discuss each of these
marks.

To say that every science has a limited field is to call
attention to a fundamental distinction between science
and philosophy. Philosophy deals with experience as a
whole, in its completeness, its unity, and its totality.
A philosopher has to consider all facts and all points
of view in his search for truth. Not so the man of
science. A physicist limits his attention to objects in
space and their movements. He is not concerned with
human feelings or values; he does not deal with the
problems of morality and religion so long as he is a
pure physicist.[14] Likewise, the biologist limits his attention to the phenomena of life and to other phenomena
only from the point of view of their relation to life.
Since the physical and social environment affects life
as intimately as it does, the biologist uses the results of
the physical and social sciences freely; but the real
subject of his investigation is always restricted to life
and its processes. On the other hand, the astronomer,
who confines his research to the laws of the heavenly
bodies, must neglect the phenomena of biological life
and of consciousness as irrelevant to his science. It is
true that astronomers are often asked by the eager
public to tell them whether or not there is life on Mars

---

[14] F. Schroedinger, the physicist, asserts that personality cannot
be proved to exist by the methods of exact science; the proof, he
holds, is ethical (*Vossische Zeitung*, Dec. 25, 1930).

or elsewhere in the stellar universe; but in such speculative answers as the astronomer may give, he has to
rely on the biologist for information about criteria for
the presence of life. Psychology (as distinguished from
behaviorism) is primarily concerned with the structure
and function of consciousness and with the physical
and biological facts only in so far as those facts stimulate or retard conscious processes. What is irrelevant
to consciousness it excludes.

Thus we see that, while the sciences are more or less
interrelated and interdependent, each particular science
deals with a particular subject matter. This subject
matter is selected somewhat arbitrarily, for purposes of
convenience in the division of labor. But, in order to
avoid confusion and conflict, each science has to define
its field precisely. In defining this field, other fields
are, for the moment, set aside. The fact that physics,
say, sets aside from consideration the facts of psychology and biology, and that other sciences act similarly,
is called by Hegel abstraction. The sciences, in this
sense, are all abstract, while philosophy is concrete, in
that it tries to unite and relate together what the special
sciences have artificially separated.

A second trait of all sciences is that they employ
methods of observation. It is true that the kind of
observation that lies at the basis of mathematics is
very different from observation in physics. In one
case it is the observation of abstract terms and relations only, while in the other it is observation through
sense-perception. In psychology it is still different,
since it rests ultimately on introspection. In history the
field of the science is mainly the past, which in the nature of the case can never be observed directly, but only
inferred from observation of present data. The nature
and the methods of observation must vary with the sub-

ject matter of the science.[15] However, in all cases the science builds on observation of some sort of experience.

Finally, all science aims at the formulation of laws. The laws of mathematics, while utilized in physics, are very different from those of physics, for they contain no reference to real time or space; geometrical space is ideal, while physical space is real. The laws of physics all refer to relations in real space and real time. The laws of psychology are different in type from the laws of chemistry. The laws of logic are not the same as the laws of economics. But all sciences aim at laws or generalizations on the basis of the observations made.

Accordingly, whatever the differences among the sciences may be in detail, all are alike in having a limited field, in employing methods of observation, and in formulating laws. If ethics is to be a science at all, it must conform to these conditions. We have some ground for hoping to build up a science of ethics when we reflect that law was found to be one of the basic concepts of ethics. But we need to examine more closely the kind of science that ethics aspires to be before we are warranted in going ahead with the construction of the science.

5. What a Normative Science Is

As has become evident in the foregoing discussion, there are great differences among sciences, as well as certain fundamental resemblances. The resemblances unite the various investigations as sciences; but the differences reveal the wide variety of experience. In seeking truth we need to give full weight to differences of subject matter and of method.

[15] See E. S. Brightman, "What Constitutes a Scientific Explanation of Religion?" in *Jour. Rel.*, 6(1926), 250-258, for a discussion of difficulties which arise when this is overlooked.

As was pointed out earlier in the chapter, ethics is differentiated from a large number of the sciences by being normative rather than descriptive. The brief statement of the distinction between descriptive and normative sciences given at that time now needs to be supplemented. It was then said that descriptive sciences deal with the actual and the necessary, while ethics and other normative sciences deal with the ideal and the possible. This is not, however, a sufficient distinction between the two types. A descriptive science, like physics, defines its laws in ideal terms (frictionless motion, for example, is an ideal) and shows what is possible in the physical realm as well as what is necessary. On the other hand, a normative science, like ethics, must build its laws on a knowledge of the actual and necessary facts and conditions of human life. For these and similar reasons, some, like W. G. Everett,[16] think that there is really no distinction between the two classes of sciences, and that ethics is simply a descriptive science of value.

The mutual interdependence of the descriptive and normative, however, does not destroy the difference between them. The interest of a descriptive science is in the statement of facts, their order and causal sequence, and (if determinable) their quantitative relations. A science is descriptive whether its subject matter is mechanical motion or conscious purpose, if only the aim of the science be strictly confined to telling what the facts are and in conformity with what causal laws they occur. This is equally the aim of physics, of chemistry, of sociology, of economics, and of psychology. But a normative science, while it presupposes the knowledge furnished by the descriptive sciences, goes beyond a mere description of given facts. It is not causal, but

---

[16] Everett, MV, Chap. I.

teleological; that is, it asks what purpose the facts
serve and whether it be a worthy purpose or not.   It is
not a merely quantitative measurement, but a qualitative estimation.   It evaluates the facts by reference
to some ideal of true worth.   Moreover, it may, and
often does, confront the facts with the judgment that
they ought not to be as they are and that a different
set of facts ought to be produced.   A purely descriptive
psychology gives us the facts of mental health and
mental disease without expressing any preference for
health over disease.   It reports, it is true, that most
people prefer health, yet this report is not accompanied
by the judgment, "And they are right."   But as soon as
we assert that health is really better than disease,
knowledge better than ignorance, beauty better than
ugliness, and the like, we are in the realm of the normative sciences of ethics or æsthetics.   A descriptive
science will have to tell us what the human experiences
of value are in the various realms of knowledge, morals,
beauty, and religion; but a normative science will
undertake to discriminate among these experiences of
value to determine higher and lower, true and false.
The descriptive psychology of thought will tell us how
we actually think (but will not add that we ought to be
ashamed of our bad intellectual habits) ; the normative
logic of thought will show us what thinking processes
are false and what are true—or, at least, will show us
how to move gradually in the direction of truth.

6. Ethics as a Normative Science

As was stated in the previous section, there are those
who regard ethics as a descriptive science.   Many texts
on ethics consist largely of psychological, sociological,
and anthropological data, which are pure description.
A writer like Schlick views the science as consisting

solely of knowledge (that is, description) of the good;[17] in criticism of which it must be said that the selection of a "good" to be described presupposes some normative science to guide one to its discovery. Again, as we have also intimated, there are those who would deny that ethics is a science in any sense of the word. In opposition to both of these views the present investigation undertakes to show, by the method of construction, that ethics is truly a science and a normative one.

The only ethics worth having would be one that would enable us to distinguish between right and wrong, good and bad, value and disvalue. To be more precise, it would give us principles by which we might confront the many conflicting value-claims of our daily experience and show us where the true value of life lies.[18] Or, as Schwarz puts it in the German, it would discriminate between *Wertschein* and *Wertsein*—"the appearance of value" and "the reality of value."[19]

In our introductory approach all that can be done is to raise the problem of whether such a normative science of ethics as we need can be developed. That such a science does not yet exist in satisfactory form is obvious even to the superficial student. The descriptive sciences are universally recognized. Physicists, chemists, astronomers, geologists, biologists, anthropologists, and even psychologists are called to the public service in time of war. We have yet to hear of a similar call to specialists in ethics. There may be reasons for this which are more creditable to ethics than to government; for the ethicist, if true to his science, would have to criticize the aims and policies of his own govern-

---

[17] Schlick, FE, 2. "The central problem of ethics, then, is solely the question of the causal explanation of moral conduct." *Ibid.*, 20.
[18] Brightman, RV, Chap. III.
[19] Schwarz, ETH, 7.

ment as well as those of the enemy. But it must be admitted that ethicists do not yet speak with a voice of scientific authority comparable with that of the descriptive scientists.

This means that in the field of ethics we are still in the pioneering stage. Hence ethics is especially interesting to all who wish to participate in the actual growth of civilization. If our culture is to live, it must live for what it can sincerely and intelligently believe to be worth living for; that is, it must live by ethical laws. The normative science which a rational individual and society require must have at least two characteristics if it is to meet the needs of man, namely, it must be genuinely universal and also genuinely progressive.

We shall, then, seek for genuinely universal ethics. This means a search for principles of right which are superior to circumstance, and apply in all times and places. Such principles must be free from all provincialism, especially from national provincialism. They must be super-American, super-French, super-German, super-Chinese, super-British. If not, they afford no basis for world-wide human relations or for an appeal to reason. The greatest systems of past and present have often been deficient at this point. After all, the ethics of Confucius was essentially the ideal of the Chinese gentlemen; that of Aristotle was the Athenian gentlemen; in modern times, that of Rashdall, the English gentlemen; and that of Paulsen, the German gentlemen. Some will assert that the attempt to have any ethics at all is inevitably a restriction to the point of view of the Puritan gentlemen (if such critics would admit that Puritans ever were gentlemen). But in opposition to every such provincialism of ethicist or critic of ethics, the serious investigator will be at least as disposed to seek universal principles for the guidance of life's values as to seek universal laws of matter.

Not only will the normative science of ethics be genuinely universal; if it exists at all, it will also be genuinely progressive. Both theoretical and practical reasons point in this direction. It is, as a matter of theory, necessary for a science to be progressive. If it is not, it is a static dogma. A science cannot be a set of fixed and unchangeable conclusions; it must have a method which renders further investigation, further discoveries possible. Practically it is even more necessary for a science to progress. Life moves on; new problems arise, and science must discover how to cope with the new problems—or die. These two attributes of universality and progressiveness should be used by the reader as criteria for estimating the success of the system of moral laws here proposed. If this book is a contribution to the normative science of ethics, it should arrive at universal laws by a method which renders subsequent criticism and improvement possible; and the laws themselves should, without compromising their universality, make definite provision for the free creative progress which is one of the most characteristic traits of humanity at its best. Whether or to what extent these ideal requirements are fulfilled by the system here developed, remains for each reader to decide.

SELECTED BIBLIOGRAPHY

(Note that abbreviations are explained in the bibliography at the back of the book.)

On the nature and field of ethics: Aristotle, *The Nicomachean Ethics,* Book I; Dresser, ETH, Chap. I; Everett, MV, Chap. I; Leighton, ISO, Part I; Seth, SEP, Introduction, Chaps. I and II; Sharp, ETH, Chap. I; Urban, FOE, Chap. I.

On the chief types of ethical theory: Dewey and Tufts, ETH, Chaps. VI, VII, VIII, and XII; Everett, MV, Chap. II; Fung, CSLI, entire; Hyde, FGPL, entire; Leighton, ISO, Part II; Paulsen, SOE, 33-97; Sharp, ETH, Chap. XVI; Stoops, IC, entire.

On ethics as a normative (or descriptive) science: Everett, MV, 14-20; Palmer, FOE, Lecture I.

CHAPTER II

TYPES OF LAW

1. THE CONCEPT OF LAW

MANUALS of ethics often deal with moral law as one of various types of law, but their discussions suffer from at least two defects. First, they are usually too narrow in their scope; they cover at most three types of law— natural, civil, and moral. Secondly, they stand in no close relation to the general theory of ethics that is proposed; that is, they assert emphatically that there is moral law as distinguished from other types of law, without giving any clear light on what the moral laws are. If the present treatment is to avoid these pitfalls, it must offer a more comprehensive survey of the types of law and a more systematic presentation of the moral laws. Such will be our aim.

First of all, let us consider what is meant by law in general. It is obvious that there are great differences between laws which are enacted by legislatures and the laws of physics. The use of the same term for both kinds may lead us to look for a real resemblance when there is only a verbal one. However, the established use of words reflects the judgment of many generations, and this judgment is at least worthy of our careful investigation.

The English word "law" (Anglo-Saxon *lagu*) means originally custom, being thus identical with the etymological meaning of the word "moral" itself. The German equivalent, *Gesetz*, has a similar social origin; it refers to what is laid down, or "set" (*gesetzt*) as a prescription for the guidance of conduct. The Greek νόμος, also, means custom. Thus the word primarily refers to what men customarily do or are expected to do.

In its modern extended usage, under the influence of the development of science and civilization, law has come to signify far more than custom. We usually mean by it a principle which is, or is intended to be, universal in its application. By universal is meant applying to all cases alike and valid for all persons alike. Universality in this sense is the ideal of justice in the administration of civil law, of science in the formulation of natural law, of logic in its treatment of thought, of religion in its conception of a divine will, and of ethics in its search for moral laws. In so far as thought is unable to attain universality, there is no law, but, rather, a state of compromise or guesswork or muddling or emotion. In every field the question must be raised as to whether laws can be found.

The attitude of the modern mind toward the concept of law is apparently contradictory. On the one hand, our times have been called a period of "the reign of law." On the other hand, the present is often described as an "age of doubt." We seem to doubt everything except law, if we are to believe both of these labels. Yet, despite the fundamental character of the concept of law in science and in society, there is more doubt about established, or supposedly established, law now than ever before. Civil law is disregarded and the very constitution is openly violated, especially in the United States and in Germany, without the infliction of corresponding penalties. Question is being raised by physicists not merely about the adequacy of Newton's laws, but even about the very principle of causality itself. The nature and significance even of logical law is in question; while the established forms of religious and moral law are being subjected to radical criticism, as

Walter Lippmann has pointed out in his *A Preface to Morals*.[1]

In this, as in other respects, our age is rather strikingly similar to the age of the Greek Sophists, when all previous standards were in the melting pot and man was "the measure of all things."[2] It was Socrates who had the wisdom to admit the truth of the assertion that man is the measure of all things, but to point out that this could be true only because there was something genuinely universal in man. He taught that if a man defines clearly what he means, taking into account what others offer in criticism, he will arrive at a universal principle which is true. The question which the present situation forces on ethics, as well as on all other formulations of law of any kind, is whether Socrates was right in his confidence that human nature contains something universal, which both justifies and requires the acknowledgment of law. The concept of law is central to the practical situation as well as to the scientific investigation of the present time.

2. CIVIL LAW

We begin our survey of the various types of law with civil law, since it is most closely allied to the earliest meaning of the term. Law, as we found, originally meant social custom. Civil law is a form of sanctioned social custom, or of socially sanctioned changes in custom. It may be defined as a body of prescriptions for conduct, imposed and enforced by constituted authorities, and usually accompanied by penalties for violation.

There are various views regarding the aim of law. Saint Thomas says, "Lex est ordinatio rationis ad bonum

---

[1] Lippmann, PM.

[2] ἄνθρωπος μέτρον πάντων, Protagoras.

commune ab eo, qui curam habet communitatis promul-
gata."[3] This definition, satisfactory as it is on the whole,
is somewhat confusing in its use of the term *bonum
commune,* "the common good." The term suggests the
moral improvement of the community as the aim of law.
But it is very doubtful whether legislation can ever
secure directly any moral improvement. Legislation
against theft does not create honesty; at most, it protects honest people and restrains the dishonest. Nor
does prohibitory legislation create a moral attitude
toward alcohol. Moreover, if it were possible by legislation actually to improve the moral characters of men,
it would be practically impossible to aim at any high
level of improvement, because of the difficulty in enact-
ing and enforcing a law with such an aim. While, then,
those who make, enforce, and administer civil law are
themselves subject to the moral law, it seems best to
recognize that the primary and direct aim of civil law is
either the protection of life and property or the regulation of social co-operation. This statement remains
true whatever view one holds of life and property,
whether the "capitalistic" or the "communistic." The
protection of life at its minimum is an assurance of
bodily safety; it also implies the protection of every
individual life in its development, in so far as that
development does not interfere with the development of
others. Taxation, laws of contract, and compulsory
education are forms of the regulation of social co-operation. Such general principles are extremely difficult
to carry out in practice; but that civil law is aiming,
on the whole, to carry them out seems to be true.

Yet, in spite of the fact that the primary aim of law
is not ethical, it must be recognized that civil law rests

---

[3] "Law is a prescription of reason for the common good, promul-
gated by him who has care of the community." *Cit.* Gury, CTM, 48.

on moral foundations and is guided by moral principles (however imperfectly apprehended). Unless society recognized that life and property have a right to protection, there would be no basis for law. Ideals of justice and human welfare (such as those formulated in the American Declaration of Independence in exaggerated language) have often inspired lawmakers to reforms and so-called social legislation. Compulsory education comes much nearer than does constitutional prohibition to a direct attempt on the part of the legislative power to control the moral life. But the theoretical right to impose both education and prohibition by means of civil law is to be found in the principle that, if enforced, they tend to make life and property safer and social co-operation more effective. Yet it cannot be denied that a community which was well educated and abstained from alcohol would probably tend to become better in moral character. Moreover, the kind of legislation which can be enacted and the possibility of enforcing it are both affected by the moral level of the community as expressed in what we call "public opinion." Legislation, therefore, requires moral and social insight.

It is not, however, our task at present to discuss the moral problems raised by civil law. Instead, we aim to confine ourselves to a definition of its nature. One very important question remains to be discussed. Is it genuinely universal? Now, if anything is obvious, it is that civil law is violated. In fact, law contemplates its own violation when it provides penalties for infractions.

Yet, in spite of the fact that the primary aim of law is not universal in practice, it is universal in principle, for it is intended to apply to all cases alike and to all persons alike. Justice is the name we give to the administration of law; the law courts are courts of justice.

Justice implies universality; it means that everyone is treated in accordance with the same principles. Civil law, then, although capable of being violated, is universal in principle if not in practice.

3. RELIGIOUS LAW

As far back as we can go in our knowledge of human development we find traces of the recognition of another type of law or order than the civil laws of human society, namely, the religious. Civil law rests on the experiences and judgments of human society; religious law is believed to rest on the will of a superhuman power or powers. On the belief in such powers many diverse systems of religious law have been built up, prescribing forms of individual conduct, forms of worship, and forms of social organization (churches, priests, hierarchy, castes, etc.).

As society develops, religious law comes to assume very definite forms, two of which are of special importance for ethics, namely, ecclesiastical law and theological ethics.

By ecclesiastical law is meant the system of law which any church enacts for the government of its members. Since churches hold property and are part of civil society, and since some of the subject matter of ecclesiastical legislation is the same as that of civil law (*e. g.,* marriage and divorce, war), and since in some countries the church is "established," *i. e.,* recognized, supported, and to some extent controlled, by the state, the relations between ecclesiastical and civil law may become very complicated, both for the individual and for society. The religious theory that "the powers that be are ordained of God" (Romans 13:1)—*superiores a deo constituti*—does not always serve to simplify the practical problems.

By theological ethics is meant the theory that moral
law is to be regarded as derived from religious law.
This theory takes various forms. It may assert that
obedience to God is the sole motive for morality, either
because God is the source of rewards and punishments
(Paley) or because he is the supreme object of love
(Isidor and Gregory of Nyssa[4]). Or it may assert that
our sole authoritative source of information about
moral conduct is divine revelation. This view was
expressed by Robert Blakey in the early part of the
Nineteenth Century, when in his *History of Moral
Science* he made "observations on the moral theory
which seems to square best with divine revelation" and
wrote further that "we are to look upon the commands
found in the Bible, as clothed with moral obligation,
from the mere circumstance of their being commanded." Indeed, Blakey went so far as to assert that
"no reason can be found for their [the moral laws']
existence, than that it has so pleased Him [the
Almighty] to make them as we find them."[5] It may
hold that the moral principles discoverable by reason
(the cardinal moral virtues of prudence, justice, courage, and temperance) need to be supplemented by those
derived from revelation (the theological virtues of
faith, hope, and charity).[6] Again, it may be concerned
chiefly to teach that all moral law is derived from the
will or nature of God, on the theory that "Deus solus est
legislator supremus et universalis"[7] ("God alone is
the supreme and universal legislator").

The variety of forms assumed by religious law in
both of its types—ecclesiastical law and theological

---

[4] See Simmel, MW, I, 24.
[5] Blakey, HMS, I, 313; II, 338, 340.
[6] So Saint Thomas. See Gury, CTM, 96.
[7] Gury, CTM, 49.

ethics—makes it difficult to define specifically, and raises a question as to its universality. Can religious law be said to be law in the true sense? Is it universal?

The same obvious objection to regarding it as universal applies here as in the case of civil law. It is not universal in the sense of being inviolable; both ecclesiastical law and theological ethics are violated every day. Can the same answer be made, namely, that religious law is universal in intent, if not in practice? Only with some reservations. Ecclesiastical law is universal in intent only for the members of the legislating church; while theological ethics, although believed by its defenders to be universal in intent, is not so universally recognized as is civil law. It may be said that the universality of religious law in this latter sense is dependent on whether a superhuman Divine Being is believed to exist or not, a question which we need not discuss here.

Of undoubted significance for ethics, however, is the fact that very large numbers of human beings in every civilized and uncivilized country of the world are firm believers in one or both forms of religious law and that religious law is a social force of prime importance. Any writer on sociology, politics, or ethics who neglects or minimizes this fact betrays provincialism of interest. Ethics must consider the problem of religious law. Further discussions of it will occur later in the chapter.

4. NATURAL LAW

Almost contemporaneously with civil and religious law, yet (as a separate principle) somewhat later, there grew up among men the idea of a moral law—of what was better or worse for the group and the individual. But we shall interrupt the historical order of development at this point in the interests of the logical. Since our chief aim in the present investigation is to understand moral law and its relations to all the other types, we shall postpone the discussion of it until we have taken up the natural and logical types.

After moral law the next major type to be recognized historically was natural law. Knowledge of the laws of nature developed considerably later than did civil or religious or moral law. The most primitive races had to have some civil laws—some recognized customs—in order to co-operate in the simplest social activities. But, although primitive man obviously had to deal with the forces of nature, he seemed to be more impressed with their irregularity than with their regularity. For him, nature was neither the steady ongoing of one system of uniform laws nor the work of a single wise Providence. It was, rather, the scene of capricious events, the play of demonic powers and magical forces, which can be outwitted only by recourse to "medicine men," Shamans, or by the use of fetishes, charms, amulets, and the like. On the other hand, it was not long before some regular habits of nature forced themselves on human attention. The seasons, the heavenly bodies, and the facts of birth, adolescence, marriage, and death, were observed both because of their importance in religious rites and also because some knowledge of them was necessary to human survival. Yet it was surprisingly long before a strictly secular, objective, and systematic study of nature began. Such a study may be said to have had its inception in ancient Greece and its first great representative in Aristotle, who was almost as truly the founder of natural science as of ethics and logic.

Moreover, a new meaning of the word "law" emerges here. In the cases of civil and moral, and even religious law, we have to do primarily with prescriptions for the conduct of human beings, although it is true that religious law is regarded as a command ultimately resting on superhuman authority. Natural law, however, is, so to speak, wholly superhuman; that is, its point of view is not merely universal, but is entirely impersonal and above all human choice. It is not imposed by human beings on themselves; it is not a command that they shall behave in any particular way; it is simply a formulation of fact. It is no account of human customs, but, rather, of the customs of the universe.

Natural law, then, may be defined as a formulation of causal principles. By causality, science means only uniformity of sequence. The cause of an event is its invariable antecedent; its effect is its invariable consequent. Whenever sufficient ether is administered to a patient, the patient loses consciousness. Administration of ether, therefore, is, in such a case, the cause of loss of consciousness. The law would describe under what conditions ether is to be administered in order to secure anæsthesia without endangering the patient. It would be a universal rule.

So far as science and observation go, a genuine natural law—that is, one based on sound experiments and correctly defined—is incapable of being violated. If it admitted of exceptions, it would not be a law. Popular language, it is true, often speaks of the bad consequences of violating the laws of nature. John Jones had insufficient nourishment, no systematic exercise, irregular sleep, and a great deal of alcohol. Before many years he lost control of his nervous system, then he wasted away, and died. Did he violate any laws of nature? He certainly violated principles of hygiene; but hygiene does not consist of natural laws alone. It rests on the ethical law that a man *ought* to care for his own health as much as is possible in harmony with his other duties. It was this moral law that John violated. But as for the laws of nature—the physiological laws— he violated none of them; he simply offered his body as a laboratory in which to demonstrate them. All that the natural laws predicted occurred without exception or violation; the death of our hero was due to the fact that he violated the commands of the moral law.

5. LOGICAL LAW

It is strange how often a survey of the great principles of human thought has to go back to Aristotle. It was he who first formulated a science of logical laws. Logic consists of the fundamental laws of thought and of the inferences to be made from them. It is a result of a high degree of generalized and abstract reflection and is naturally a relatively late result of human culture. Aristotle could not have created the science of logic had not a great deal of intellectual work preceded him, especially the work of Socrates.

Let us define logical law somewhat more in detail. The three fundamental laws of thought, according to the Aristotelian logic, are the law of identity (A is A); the law of contradiction (A is not non-A); and the law of excluded middle (A is either B or non-B). It seems obvious that anything is itself; that it is not its contradictory; and that it either is or is not whatever you happen to be saying about it. But precisely obvious truths are in practice most commonly ignored. We violate the law of identity when we begin to praise the record of the Republican Party, and later in our discussion show that we did not mean the whole record of the Republican Party, but only such parts of it as we liked. We started to talk about A and shifted to A minus X. The sum and substance of the three laws is that we shall be absolutely consistent in our use of terms. The whole science of logic, both in its simpler Aristotelian form, and in the more complicated modern forms of Hegelian, symbolic, and mathematical logic, is nothing more nor less than an elaboration of the rules of precise and consistent thought. It is true that some regard logic, not as a science of thought, but as a science of the most universal objective relations; but for the purposes of our discussion this would make no more than a formal difference.

There is fairly general agreement that the laws of logic are universal, and, in fact, constitute the most certain body of universal knowledge that we possess. Logic remains true through all changes of our experience.[8] It is equally certain that our actual thinking does not conform to the laws of logic. As was pointed out, the *A* that we start out with changes, through carelessness or hidden intent, to a *non-A;* and we try to make ourselves or others believe that the same *A* is both right and wrong, both *B* and *non-B*. If we take the view of those who see in logic a system of objective relations, then, it is true, logic is never violated; but whatever our theory of logic may be, inconsistent thinking occurs in human minds and needs correction. On the view of logic as a science of thought (which we adopt), logic is a normative science. On the view of logic as an account of objective relations, it is descriptive. On either view, logical laws are universal and permit of no exceptions to their truth, whether human thinking conforms to them or not. The obligation of conformity to logical law underlies all other types of law; without it, the mind would be in a perpetual, whirling chaos. Hence logic is often called *die Moral des Denkens,* "the

[8] "Wherever I meet a proposition which is true, independently of all experience, I am in the realm of logic." Schlick, FE, 81.

ethics of thought." A consideration of logical law, then, involves a transition to moral law.

6. MORAL LAW

With moral law we have reached the main subject of our investigation. Our immediate discussion must necessarily be incomplete. The aim will be to describe moral law as related to other types of law. We shall first seek to define what is meant by moral law (what it is and what it is not) ; then, raise the question whether there really are moral laws; next, take up the relations of moral to civil, religious, natural, and logical law; and finally discuss the relation of moral law to moral experience.

What, then, do we mean by moral law? A moral law is a universal principle to which the will ought to conform in its choices. If it is not a universal principle, it is not a law; and if it does not apply to the obligation of the will in choosing, it is not moral. Both conditions must be fulfilled by a moral law. Moral law, therefore, needs to be clearly distinguished from social codes and conventions. Codes are sets of principles in accordance with which society expects or demands that the individual shall choose. It may be, and perhaps usually is, in accordance with moral law to choose to act as the code or social convention prescribes, especially if the code has been thoughtfully prepared by and for moral persons. But no act is moral because it conforms to a code. It is moral because it conforms to moral law. Every code is subject to criticism by the moral law. Convention is sometimes an aid and sometimes a detriment to morality. The fact that others expect us to do something creates no obligation, although it creates a situation and a problem. What creates obligation is a subject for later investigation.

The confusion between social code and moral law is illustrated by the double meaning of the word "duty." On the one hand, a duty means a demand that society makes on me. In this sense a duty may not only be an act which I do not choose; it may even be an act from which my whole moral judgment revolts. On the other hand, a duty means a demand which my own enlightened conscience makes on me; it is what I judge that I ought to do after having consulted my own experience and reason in the light of my highest ideals. One's social "duties" and one's moral "duties" would ordinarily coincide, especially in cases of the socially recognized standards of a profession or trade, in matters of social etiquette and the conventions of courtesy, and in many other instances. But to accept the duties imposed by society as if they were all and always moral duties and to recognize no duties save those definitely prescribed by the group, is to surrender the whole task of morality. If all moral law were derived from social prescriptions, then it would be impossible for a social prescription ever to be subjected to intelligent criticism. There would be no way of distinguishing between good social prescriptions and bad ones. Social duties, then, must be judged in the light of moral duties. As Kant put it, "the essential characteristic of all moral value in our acts depends on whether the moral law determines the will immediately."[9] If the person chooses determination by moral law, he is moral; but if he is compelled by social authority, military power (or by hypnotism or the will of God or any other form of superior force), his act has no moral quality. It was not determined by moral law. It was social duty or compulsion; it was not moral duty.

We have been speaking about moral duty and moral

---

[9] Kant, KdpV (Reclam S), 101.

law as if it were very sure that there is such a reality as moral law. Men as different from each other as Benedict Spinoza, Ralph Cudworth, Immanuel Kant, and Jeremy Bentham shared the conviction that there is moral law. Spinoza demonstrated his ethics *more geometrico* ("in a geometrical manner"). Cudworth wrote *A Treatise Concerning Eternal and Immutable Morality*. Kant called the moral will "practical reason" (with the accent on the "reason") and held that moral law must be universal and necessary—*a priori*, as he called it. Jeremy Bentham developed a calculus of pleasure with a very definite system of moral laws. But these defenders of law differ among themselves, and there have been eminent thinkers who have questioned the universality of moral law, and so its character as law.[10] Consequently, without taking up the absurd views of unreasonable extremists, let us consider three of the main criticisms that have been leveled against moral law.

The first of these criticisms may perhaps better be regarded as a caution than as a criticism. The great Aristotle taught that in ethics no absolute accuracy is to be demanded, by reason of its inductive method.[11] This caution was admirable in the founder of a science. Moreover, as a perpetual warning against dogmatism and misguided feelings of absolute finality, it will always remain wholesome advice. Yet if it were to be taken as a prohibition of a search for accuracy, it would prevent ethics from ever becoming a science and would encourage loose thinking, not to mention loose living. As a reminder that ethics is derived from moral expe-

---

[10] See the discussion of moral skepticism, Everett, MV, 320-334.

[11] Aristotle, *Nicomachean Ethics*, I, vii. The scholastics hold the same view. "In rebus moralibus non est absoluta certitudo in omnibus quaerenda." Gury, CTM, 31.

rience, it calls attention to a truth that some abstract
theories are in danger of overlooking. But as an assertion that a science derived from experience can expect
to attain no universal laws, it contradicts the history
of inductive science since the days of Aristotle, and
rests on too narrow a view of experience; for experience includes rational thought as well as particular
facts.

The second criticism is an application of the maxim,
"Life is more than logic" (Lotze, James, Bowne), to
ethics. The point of this criticism is that moral life is
too rich and creative to be grasped adequately in any
law. "The good," says Romano Guardini, "is no dead
law. It is infinite life."[12] Similarly, Georg Simmel
wrote, "No one can cite a single act or a single universal
law which, under special conditions, we should not
sometimes have to refuse to acknowledge as *our* duty."[13]
This point of view is fairly familiar; and, if it be pressed
to the limit, it is hard to distinguish from the standpoint of the ordinary wrongdoer. Life urges him to
violate law. Yet, despite the possibility of abusing this
principle, it must be recognized as containing a truth.
Moral life is certainly more than a formula; and moral
choices are not so completely and unambiguously determined by moral laws as are mathematical conclusions by mathematical premises. There is something
individual in every moral situation. This means that
moral laws should be so formulated as to take account
of the individual character of life; but it does not mean
that moral law is impossible. If it did mean that, then
Lotze, James, and Bowne, Guardini and Simmel, would
have no right to which they could appeal when they
go beyond logic and law to life; they would have

[12] Guardini, GGS, 24.
[13] Simmel, LA, 224.

abandoned reason—and this they certainly did not
mean to do.

The third criticism is more radical. If the first was
the revolt of induction against deduction, and the
second the revolt of life against logic, the third is the
revolt of sociology against ethics. It has been most
brilliantly stated by L. Lévy-Bruhl,"[14] who argues that
theoretical ethics is impossible because sociology has
destroyed the presuppositions on which it rests. He
holds that these presuppositions are: (1) "Human
nature is always identical with itself in every time and
at every place," and (2) "The content of the moral consciousness forms an harmonious and organic whole."
He is able to show that the study of social evolution has
refuted both of these presuppositions, and he infers that
there is no moral theory and no moral law.

The trouble with Lévy-Bruhl's argument is that his
statement of presuppositions is incorrect. On the first
one, two comments are necessary. First, moral law is
not intended to be universal in the sense of being binding on human beings at every stage of evolution and
development, any more than it is binding on apes; it is
universal for moral beings such as we know ourselves
to be. Secondly, identity is not necessary for law in
morals any more than biological identity is necessary
for biological law. Moral law should be so formulated
as to recognize those differences (note especially the
Law of Autonomy, the Law of Specification, and the
Law of the Best Possible). Lévy-Bruhl's second presupposition rests on a failure to distinguish clearly between uncriticized moral experience and the same
experience after it has been rationally interpreted. Of
course the actual moral consciousness is a mass of contradictions, just as is our sensory consciousness of the

---

[14] Lévy-Bruhl, MSM, 66-96, esp. 67, 83.

outer world. Lévy-Bruhl, it is true, urges that a conflict of duties often remains in spite of the best our reason can do. However, there can be no conflict of duties if there are no duties; and there can be no duties if there is no moral law. Conflict of duties proves only that moral law is difficult to apply; instead of disproving, it presupposes moral law. It cannot, then, be justly said that the existence of moral law has been refuted. It has only been shown hard to apply.

If we may now go ahead on the assumption that moral laws are to be found, we shall understand their nature better when we compare them with the other types of law and consider the mutual relations of the various types. The present treatment must, of course, be preliminary, and consist far more of the raising of problems than of answers to them.

There are certain respects in which all five types of law are alike, despite obvious differences in their subject matter. All are in some sense universal. All, in order to have any sort of universality, must be reasonable, *i. e.*, must conform to logical law. All are enforced or sanctioned by some "authority";[15] civil by the state, religious by the church or God himself, natural by nature, logical by intelligence, and moral by the rational will. All, except the natural, are in the form of commands which are capable of being disobeyed.

While the moral law, as a consciousness of genuine individual responsibility, is a rather late development, from the point of view of our present knowledge and experience it must be said that civil and religious law are both logically dependent on the moral. If we did not know something about the good, there would be no criterion for just legislation and no basis for acknowl-

[15] See Brightman, POI, Chap. IV, "Sources of the Authority of Ideals."

edging a good God.[16]   Indeed, all search for law presupposes ethics, for the desire to be reasonable is an
obligation, and the formulation of natural and logical
law is itself a moral enterprise.   I ought to know nature
and I ought to think logically.

But, despite these interrelations, there are conflicts.
That moral law sometimes conflicts with civil law is a
tragic experience of passive resisters and conscientious objectors; that the relation between the two is at
least highly problematic is proved by the firm and justified belief of the German nation that the Versailles
Treaty rests on an untruth, namely, the assertion of the
sole guilt of Germany for the war, as well as by the
refusal of many American citizens to obey prohibitory
legislation which they consider unjust.   In one direction, anarchy threatens, if civil law is wholly subordinated to the moral judgments of individuals; in the
other direction, unendurable tyranny and injustice
threaten, if moral law is wholly subordinated to civil
law.   The problems of ethics here are the very central
problems of civilization.

There are also conflicts between moral and religious
law.[17]   What religion has approved has often been condemned by the moral law, as in Plato's criticism of the
morals of the Homeric gods.   On the other hand, what
religion has condemned has often been approved by
morals; moral law would disagree with the religious
denunciation of purely ritualistic sins and there is
serious question about the moral validity of the
church's traditional attitude toward divorce.   Yet it
should be remembered that the lower ethical standards

---

[16] See Brightman, RV, Chap. II, "The Moral Basis of Religious
Values."

[17] See Everett, MV, Chap. XIII.   See also Diamond, RC, *passim*,
and Urban, FOE, Chap. XIX.

of religion have often found their correction from within religion itself. The so-called prophetic movement in world-wide religion, from about the Eighth to about the Fourth Century before Christ, in China, India, Persia, and Greece, as well as in Israel,[18] was essentially a moral criticism of traditional religion by the greatest religious geniuses of the times. But the relation between morality and religion is in almost constant need of readjustment.

There can be no direct theoretical conflict between natural and moral law because they move in different spheres—one being descriptive and the other normative. Yet the practical conflict between the workings of natural law and the demands of moral law is an ancient experience of the race. It is not merely the struggle between "flesh" and "spirit." It is also the profound realization that things as they are are not as they ought to be. In one sense, of course, natural law is the necessary ally of moral law; knowledge of natural law is necessary in order to make moral law effective and to secure a state of affairs in the world that will render moral development socially possible. But morality is never exhausted by mere knowledge of natural laws; the laws must be used for the realization of chosen ends. That use involves struggle and conflict. There is, then, a practical, if not a theoretical, conflict between the natural and the moral.

The cases of possible conflict between the logical and the moral are all of one type. It would be absurd to subject logic to moral criticism. We cannot say that the logical is immoral; we can only say that the moral is illogical. When we see a person logically carrying out wrong principles with cold-blooded calculation, we are inclined to pass the judgment that logic is immoral.

---

[18] *Cf.* Galloway, POR, 131-138.

But there is nothing morally wrong in the logic; the trouble is in the wrong moral principles with which the man starts. What is the nature of that trouble? In the last analysis, if we are to show that there is any trouble with his principles, we must do so by showing them to be, in some way, unreasonable, that is, illogical. If we cannot do this, and if it is equally reasonable to be good or bad, it is difficult to see why a person with a mind should care anything about being moral. Moral principles, then, may be illogical; and if they are, logic has the right to assert that they need revision. Sound moral principles are logical; unsound ones are in some way illogical. We therefore perceive the rule of reason over moral law.

In conclusion, something should be said about the relations of moral law to moral experience, a subject which has already emerged both in the criticism of Lévy-Bruhl and also in the discussion of the relation of logical to moral law, as well as in the treatment of ethics as a science in Chapter I. Moral experience occurs wherever there is a feeling of obligation or a choice between what is felt to be better and what is felt to be worse. But these moral experiences are usually unsystematic, confused, and often contradictory; where they are not confused, but perfectly clear, there they are in danger of being most wrong. A science of ethics could not possibly exist and moral laws would not be derived if we were to confine ourselves to a mere description of the variegated individual and social hodge-podge of moral experience. It is only by a rational criticism and systematization of moral experience that moral laws can be discovered. As Kant puts it, "Die praktische Regel ist jeder Zeit ein Produkt der Vernunft" ("the practical rule is always a product of reason"); or, to quote Bergmann, there is, in moral law, "an identity of the law-giving will and the practical reason."[19]

Therefore the problem of ethics is to examine the facts of moral experience in order to discover what laws of obligation it implies. Chapter III will outline the data of experience, and the remainder of the book will be concerned with the moral laws.

SELECTED BIBLIOGRAPHY

Bentham, DE; Dunham, POE, 493-508; Everett, MV, Chap. XI; Palmer, FOE, Lecture II; Pound, LAM; Urban, FOE, 23-25, 177-182.

---

[19] Kant, KdpV (Reclam S), 26. Bergmann, UR, 54ff. See also Hobhouse, RG, and Paton, GW, for a defense of morality as rational.

CHAPTER III

THE DATA OF ETHICS

1. EXPERIENCE AS THE SOURCE OF ETHICAL KNOWLEDGE

ALL sciences deal with objects either given in or implied by experience. Psychology deals directly with consciousness; behaviorism deals with the organism and its responses to stimuli. Both, however, are derived from experience, despite the fact that behaviorism has tended to deny the very existence of those aspects of experience in which it was not interested.[1] It is true that some sciences have to go beyond any possible present or future experience. History deals with past experience; and since the past is inaccessible and unverifiable, it might almost be called experience by courtesy. History has to infer its not-now-experienced objects from their traces in present and future experience. Mathematics deals with concepts that can never be completed in experience, such as the infinite series. Even psychology speaks of the subconscious, which we do not experience, but only infer; while the electrons and protons of physics or the Einsteinian curvature of space can be said to be objects of experience only in a very remote sense. Nevertheless, no matter how far the sciences may march, their base of supplies is always the same. All sciences are attempts to explain what is given in experience.[2] Art, religion, daily life, and philosophy, as well as science, can be nothing else than ways of dealing with experience. Particularly is this

---

[1] Roback has rightly differentiated behaviorism from psychology (BAP). On the relation of behaviorism to experience, see Brightman, "Behaviorism and Experience" in King, BBL, 307-330.

[2] See Chap. I, § 3, of *Moral Laws*.

55

true of ethics, which might be defined as the science of the proper control of experience.

Unfortunately, our fundamental term, experience, is vague. It has had a checkered career. Some (like the late Theodore de Laguna) regard it as meaningless and would like to do away with it. In the eighteenth century, Hume thought of experience as consisting of sensations, which he called "impressions," and their paler copies, "ideas." If experience is indeed nothing more than material furnished by sense, it is hard to find any experiential basis for ethics. Why should one sensation or group of sensations call another good or bad? Yet, so great was the force of actual experience as distinguished from any theory about it, that Hume clearly recognized the moral data. In Section I of *An Enquiry Concerning the Principles of Morals,* Hume says: "Those who have denied the reality of moral distinctions, may be ranked among the disingenuous disputants. . . . Let a man's insensibility be ever so great, he must often be touched with the images of right and wrong."

It would lead us too far astray to go on to consider the detailed history of the term "experience," as used by Kant and by Hegel, by Bradley and by Royce, by Bowne and by Dewey. It is, however, essential to tell how it is to be used in the present discussion. Experience, here, shall mean the whole field of consciousness, every process or state of awareness within it; not sensation alone, nor scientifically interpreted experience alone. It is not to be taken in contrast with reason or speculation, but, rather, in contrast with the absence of experience, or unconsciousness. It is *Erlebnis,* not the Kantian *Erfahrung* alone. Experience is always complex, ongoing conscious activity; thought and will belong to it as truly as do sensations and memory images. Hence, in the broad sense in which we use it, experience contains both what have been called empirical and what have been called transcendental (rational) factors.

Kant's attempt to make a sharp distinction between the empirical and the transcendental is, for some purposes, useful; yet it leads to an artificial view of experience. Kant said that his critique was to give principles "ohne besondere Beziehung auf die menschliche Natur"[3] ("without special reference to human nature"). But principles of conduct have to be derived from a study of human nature and cannot float in the air. Eduard von Hartmann was right in saying that the question whether there is an ethical consciousness is a purely empirical one, a *quaestio facti*.[4] We cannot derive ethical knowledge from any remote realm inaccessible to experience. It goes back to our actual experiences of the problems and the values of life. Ethical knowledge is based on moral experience. Normative science rests on descriptive science for its facts.

2. WHAT IS MORAL EXPERIENCE?

In Chapter I we found that ethics is a science of conduct. Moral experience, therefore, consists of conduct. Conduct we have defined as voluntary behavior, but this definition needs fuller explanation. As it stands it is somewhat too narrow. The term "behavior," as ordinarily used, refers to actual overt movements. The behaviorist, it is true, has theories about "implicit" movements, which no one can observe. But a definition of the subject matter of a science ought not to have to rely on questionable theories or unusual uses of words. Most psychology agrees with common usage in distinguishing between purely physical acts of the organism and acts that are primarily mental in character. An

---

[3] Kant, KdpV (Reclam S), 11.
[4] Hartmann, PSB, 105.

unconscious reflex is an instance of the former and thinking of the latter. Both types of act are more or less susceptible to voluntary control. Much behavior of the organism, however, is not conduct, because not voluntary; so, likewise, many mental states are not conduct (such as impulsive desires). But both mental and physical acts may be conduct. If I choose to think, or to indulge in mental imagery, or to assume an attitude toward a person, a group, or a cause, I am having a moral experience as truly as though I expressed my mental life in my overt behavior. Thus conduct includes more than behavior. Indeed, behavior always derives its moral significance from the fact that it is voluntary, that is, from its relation to the mental.

Moral experience, in the broad sense, includes not only the act of voluntary choice, but also the experiences chosen—the consciousness of value, of obligation, and of law to which reference was made in Chapter I.

Moral experience occurs only in persons. In fact, a person may be defined as a being capable of moral experience. If so-called lower animals have moral experiences, as in some instances appears possible, they are persons. Moreover persons, whether human or sub-human, develop only in social relations. Their birth is the result of a social act. Without social care they perish. Human customs and languages are a social heritage. Hence the data of ethics are to be found in the sociological and the psychological sciences. The psychological data are, however, more fundamental than the sociological for various reasons. Sociological phenomena can be known to be ethical only through the psychological approach. The presence or absence of voluntary control in a social situation can be ascertained only by psychological methods. Psychology is broader, in that it is both social and individual, while

sociology is purely social.   Psychology also has the
advantage of being better established and more scientific than sociology.   The ensuing treatment will therefore begin with the sociological, but will be chiefly occupied with the psychological data.

3. SOCIOLOGICAL DATA OF ETHICS

The sociological facts of importance for ethics have
been described in so many books and articles that they
need not here be repeated in detail.   Herbert Spencer's
Data of Ethics treats moral consciousness as wholly a
social product.   The works of Hobhouse and Westermarck give abundant data; briefer accounts, for the
purposes of ethics, are to be found in Wundt, Dewey
and Tufts, Sherman, Drake, Fullerton, and others.   It
would be pointless and unjustifiable to do more than to
outline the material here.

The data of ethics include all of the subject matter
of all of the social sciences, *i. e.*, sociology, anthropology,
ethnology, criminology, economics, political science, and
history, in so far as these sciences study voluntary behavior.   Even social phenomena which confront the
individual as brute facts that he did not choose are
moral phenomena in at least two senses.   A declaration of war, for example, in its relation to a citizen
opposed to war is a moral phenomenon for that citizen,
in so far as he assumes any voluntary attitude toward
it; and in itself it is moral, in so far as the momentous
declaration involved decisions on the part of responsible
statesmen.   Many writers, especially in Germany, tend
to regard all great social phenomena as due to the
hand of fate (Spengler) ; and it cannot be denied that
when the situation reaches a certain point, catastrophe
is inevitable.   For the individual all such phenomena
which he did not share in making seem like sheer des-

tiny. Yet it is needless pessimism to overlook the possibility of voluntary control of social behavior. Even war might be averted if the right persons made the right choices.

As the sociologist studies human group behavior, he finds first of all a great variety of phenomena. What some groups idealize as the highest virtue, others condemn as vice. Suicide, under certain conditions, has been regarded as heroic in Japan, whereas in the Catholic Church it excludes the person from Christian burial. Attitudes toward sex are amazingly contradictory. Some writers go so far as to say that almost every act which is condemned anywhere is praised somewhere else.

The impression of variety in the *mores* is heightened when one takes the evolution of morals into account. Anthropology carries us back to the dawn of morality in the race. While our actual information about the origins of morality is very meager, being largely imaginative deduction, it appears clear that such forms of primitive social behavior as tended toward the survival of life would be maintained. If we picture a time when the remote ancestors of man still lived in trees, like the apes, then the moment when they descended from the trees and took to homes on *terra firma* was a turning point in the history of morals, for life on the ground was more dangerous, more exposed to attack, and therefore more dependent on social co-operation than was arboreal life.[5] Sutherland believes that the development of morals centers about the maternal instinct, which doubtless was and is an important factor. Tarde is of the opinion that imitation is the great social force, "inventors" being few and imitators numerous. It is well established that individual moral independence is a

---

[5] This is suggested by Thomson in WM.

later development than social standards.[6] Early man lives only in and for his group, and independent thought and action require personal courage and maturity. Types of approved behavior become rigidly standardized; yet, as contacts among groups increase and their conflicting standards clash, the rigidity tends to break down, and after a period of moral chaos new standards are slowly formed. This is illustrated in historical times by the rise of the Sophists during and after the Persian Wars in Greece; by the Renaissance, related as it was to wars between Turks and Christians; and by the moral turmoil of the present, following the World War. The evolution of morals is a picture of conflicting and changing social and individual standards.

The organization of social institutions gives rise to a mass of moral data. We have already (Chapter II) spoken of moral problems growing out of the institutions of the state (moral and civil law) and the church (moral and religious law). Economic institutions are the sources of some of the most acutely pressing problems of the moral life. Karl Marx, with his theory of historical materialism, believed that economic conditions determine the whole course of history; and this theory is believed by millions today. Whether one accepts or rejects the theory, its existence is a social fact of the utmost importance for morals. Various types of organization of labor and of capital enter into all degrees of co-operation and conflict with each other, and programs of strike leaders and strike breakers, and of advocates of communism, industrial democracy, and "wage slavery," are pressing moral data of the modern world.

Race differences are also a source of moral conflicts. The theory of Anglo-Saxon or of Aryan supremacy is

----
[6] Simmel, MW, I, 173.

met in the Orient by an equally proud sense of the superiority of the Japanese, the Chinese, or the Indian. To be born a Jew is to enter into a social situation which compels the individual to carry the burdens of two millenniums of hatred, irrespective of his individual merits, as well as to be exalted by pride of race. To be born a Negro, at least in free America, is to find oneself in many respects a social outcast, even though one's skin be so white that expert research is required to prove the presence of Negro blood.

Similarly, sex is a source of social phenomena of great importance for morals. It is the basis of the family; it inspires the lowest and the highest passions of men and women, so that all other considerations are forgotten for its sake. The biological and psychological differences between the sexes, which survive no matter how far the emancipation of woman goes, create special moral problems for each sex.

It is not the task of theoretical ethics to offer a specific solution for each of the problems arising from the sociological data, any more than it is the task of theoretical physics to tell just how a tunnel under the English Channel should be constructed. A theoretical science must, however, formulate laws which will be true for all possible situations, while the art of living consists in the application of theory to the actual situations which arise. But theoretical ethics never removes from the individual the responsibility of acquainting himself with the situation and of deciding for himself the form which the application of moral laws will take. Physics does not build tunnels nor ethics create a just social order.

4. PSYCHOLOGY OF VALUE

When we turn from the sociological to the psychological data of ethics, we are moving from visible social behavior to its causes in the inner world of mind. As Elsenhans has said, "The fixed starting point of ethics as a science . . . can . . . be nothing else than the psychological fact of the moral consciousness."[7]

In Chapter I we found that the fundamental concepts of ethics are value, obligation, and law. If these concepts are not mere artificial abstractions, they must have a basis in experience. Let us, then, seek for the psychological basis of each of these concepts.

There is no doubt that experiences of value occur. An experience of value is any consciousness of attainment of desire or any experience that satisfies or is approved of. It may be called a realized ideal; for an ideal is a concept of a plan of action or type of experience which, when realized, is satisfactory. The optimist thinks that life consists chiefly of values. The pessimist thinks that value experiences are few, but he does not deny that they occur; his complaint is that there are not more of them. All agree that at least some moments of life are worth living. Every human being can say, "I value."

A pessimist like Hartmann, for example, holds that there is "in the human consciousness an immediate, involuntary evaluation of human acts and sentiments, which has as its criterion neither egoistic interest nor mere conformity with external commands."[8] He believes, then, that there is a genuine experience of moral value. James Martineau, a very different type of man, speaks of "an irresistible tendency to *approve and disapprove*";[9] while Brentano calls "love" and "hate" the fundamentals of value experience.[10] At the close of a

[7] Elsenhans, WEG, 331.
[8] Hartmann, PSB, 105.
[9] Martineau, TET, II, 17.
[10] Brentano, USE, *passim*.

volume devoted to a survey of "the facts of the moral life," Wundt summarizes his conclusions by saying that, in all stages of the moral life, there are judgments of approval and disapproval, and that values which bring permanent satisfaction are sought.[11]

There are, it is true, differences among psychologists about the analysis of the value experience. Some make desire paramount (voluntarism); others make pleasure the essential value-factor (hedonism); while others make conformity to ideals the chief mark of value (idealism).[12] For the study of the data of ethics, however, these differences are less important than the universal agreement that value experience exists. It is also agreed that value is a fulfillment or development or extension of what have been regarded as man's basic interests.[13] Hence the psychological data of most significance for ethics are not found in the writings of scientific psychologists so much as in literature, biography, and history.

5. PSYCHOLOGY OF OBLIGATION

When we move from experiences of value to experiences of obligation, we are drawing closer to the heart of the moral life. One might enjoy values, as does the æsthete, without regarding them from a moral standpoint; but when one feels obligation, one is distinctly in a moral situation, even though the feeling of obligation be unjustified. Obligation addresses itself more directly to will than does value.

First we note that feelings of obligation certainly exist. Everyone who knows human nature has observed

---

[11] Wundt, ETG, I, 279.

[12] See Brightman, ITP, Chap. V, for a brief survey; and Perry, GTV, for a fuller discussion from a different point of view.

[13] For a brief statement of this aspect of value, see Urban, FOE, 166-169.

them. The sense of duty, the feeling, "I ought," and the pangs of conscience when duty is violated, are all evidence of the existence of such an experience. It is, however, no more capable of being defined than is any other ultimate, such as space or time. Only experience shows what space, time, and obligation are. If a man were blind and paralyzed from birth, you could not tell him the difference between walking and running. Likewise, in the moral realm there are a few who are in an analogous state; they simply lack a sense of obligation. No one can explain to such persons what is meant by a sense of duty. But most supposed cases of this sort are either instances of unconventional and unusual feelings of obligation toward certain supposed values, so that the socially recognized values are not acknowledged as obligatory by such persons; or else they are instances of mere dislike for the words "duty" and "obligation." In both cases there is a real experience of obligation.

We have said that obligation cannot be defined any more than space can be defined; but this does not imply that either obligation or space is meaningless. Rather, they are both so full of concrete meaning as to be unique. There is nothing else like duty; and yet every normal mind knows what is meant both by space and by duty. Any so-called definition of either term really moves in a circle by presupposing that which is to be defined. But we can identify or "point out" either one so that all will know what is meant. In this sense we may say that obligation is the unique feeling, not identical either with desire or with social prescriptions, which arises when I consider that which I take to be the highest value for me, or, as we ordinarily say, "the best thing for me to do," and which leads me to say, "I ought to do this."

Not all will agree with the theory of the psychological uniqueness of obligation here defended.[14] Therefore, in order to bring out more fully the meaning of the experience of "ought," let us ask two questions which are often raised by critics of our view. (1) Is the feeling of obligation analyzable? (2) Is it capable of evolutionary explanation?

In answer to the first of these questions, Mr. Bertrand Russell has said that the "ought" is simply what other people desire me to do. But this facile analysis is refuted by the fact that men often feel that they ought not to do what others desire them to do and that they ought to do what others do not desire them to do. It has also been suggested that obligation is a feeling of controlled or inhibited desire. But, on the one hand, an obligation may be recognized without the slightest desire to fulfill it; and, on the other, there may be control of desire out of fear or other motives that have nothing to do with duty. Let us grant for the moment that obligation is analyzable and that it can be broken up into constituent elements; even then it would remain true that the compound of those elements, the actual experience of obligation, would have properties that its parts do not have, just as salt has properties that sodium and chlorine do not have. "Ought" means more than that desires are being controlled or inhibited. It is a unique kind of inhibition.

The second question is much easier to answer than was the first. There is no reasonable doubt that obligation is capable of evolutionary explanation. But what does this mean? Evolution presupposes that variations occur, or, to use language popular among recent philosophers, that there are emergent qualities—new qual-

---

[14] Various views of obligation are discussed in Brightman, RV, Chap. III.

ities which arise from time to time. It is necessary to remind ourselves in this connection of Bowne's statement that evolution describes the survival of the fit, but does not account for the arrival of the fit. To say that obligation has had an evolutionary history, then, is to say nothing about the nature of obligation, certainly not to deny its uniqueness.

It is true, however, that the unique and indefinable character of obligation has sometimes been stated in such a way as to seem to separate the "ought" entirely from the evolutionary process. The frequently repeated idealistic thesis that the *ought* cannot be derived from the *is* is ambiguous. What this properly means is that no consideration of sensations or of any type of non-moral experience would enable us to infer what is meant by obligation. It is like saying that no examination of color would enable us to infer what sound is like. This was plainly Kant's intent when he called obligation "a fact which is absolutely inexplicable from all the data of the sense world and from the whole range of the theoretical use of our reason."[15] But Donald Cary Williams takes such a statement, although he does not quote Kant explicitly, to be a form of "the threat to isolate ethics from the natural world of fact and concept."[16] It is, indeed, a recognition of the difference between sensory and nonsensory experience; but only exaggerated polemics could characterize the recognition of a difference as a threat of isolation. No one ever supposed that duty was so isolated from the sense world as to stand in no relation to it. Obligation is a fact of experience to which the full weight of its unique import should be given. Every experience has its rights.

---

[15] Kant, KdpV (Reclam S), 60-61.
[16] D. C. Williams, *Jour. Phil.*, 27(1930), 515. The article is a plea for "naturalism."

In closing our treatment of this topic, we should note that a feeling of obligation is not sufficient to constitute a real obligation, any more than our feeling that railroad tracks meet at a distance proves that they really meet. Sense and moral experience alike need criticism and interpretation.

6. PSYCHOLOGY OF LAW

We have just said that experience needs interpretation. Many of our experiences are loosely connected and confused. But experience is not mere nonsense. One ancient writer said that the earth was without form and void, and the Spirit of God moved on the face of the waters. Then the formless took form. Myth-makers saw the universe as a combat between chaos and cosmos.[17] Naturally; for experience certainly contains both the rational and the irrational. Every person finds facts given in his experience and every person builds up some generalizations. "I universalize" is as surely the experience of all men as "I value" or "I ought." Sometimes we feel blindly, but sometimes we think. This rational factor in moral experience we call moral law.

There have been those who have overemphasized the rational factor. Socrates taught that knowledge is virtue; yet common experience shows that knowledge does not generate virtue. A university library reports that books on theoretical ethics are more frequently stolen than those on any other subject. But, for the strongly disciplined will of Socrates, knowledge of the right led directly to right action. Schelling shared the psychology of Socrates when he wrote, "Give man the consciousness of what he is and he will soon learn

---

[17] See Brightman, "Pre-scientific Conceptions of the Universe," in Cleveland, MSK, 15-30.

to be what he ought to be."[18] Many hopeful idealists have come to disillusionment through reliance on this estimate of the magical power of reason.

The deepest insight into human nature leads to a different view. Whatever one may think about the technical theology involved, the Christian doctrine of original sin expressed the truth that there is something fundamentally unreasonable about man. Who will say that there is no basis for Karl Barth's statement that "the problem of ethics is the sickness of man, yes, his sickness unto death"?[19] Kant, with all his respect for reason, pointed out *das radikale Böse* ("the radical evil") in human nature, which deviates from the maxim of morality even when we know that we are doing it. Edgar Allan Poe's essay on "The Imp of the Perverse," the tendency in us to be unreasonable simply for the sake of being unreasonable, expresses the truth. Politicians, conservative religionists, emotionalists, pragmatists, mystics, artists, poets, sinners, and cynics, often tend to doubt the significance of reason, although in different degrees and on different grounds. The fact of this doubt, however ill-grounded it may be, is just as truly a fact as is the existence of science and philosophy. Psychology treats it as a complex of impulses, reflexes, instincts, and habits, largely due to our animal ancestry, our social environment, and our subconscious depths.

But it is just as erroneous to overemphasize the tendencies to irrational lawlessness in human nature as to overemphasize the tendencies to be guided by rational laws. Sometimes, if not always, rational processes control the irrational. They can inhibit the undesirable,

---

[18] Schelling, *Werke*, I, 81.
[19] Cited in *Jahrbücher der Philosophie*, 3(1927), 177, by Kurt Kesseler.

select the desirable, and guide the movement of consciousness toward a chosen goal. Were this not so, the simplest act of taking a book out of a library and reading it, or of crossing the street, would be impossible.

Now, ethics is based on this fact of purposive control by rational principles. Wherever such control exists, it is possible to discover the reasons for it and to criticize and examine them. Critical thought about rational control is among the most important data of ethics. The fact that human beings sometimes guide their conduct by ideas and ideals is just as certain a fact as is sense experience. As R. B. Perry rightly remarks, moral life is impossible without a degree of intelligence. Hence control by rational laws belongs with value and obligation as empirical subject matter for ethics. Those who reduce ethics to mere convention or tribal *mores* omit these experiences from consideration.

7. AFFECTIVE CONSCIOUSNESS

An important part of our consciousness of value, of obligation, and of law is our affective consciousness, the awareness of pleasure and pain, or, as it used to be called, the sensibility. The psychology of the affective or emotional consciousness is far from thoroughly understood, but certain aspects of it are of great importance for ethics.

First of all, we should note the theory of psychological hedonism.[20] It was made famous by Jeremy Bentham, who said, "For a man not to pursue what he deems likely to produce to him the greatest sum of enjoyment, is in the very nature of things impossible."[21] While

---

[20] Not to be confused with the hedonism mentioned in Chap. I. That was ethical hedonism, a theory about what we *ought* to do; this is psychological hedonism, and is a theory about what we *must necessarily* do.

[21] Bentham, DE, I, 13.

ethical hedonism teaches that pleasure is the only good end, psychological hedonism holds that it is the only possible end of action. According to it, the only motive a man can have is his own pleasure. Psychologists and ethicists (including hedonists) now almost unanimously agree that this is false. While it *may* be that an awareness of pleasure accompanies all our choices, yet some choices are so painful that this is questionable. At any rate, it is certainly not true that our actual motive is always our own pleasure. Often we think nothing about our own pleasure in making a choice; if it be said that pleasure is our subconscious motive, it may be replied that we are concerned in ethics only with our conscious choice and its conscious motive. We cannot be held responsible for the subconscious, except in so far as it is influenced by conscious choice. In actual conscious experience man sometimes, as in acts of sacrifice, deliberately chooses what he believes is not pleasurable. Often our interest is in the act itself or the end sought or in the person or persons to be affected rather than in the way we are going to feel ourselves. Psychological hedonism, then, is false and its supporters have to maintain, as G. K. Chesterton points out, such absurdities as that a man is self-indulgent if he wants to be burned at the stake.[22] The assertion that everyone desires his own happiness really boils down to the truism that everyone desires what he desires.[23]

A second important fact about affective consciousness is the distinction between pleasure and happiness. When we speak of pleasure, we think of immediate, present, and (usually) sensuous satisfaction. When we speak of happiness, we mean a consciousness of the enduring satisfactions of our whole nature. Pleasure is

---

[22] Cited by Urban, FOE, 80.
[23] Simmel, MW, I, 391.

a matter of feeling; happiness concerns the whole of living. Thus pleasure is called fleeting, while happiness is permanent, so long as one conforms to the conditions which render it possible. Pleasure might be exclusively sensuous, but happiness could not be; for it includes the spiritual life—knowledge, imagination, worship, appreciation of beauty, and character. Pleasure and happiness are, however, alike in one respect, often called the paradox of hedonism, namely, that each comes most satisfactorily to those who are not seeking for it directly. We become happy, not by determining to be happy, nor by aiming at happiness, but by doing things that are worth doing and forgetting ourselves. It is not obvious *why* a person who is trying to be reasonable should find happiness in his reasonableness, and should cease to be happy if he sought happiness at the expense of reasonableness. But, although the *why* is not clear, the fact is there. It is an ultimate reality of experience.

A third aspect of the affective consciousness is the part that painful experiences play in moral development. Some critics believe that pain predominates over pleasure in the life of those who have done the most for mankind. Saints, philosophers, scientists, reformers, and liberators have been abused, ostracized, or killed by an unappreciative world. Everyone who advocates an unpopular minority opinion is made to suffer for it in one way or another. It is almost impossible to be honest in modern civilization without having to pay for it by much personal misery. Paul Rée found it hard to decide whether goodness or evil is more painful.[24] But there is a radical difference, in meaning for the sufferer as well as in results, between pain that leads to personal

---

[24] Rée, UME, 132. The hedonist Schlick recognizes that pain has the function of preserving men from shallowness. FE, 100.

and social values and pain that destroys them. It is harder to bear meaningless and needless pain than to endure any amount of suffering that actually is leading one's cause to success.

8. PSYCHOLOGICAL MECHANISM

Thus far we have spoken of specific psychological processes which are data for ethics. An additional datum of very great importance is the well-grounded fact that a large part of our conscious life consists of involuntary psychological mechanisms, and is influenced by other mechanisms, both physiological and unconscious.

The mechanistic aspect is illustrated by the influence of the physiological organism on consciousness (physiological psychology), the fact that the control of consciousness over the organism is limited by the habits of the organism (e. g., "conditioned reflexes"), and the (not yet clearly determined) extent to which the so-called subconscious and unconscious processes affect normal consciousness. The volume of fact thus briefly indicated is vast and is being increased by investigators in endocrinology, behaviorism, psychoanalysis, and abnormal psychology. Let us take a single illustration, the familiar case of posthypnotic suggestion. The hypnotized subject is told to appear in a public place and perform a ridiculous act at a set hour tomorrow. He does so, but he believes he did it freely and assigns a false, if fairly plausible, set of reasons for his act (rationalization).

The mass of evidence for psychological mechanisms has made a great impression on the modern mind and raises the question whether voluntary choice in accordance with "value, obligation, and law" really plays any causally directive part in life. Is it all mere rationalization? The problem takes the form: Is free, effective, voluntary, rational choice possible?

9. WILL AND FREEDOM

If choice is not possible, the science of ethics is not possible. If rational, purposive choice is not effective in the control of life, goodness is not possible. When we discuss the nature of will and freedom, therefore, we are dealing with an absolutely central and essential foundation of ethics.

For an act to be moral it must be voluntary. Voluntary choice, or will, is the heart of every ethical situation. There are many consequences which follow from an act of choice without being themselves chosen. When Austria sent her ultimatum to Serbia in 1914, she did not deliberately choose the state of Austria in 1931. When the United States adopted the Eighteenth Amendment to the National Constitution, she did not choose to create the business of bootlegging. It cannot be denied that these unchosen consequences are of ethical importance, for as soon as they arise or can be foreseen they create a problem toward which an ethical attitude may be taken. But until such an attitude is taken, that is, until some choice is made, there is nothing ethical (morally good or bad) about the situation, so far as the agent's responsibility at the time of the original act is concerned. The Austria of 1914 or the United States of 1918 cannot justly be held responsible for what it could not foresee and did not choose.[25] There is no moral situation where there is no choice. The essence of a moral situation is will, and the essence of will is choice.

Now will is a fact, whatever our theory of it may be. It is the experience of choosing from among real or

[25] See Chap. VIII.

supposed possibilities one which becomes the actual purpose or goal of conduct. The scholastics defined liberty as the *facultas eligendi* ("the faculty of choosing"). If we substitute the more fashionable term "function" for the less fashionable "faculty," the scholastic phrase expresses exactly what we mean by will. The recent tendency to define the will as the mind in action is a case of obscurantism; for the term "action" is ambiguous and question-begging. If it means all action whatever—sleepwalking, reflex action, habit—it is incorrect as a definition of will, for the acts named are not willed. If it means only action which is consciously chosen, it conceals that meaning under a misleading label. There is aversion on the part of some psychologists to recognizing the rôle of choice, partly because choice is not behavioristically observable and partly because it conjures up the problem of freedom of the will, which leads to philosophy; and some psychologists will pay almost any price to avoid being led thither. But choice reëmerges as attention or set or attitude or selection and we are back where we were, namely, in choice.

Lotze holds that approval is an essential element in will. You choose, he thinks, what at the time you approve; although in the case of the most perverse choices, the word "approve" must be given a very special meaning. Certainly, not all choices are in agreement with what our best judgment, even at the moment of choice, approves.

Driesch has recently proposed the simple theory that a free will is the act of saying "yes" or "no" to a given content.[26] Whether this is an oversimplification or not, it represents a factor in every genuine act of will. The consent which one gives or refuses to give to a situation determines both the moral quality of one's act and the

---

[26] Driesch, MET, 40-69, and his paper in Brightman, P6IC, 1-9.

direction of one's further development. Driesch's theory appears acceptable to the present writer, although it has been criticized[27] as not giving sufficient place to the creative power of will. But the fact seems to be that our will has powers of selection and therefore of direction, without possessing the divine attribute of creativeness.

An important trait of acts of will is their unique combination of necessity and possibility. The necessity is implied in the givenness of the situation, the psychological mechanisms involved, and the necessary consequences of the act. Unless there were a situation with a definite structure, knowable psychological mechanisms, and causal laws guaranteeing connections with the past and effects in the future, our will neither would have anything to deal with, nor could it deal with what it had in any effective or responsible way. But in addition to necessity, possibility is also a feature of experience. When one makes a voluntary choice, there is normally first an inhibition of impulsive tendencies, followed by deliberation regarding possible courses of action, and then by a decision to select one possibility for actualization.[28] The highest moral experience would consist of a continual choosing of the "best" possibilities. Some theories emphasize possibility without necessity, and thus have a romantic and unscientific character; others emphasize necessity without possibility, and thus ignore the central fact of moral experience. Both elements are essential.

Determinism—the exclusive belief in necessity, which regards all supposed possibility as disguised necessity—was the predominant view in the Nineteenth Century

[27] By R. T. Flewelling.

[28] "Every idea of freedom rests on this fact that a possible is thinkable in addition to the actual." Simmel, MW, I, 286.

after the freewill theories of Kant and Fichte had
yielded to the advances of mechanistic science. But the
number of advocates of freedom has greatly increased
of late. Palmer, Bowne, James, Hudson, Spaulding,
Hocking, Urban, Simmel, Bergson, Driesch, and Haeber-
lin are some of the recent writers who defend freedom.
Heisenberg and others are leading physicists to doubt
the absolute validity of mechanical causation. On the
other hand, determinism has continued to exert a wide
scientific and popular influence through its methodolog-
ical place in the sciences, especially in the popular sciences of sociology, psychoanalysis (except for Jung
and Adler), and behaviorism.

The effect of the theory of freedom on the general
theory of ethics has been exaggerated both by determinists and by their critics. It is true that only a
freedomist could hold to Fichte's ethics and only a
determinist could build an ethics on psychological
hedonism. But one's theory of freedom often makes
strangely little difference in the type of ethical theory
developed. George Herbert Palmer believes in freedom
and Walter G. Everett in determinism; yet both are wise
and good men and their ethical theories are indistin-
guishable. Epicurus held to freedom and had a less
elevated ethics than did Spinoza, who held to determinism. But Kant, who held to freedom, had an ethics
still loftier than Spinoza's.

Freedomists and determinists have both pointed with
horror to the calamitous ethical consequences which are
bound to follow from a rejection of the true theory.
But we keep on making choices, whatever our theory,
and it must be granted that the evil consequences have
often failed to occur as predicted. Some believers in
freedom are good men and some are bad. Some determinists are good men and some are bad. A Spinoza or a

Calvin lives as though he were free to be his best; and a Kant or a James lives as though he were determined (by moral idealism). The most significant fact for ethics is that men make moral choices, regard themselves and others as responsible, recognize distinctions between better and worse, and, in short, act as if they were free. At this stage in our investigation, then, it suffices to point to the actual experience of purposive choice as fundamental to morals, leaving to Chapter XVI a more metaphysical consideration of the place of freedom in ethical theory and moral living.

10. The Unity of Consciousness

If we turn now from the various specific processes and traits that we have been considering to a view of personal consciousness as a whole, the first impression is one of its complexity and even disconnectedness. Not only are there cases of multiple personality, but even in so-called normal consciousness there are inner conflicts, contradictions, and irrational impulses. In a sense, it is this very variety and contradiction that is the basis of the moral life. We are able to take an attitude which surveys this whole variety and reduces it to a semblance of order, by virtue of "the power of the self to divide itself, as it were, into different parts."[29] Moral issues arouse a wide range of passions and one is often almost torn asunder psychologically by the complexity of the moral consciousness. Moreover, the differences among individuals due to heredity, environment, habits, choices, and psychological type, add to social complexity and so to the complexity of each person's consciousness.

But complexity and confusion are not the whole story of the human mind. Each individual mind is a unity

[29] Simmel, MW, I, 181.

in some sense. This statement is only confirmed by dual or multiple personality, for each of the two or more personalities in such a phenomenon is itself a unity; if not, there would be no sense in talking of two or more personalities.

Every conscious being is a complex unity, a *unitas multiplex,* to use William Stern's phrase. All of the complex data of any particular conscious being belong together in a unique way; "my" experience is mine only and cannot be handed over to anyone else. Not only do the present data hang together uniquely, but they are also connected uniquely with past and future data by linkages of memory and of anticipation. A present complex consciousness may be called a datum self. The whole self is the whole range of present, past, and future experiences that belong with a datum self by virtue of conscious linkages. Morality may be said to consist largely in an intelligent interest in the whole self on the part of the datum self. A person is a self capable of moral experience. Without the personal unity of a whole self, moral responsibility and moral development would be alike impossible. In this sense all ethics must be personalistic. The unity of each individual person is, of course, developed in a social environment in interaction with a physical world. But in all its changes the self continues to be the same self, not in the sense of possessing an unchangeable character or essence, but in the sense of experiencing its own unity-in-diversity. The emphasis on the unity of the self in this discussion is in harmony with self-psychology, purposive psychology, and *Gestalt* psychology.[30]

---

[30] Fuller treatments of the nature of the self are found in the following discussions by the present author: ITP, Chap. VI; POI, Chap. I; "The Dialectical Unity of Consciousness and the Metaphysics of Religion," in Ryle, P7IC, 70-77; and "The Finite Self," in Barrett, CIA, 169-195.

Selected Bibliography

Note: It unfortunately happens that the conscious processes of most importance for ethics have been least satisfactorily investigated by psychology.

Allers, WSP (excellent recent survey in German); Drake, PC, Part I; Dresser, ETH, Chap. IV; Garvie, CIHS, 209-258 (from the Protestant standpoint); Hadfield, PAM (a good treatment of applications of psychoanalysis); Hartmann, PSB (a thorough study in German); Leighton, ISO, Part III; Mezes, EDE, Part I; Seth, SEP, Introd., Chap. II; Sherman, MS (a good general survey); Sutherland, OGMI (one of the older standards); Urban, FOE, Chap. II; Westermarck, ODMI (a great sociological study); Wundt, ETG (also in English translation).

CHAPTER IV

THE SYSTEM OF MORAL LAWS

1. How Moral Laws Are Derived from Experience

THE present age is one in which laws of all kinds are being criticized, whether Newton's or Volstead's. This empirical and pragmatic era questions all universal rational principles. But the tendency to deny law and to reduce experience to a series of particular facts without universal meanings does not do justice to actual human life. Embedded in all human consciousness, as far as our knowledge goes, there have been universal principles as well as particular facts. We do not seem to be able to experience without generalizing. While our generalizations need correction, so also does our view of the facts, as experiments in the psychology of the witnessing of crimes or unusual events have repeatedly proved.

This trait is especially true of our moral experience. We not only experience this X to be good, but we also experience the moral law: All X's are good. If there is to be a science of ethics, it must discover and correlate the moral laws which are true.

Such laws must at least be consistent with each other and with the rest of experience. Hence those who, like Wundt, hold that ethics has to *find* the norms to which the phenomena of the will conform, rather than to prescribe them, are only partly right.[1] That they are partly right follows from the fact that all science must be derived from experience, and that the moral values, laws, and "norms" must, in some way, be found in

---

[1] Wundt, ETG, III, 132.

experience, if we are to know anything about them at all. But that they are only partly right follows from the fact that our actual experiences of value, obligation, and law are contradictory. Our will does not naturally strive for a single consistent good nor in a consistent way. The task of ethical science, then, is to construct, out of the data of experience, a coherent system of laws which does not lie in the mind ready for use, but which needs to be created by scientific thought. As in all cases of the progress of science, hypotheses will need to be devised for the consistent understanding and control of experience. When by this method a system has been built, however tentatively, it becomes our moral ideal and has a right to *prescribe* the direction of further development. Ethics, as we showed in Chapter I, is normative. It prescribes; it does not merely describe. But the prescription must follow and be based on an objective description of the facts of experience.

If normative prescription were not necessary, we should have only to take the goals of conduct from un-criticized experience. There have been attempts to do this. Many have held that the mind contains funda-mental, self-evident intuitions, or immediate insights into basic moral principles, so that the ethical scientist has only to "read off" these intuitions in order to arrive at a knowledge of right and wrong. This theory—intuitionalism, as it is called—very often regards the fundamental intuitions as the voice of the Divine Being, or as the reflection of eternal values. But, while intui-tionalism is based on the truth that experience is the source of all knowledge, it overlooks the fact that think-ing is one of the most significant aspects of experience and that no intuition, whether moral or mathematical or sensory, can be trusted as leading to truth about

conduct or fact until it has been criticized and tested by
the way in which it fits into the rest of our experience.[2]
Appeal to intuition, even when made by a Max Scheler,
really reduces to appeal to the deep-rooted present convictions of the individual and society. These deep-
rooted convictions may be no more than the predominant social practice of the age. In this case, the appeal
to intuition is simply a disguised form of the appeal
to social authority, which, as every thoughtful person
recognizes, needs criticism by the independent mind.

A curiously opposite turn occurs when thinkers like
Mr. Bertrand Russell, who wish to break away from all
fixed intuitions and petrified authorities, assert that
the moral end is given in the desires of man. This view
is naturally acceptable to the average person who
"wants what he wants when he wants it," as well as to
the psychoanalyst who knows the evils of suppressed
desire. But to find the end and aim of moral living
in the realization of our desires must mean one of two
things: either the realization of all of our desires or
the realization of some only. It is unnecessary to abuse
the person who wishes to realize all of his desires by
telling him that his aim is base, depraved, sensuous, and
egoistic; rather, it is sufficient to show him that it is
impossible. Our desires are so contradictory that they
could not all be realized without canceling each other
and destroying us in the process. Hence the realization
of some desires only is the sole possible course. But
then we have to choose among our desires; and if we
are to choose solely on the basis of the strength of the
desire, we are back in the realm of intuition. What
we desire most strongly, however, may turn out to be
the worst thing for us. To speak in vulgar American,

---

[2] For "Sources of the Authority of Ideals" see Brightman, POI,
Chap. IV.

our "hunch" may be fatal, and in the stock market usually is. What gives us the greatest "kick" may be, both individually and socially, despicable. If there is to be any approach to reasonable living, there must be a rational selection and criticism of our desires with inhibition of some and stimulation of others. Somehow reason has to prescribe "measure," as the Greeks said, to our desires.

Moral laws, then, cannot be based on intuition, authority, or desire alone. All intuitions, authorities, and desires—in fact, the whole field of our actual and possible experience, as far as may be—needs to be surveyed and criticized by reason if we are to have the slightest hope of attaining moral truth. As Haeckel (who was not always wise) wisely said, "Reason is the highest good of man."[3] Or (quoting von Hartmann), "Reason is the highest criterion which stands at the disposal of man, the highest subjective court."[4]

But to appeal to reason for our moral science is not to depart from experience. The sharp separation which Kant made between the empirical and the transcendental, going back to Aristotle's division of theoretical from practical, was useful for purposes of abstraction, but it has done much damage. The basis of moral knowledge is total moral experience; reason has no existence except in the actual conscious experience of reasonable persons.

Reason, however, is a special ideal function of experience; the function which surveys, orders, unifies, and systematizes. Because this function exists, we have built up music and art, which are structures of reason no less than mathematics and logic. In fact, music is, in a sense, mathematics made audible, as color (and so

[3] Cited by Fabricius, AG, 28.
[4] Hartmann, PSB, 325.

painting) is mathematics made visible. Sound and color and feeling without reason are not art. Through reason's work on experience, physics, chemistry, and all the sciences have been developed. To deny the right of reason is to deny the very structure of the mind and the achievements of the highest culture.

The appeal to reason is sometimes made in a very immature fashion as a pretext for the "rationalization" of desire and for independence from real reason. The chief practical need is not so much for independence as for learning how to think. It is easier to be a rationalist than it is to reason.

Let us, therefore, state briefly the essential elements of rational thought in ethics, by means of which moral laws are derived from moral experience. The first step, as in every science, is observation; in this case, observation of experiences of value, obligation, and law as voluntarily chosen or controlled, and of other experiences related to them. The next step is generalization, the formulation of such general likenesses or tendencies as appear. But the generalizations from moral experience are certain to contain contradictions, as our summary of the sociological data showed. Hence the next step is criticism, with a view to eliminating these contradictions. But mere absence of contradiction is not enough; the materials of moral experience call for action, forward movement of life, and richness of meaning. Hence there is necessary a final stage, which may be called interpretation; this consists of two phases, hypothesis and systematization. If moral experience is to be understood and interpreted, ethics, like every other science, needs to have recourse to hypothesis—a "guess" as to the probable rational connection of our experiences. The hypothesis is tested by a twofold systematization; the practical system of living and the

theoretical system of our most general and best established hypotheses, which we call laws.

The natural scientist will doubtless approve of observation, generalization, criticism, and (with some caution) interpretation; but he will miss experiment. For
two reasons, the method of experiment is not practicable
in ethics. First: it is impossible to have a genuinely
moral situation under laboratory conditions. Significant moral situations occur in the real context of life,
not under artificial control. If an attempt were made
to have a moral "experiment," the moral character of
the situation would at once be changed as soon as the
subject knew that it was an experiment; on the other
hand, if he did not know that it was an experiment, not
only would he be treated unjustly in being experimented
on, but also the scientific need of having a trained
and intelligent subject for the experiment could not well
be met. Accurate reporting by the subject would be all
but impossible. Secondly: no moral experiment could
solve any ethical problem of what ought to be done. It
could only show what is done. For descriptive science,
what "is done" by nature is the ultimate court of
appeal; but for normative science what is done is not
equally ultimate. Critical and systematic reason must
determine whether it ought to have been done or not.
Hence the relative absence of experiment in ethics is not
so serious as appears. Life itself is the ethical experiment, and it furnishes subject matter enough.

2. Moral Law as a System

If ethics is a rational account of moral experience,
it must be a system. It cannot consist of isolated propositions, even if they are true, but of a connected whole.
Reason needs to see relations. Proof consists in showing the coherent relations of a proposition to other

propositions, to experience, and to the system of which it forms a part. Wundt's great *Ethik* has a title that corresponds exactly to the aim of our present study: *Eine Untersuchung der Tatsachen und Gesetze des sittlichen Lebens* (An Investigation of the Facts and Laws of the Moral Life). But when Wundt comes to give the normative laws, he sets them up, one after another, without proof and without system. This procedure may be a statement of moral truths, but it is not ethical science. A science is more than a list of laws; it is a system. Certain types of ethical theory (such as hedonism) have been atomistic, not organic, and so have failed to develop a true system. Bentham says, for instance, that "every act whereby pleasure is reaped is, all consequences apart, good."[5] But a more rational insight perceives that no act can be judged to be either good or bad apart from the whole—the system—to which it belongs. Goodness is not a property of isolated acts. Pleasure which satisfies a good man is indeed good; but the pleasure which attends the malice of a bad man is bad. Schleiermacher criticized not only the hedonists (as most writers do) but even Aristotle for making "the *summum bonum* only an aggregate,"[6] that is, only a collection of parts instead of a living whole—a mechanical mixture instead of a compound.

Why should moral truth be viewed as a system? For the same reason that geometry is a system; or for the same reason that a human organism needs to be studied as a living whole, namely, that isolated assertions lack support, but truths functioning in living relation to other truths are understood and proved. The extreme opposite of system is chaos; and chaos is both meaningless and, as Urban points out, incapable even of being

---

[5] Bentham, DE, I, 58.
[6] Schleiermacher, *Werke*, I, 81.

communicated to others.[7]   All truth partakes of system
and of wholeness.   Lessing once said, "I do not know
whether it is one's duty to sacrifice happiness and life to
truth.   But I do know that, if one wants to teach truth,
it is one's duty to teach it whole or not at all."[8]   The
poet Uhland wrote lines which may be translated thus:

"O World, do not perish, and fall not, O Sky,
  Till we are together, my dearest and I."[9]

The poet saw that even the most passionate love needs
the support of a system, a World and a Sky—it does not
stand alone!   Generalizing, we may say that every value
needs a system.

This principle has been recognized by philosophers
of very different periods and schools.   Plato, Aristotle,
Spinoza, Kant, and Hegel were the great minds that
contributed most to its development.   It is the essence
of the logic of Bradley and Bosanquet.   Schleiermacher
expresses it well when he speaks of ethics as "a self-con-
tained whole, whose parts can be understood only from
and through the whole."[10]   Hastings Rashdall not long
ago reaffirmed the same principle, when he said that
"the supreme ethical precept must consist of an harmonious and self-consistent system of precepts."[11]   Recently, it has been excellently, although somewhat too
abstractly, explained in H. J. Paton's work, *The Good
Will*.[12]   "The ideal," says John Dewey, "means a sense
of these encompassing continuities with their infinite
reach."[13]

---

[7] Urban, IW, 432.
[8] *Cit.* Treitschke, DL, 127.
[9] Welt, geh' nicht unter, Himmel, fall' nicht ein,
  Eh' ich mag bei der Liebsten sein.
[10] Schleiermacher, *Werke*, I, 248.
[11] Rashdall, TGE, I, 111.
[12] Paton, GW.
[13] Dewey, HNC, 330.

3. The Moral Laws: Their Systematic Structure

In view of the fact that a system incompletely grasped is a system misunderstood, and of the companion fact that every system must be presented in a gradual exposition, there is always the danger that every step of the way will fix misunderstandings in mind which only the completed whole can correct; but by the time the completed whole is reached the misunderstandings have become too habitual to be uprooted. In order to avoid this danger as much as possible, we here present a preliminary synopsis of the entire system, to which frequent reference should be made as the study of the detailed laws progresses:

System of Moral Laws

(The laws are numbered consecutively, as throughout the book.)

I. The Formal Laws.
  1. The Logical Law (consistent will).
  2. The Law of Autonomy (self-imposed ideals are obligatory).

II. The Axiological Laws.
  3. The Axiological Law (consistent values).
  4. The Law of Consequences (consider and approve foreseeable consequences).
  5. The Law of the Best Possible.
  6. The Law of Specification (develop values relevant to the situation).
  7. The Law of the Most Inclusive End.
  8. The Law of Ideal Control (control empirical values by ideal values).

III. The Personalistic Laws.
  9. The Law of Individualism.

10. The Law of Altruism.
11. The Law of the Ideal of Personality (judge and guide all acts by an ideal of personality).

The foregoing table is a mere outline, lacking in content. Yet a hint has been added as to the meaning of each law, where it was not self-evident from the very name of the law; and the reader who finds himself perplexed is advised to refer ahead for explanation to the later chapters in which each law is stated explicitly and discussed.

Even at this stage certain traits of this system of moral laws may be observed. It develops from abstract formalism to concrete value and still more concrete personality. The Formal Laws have to do with the will alone, and state the principles to which a reasonable will must conform irrespective of the ends (values) which it is trying to realize. The Axiological Laws show the principles which the values that a good will is seeking ought to embody. The Personalistic Laws show what ought to follow in conduct from the fact that value is always an experience of persons. It is to be noted that each of the three divisions culminates in a theory of the moral ideal: the Law of Autonomy asserts that self-imposed ideals are obligatory; the Law of Ideal Control says that all empirical values ought to be controlled by ideal values, thus both defining and refining the quality of ideals; while the Law of the Ideal of Personality makes the ideal more concrete and, as we shall see, more flexible. The Formal Laws may be called the principles of form or of subjective ethics, or the ethics of sincerity. The Axiological Laws may be called the principles of content or of objective ethics, or the ethics of achievement. The Personalistic Laws are the concrete synthesis of form and content, of subjective and objective ethics, in the ethics of personal and social idealism.

This system of moral laws is new. It is an attempt to make ethics more scientific than it has been. But it is not a mere novelty, or a fantastic invention, for it undertakes to include the contributions, to supplement the incompleteness, and to criticize the errors of previous systems of ethics. It can be shown that many systems have built on one or two laws alone, at the expense of others. Most of the differences in ethical "schools" are overemphases of special aspects of the ethical life embodied in these laws; and there is an ever-present danger of dealing with a favorite abstraction instead of with the rich fullness of life. This system seeks to profit by the lessons of the past and to move nearer to that inclusive truth which is the ideal of all science and philosophy.[14]

4. Does System Prove Ethics to Be Universal and Rational?

While, as was just said, the system here presented is new, the principle that ethics is or should be a system of law is not new. Kant said that pure reason gives man a universal law. British ethics had appealed to the judgment of the "impartial spectator" (Bishop Butler and Adam Smith)[15] before Kant. What the impartial spectator thinks, being guided by reason rather than by special interest in either party, is just and right. In ways as different as Bentham's laws and the principles

[14] Max Scheler, one of the most fruitful of recent writers on ethics (although not the clearest or most precise), has made the mistake of trying to substitute intuition of concrete values for law or system as the basic ethical principle. See his treatment in *Jahrbücher der Philosophie*, 2(1914), 89-90.

[15] The "impartial spectator," according to Jacobi, appears first in Butler's *Analogy of Religion*. See Dilthey, LS, 125. See also his GW, II, 1.

of intuitionists, rational universality has been asserted.
Most ethicists hold to it in some form.

On the other hand, doubts have been raised about the
existence of universal and rational ethical principles.
"There are no absolute values or norms, and no categorical imperatives in ethics"; this is the belief of two
such scholars as Ehrenfels and Adickes,[16] and their
view is typical of a fairly large body of opinion. We
have already noted Lévy-Bruhl's similar position. Let
us consider some of the reasons for an opinion of this
sort.

It is pointed out that ethics must be based on psychology and sociology and that these sciences reveal no universal recognition by all men of any absolute moral laws.
If law means agreement, there are no laws.

Moreover, it is argued that morality is always an
individual matter, and that general rules therefore fail
to do justice to the individual factor. This point was
raised by Schleiermacher[17] and is re-enforced by the
results of individual psychology, as well as by the insistence of pragmatists that every situation has a unique
value of its own which can only be ascertained by experience and not by any general formula ("moral pluralism").[18]

It is also seriously urged by some that feeling is a
better guide to good conduct than any system of ethics.
Herbart once said that "hard maxims break at the first
visible transgression, and even before they have broken
they do harm through the self-deception which they
cause, for we tend to keep our lesser transgressions

---

[16] From Adickes' article in *Zeitschrift für Philosophie und philosophische Kritik*, 116(1899), 7.

[17] Schleiermacher, *Werke*, I, 111.

[18] S. P. Lamprecht, "The Need for a Pluralistic Emphasis in
Ethics." *Jour. Phil.*, 17(1920), 561-572. Compare Chap. X of *Moral
Laws* on "The Law of Specification."

away from the maxims. But we do not need to keep anything away from tender feeling, which is able to divine the smallest needs and to overcome the greatest obstacles."[19] The same point of view is expressed by Paul Ernst in an imaginary dialogue between Immanuel Kant and an unmarried mother, in which the latter says: "There is no law of morality, but God tells each one what he may and what he may not do."[20] Eduard von Hartmann often raised the question whether woman's emotional nature allowed her to have a rational ethics; but there seems to be no cogent reason, save masculine prejudice, for confining this question to woman.

Are these arguments conclusive? Only a preliminary answer can be given now; the laws will speak for themselves as they are expounded. But the objections on their face are not final. If, despite the facts to which they refer, other sciences, including psychology and logic, have been developed, why is ethics impossible? The fundamental questions at stake are: Whether intelligent conduct is better than unintelligent, and Whether any principles of intelligence in conduct can be defined. All of the considerations just mentioned show that there are difficulties in being intelligent, which is no new truth. But is not the only remedy for these difficulties more intelligence?

It is important to guard against a misunderstanding in this connection. When we use words like "system," "universal," and "rational," we are in danger of being taken to mean something final, absolute, and unchangeable. Yet it would be a gross error to take the words in

---

[19] Herbart, *Werke*, VIII, 66. Herbart fails to note that tender feeling protects its favorites from moral law far more effectively than does the self-deception of the moralist.

[20] Ernst, EG, 53.

this sense. "System" means a logically connected whole or body of principles; "universal" means applicable to all cases; and "rational" means consistent and coherent. But no one who has a clear conception of the nature and function of human reason would suppose that a universal and rational system was incapable of improvement. The expression "universal rational system" is a condensed way of saying, "The most connected body of principles that I am now able to formulate, which I believe to be applicable always and everywhere." It would, however, be absurd for anyone to make his present ability, or the present ability of the entire human race, an absolute standard for all time. Humanity is accumulating new experiences and knowledge which constantly causes revision of present systems. The very nature of reason, which is to understand experience as a coherent whole, means that no finite mind can ever be completely reasonable. Rationality is a principle of growth and movement of life toward higher and deeper levels of insight. It is dogmatism and not rationalism that is static. The laws which are presented in this book are principles of rational development, not rigid prescriptions of specific acts which are supposed to be eternally right. Doubtless there are other reasonable ways of describing the moral ideal. Doubtless the laws here defined can and will be improved. It is only through confidence that reason is more than any insight which it has yet attained that a system of moral laws can be proposed.

5. Does the System of Laws Distinguish Between Good and Evil?

A further preliminary problem should be raised before we pass to the discussion of the laws in detail. If a theory of ethics is to fulfill its function, it must distinguish in principle between good and evil. We must ask whether the proposed system of laws fulfills that function.

It must be granted that some of the laws, taken by themselves, are as truly laws of evil as of good. If one wishes to be maliciously and successfully evil, one will have to obey the Logical Law; his will must be consistently evil. The Law of Consequences is observed by the prudent sinner as much as by the thoughtful saint. The Law of Individualism is very dear to egoist and lawless lover of "personal liberty." But these considerations are only proof of the central contention of the present chapter, namely, that the moral laws are to be taken as a system. Poor Richard advised the development of character by the practice of a virtue a day. But such moral atomism is futile; if one virtue is being violated while another is being developed, there is no gain. Morality is rational; and reason demands that the moral ideal shall be taken as a whole.

Now, if we take the laws as a whole or system, we have a complicated task, yet not an impossible one, and not so complicated in principle as the science of geometry or even the art of dressmaking. And we have a very useful guide for the analysis and evaluation of moral situations. The fact that it is a rational system means that it is beyond good and evil in the merely conventional sense; it makes essential reasonableness, and not custom or social approval, the criterion of right conduct. If we were to hold that right is not more reasonable than wrong, and that there is literally just as much reason for doing wrong as for doing right, then we should have given up the appeal to intelligence and placed ourselves beyond the pale of argument. But if we appeal to reason, we appeal to something that is genuinely universal and is acknowledged by every normal mind.   Rational system, then, is the only trustworthy foundation of ethics and criterion of morality.

Selected Bibliography

The problem discussed in the chapter, being a new approach to ethics, is not treated directly in the literature. However, a closely related standpoint is discussed in Hobhouse, RG (especially Chap. V), and in Paton, GW (Book V).   Everett, MV, 320-334, is a sane critique of moral skepticism.   Fite, MP, presents in admirable style a view opposed to that of the text.

CHAPTER V

1. THE LOGICAL LAW

1. THE METHOD OF PRESENTATION

FOR the sake of clarity and ready reference each Law will be stated explicitly at the outset of the chapter in which it is discussed, together with a brief explanation of its place in the system of Moral Laws, its proof, and its derivation from experience and history. The author of a book may take advantage of his readers by leading them to a destination known to him, but not to them. It is hoped that the method which is chosen may to some extent avoid that unfairness.

2. THE POSTULATE OF ALL MORAL LAWS

Underlying all Moral Laws is a postulate which should be recognized clearly, namely, that there are many selves who have moral experience in interaction with each other and with a common environment. In Chapter III the general nature of those experiences was outlined on the basis of the sociological and the psychological data. We there found that experiences of obligation, of value, and of law are the most essential moral data. We experience values; and we feel that we ought to achieve value in accordance with law. It is the function of ethics to build a rational interpretation of the situation described in this postulate. Ethics does not try to prove that there is moral experience or that there are other selves and a world; it postulates them as given, and goes on to formulate the normative laws of moral experience in such an environment as we find.

97

3. THE LOGICAL LAW AND ITS PLACE IN THE SYSTEM

The Logical Law is stated as follows: *All persons ought to will logically;* i. e., *each person ought to will to be free from self-contradiction and to be consistent in his intentions.* *A moral person does not both will and not will the same ends; this property of a moral person is called his formal rightness.*

As was pointed out in Chapter IV, the Logical Law is the first of the Formal Laws. To call it formal means that it has to do only with the will or intent, not with the act or the content of the will. Let us suppose a case in which a person's consciousness is confined to a choice between two ideas, and he has no other ideas at all. Let the two ideas be, "I will to murder John Jones" and "I do not will to murder John Jones." As far as the Logical Law is concerned, the person knows only that it is wrong for him weakly to entertain both purposes in his mind approvingly. But the Logical Law gives him no light as to whether murder is good or bad; so that he would obey the Logical Law equally well whichever way he decided. Even in real life, where the artificial conditions of this illustration do not obtain, the Logical Law alone would leave unanswered the question about the moral value of murder. It would tell us only that we ought to assume a consistent will-attitude toward murder. Its primary function is negative: the elimination of contradiction.

Thus we see what is meant by the formal character of this Law. It tells us what is wrong in our will; but the fact that a will ought not to be inconsistent does not imply that a consistent will is as good as it ought to be. The Logical Law, therefore, is a necessary part of the moral system, but it clearly needs to be supplemented by other laws if we are to have adequate standards for determining right and wrong. The achievement of purely formal and subjective consistency in our will is no mean task. But, while necessary, it is not sufficient.

4. PROOF OF THE LOGICAL LAW

In general, the Moral Laws are proved by showing that, if you assume them to be false, impossible or irrational consequences will follow. In the case of the Logical Law, let us suppose that it is not true. Then there is no obligation to will logically and there is no moral objection to a self-contradictory will. Now, a self-contradictory will is a will that chooses both to do and not to do a given act at a given time. A person who does this is in the curious position of choosing twice, yet not choosing at all. His choice is meaningless, for the same reason that +5 added to —5 equals zero. If the Logical Law were not true, there could be no real willing at all, either right or wrong. Therefore, since its contradictory is impossible, the Law is true.

5. ITS BASIS IN EXPERIENCE AND HISTORY

We have begun, in accordance with our method, by a statement of the Law. However, a law in such a form is not found in ordinary experience. It is a product of thought about experience. Hence, if we are to understand the Law, we shall need to indicate how it is derived from its basis both in the moral experience of the race and in the reflective thought about morality that has taken shape in the history of ethics.

It is evident that this Law is not based on the whole concrete range of moral experience. It is an abstraction from our experiences of will, obligation, and reason taken in connection with each other and criticized. We are justified in concentrating on the will, for all moral experiences have the trait of being instances of chosen conduct, or voluntary acts. The will is the most essential, most fundamental, most characteristic part of personality for ethics. Goethe expressed this thought when he said:

"What can we call our own save energy, force, will? If I could tell what I owe to great predecessors and contemporaries, there would not be much else to me!"[1]

Will is even more truly our essential self than are our feelings, which we think of as peculiarly intimate. But, after all, feelings happen to us; often they come and go in accordance with almost inexplicable moods and whims. A feeling is not central in our life until it is approved and chosen by our will. Then it truly becomes a part of our life purpose. But laws of feeling are, for ethics, secondary to laws of will. This may be the reason for Fichte's remark that a theory of amiability is of the devil.

It is clear, then, both that the Law is based on experiences and also that it is based on the experiences of the greatest importance for ethics.

In the history of ethics, the need of logical consistency in the will was early recognized. Socrates laid great stress on consistent definition of moral concepts, but he did not see so clearly as did the Cynics and Stoics the central place of the will. In Book III of the *Nicomachean Ethics*, Aristotle also dwells on the fact that feelings and acts are ethical only when they are voluntary; and in Book I (1099b) he defines happiness as certain activity of the soul "in accordance with virtue." Since he defines virtue as the mean between extremes, it is evident that only a will which is consistent in seeking the mean can be good.

---

[1] *Cit.* Dünnhaupt, SSRK, 28.

Yet the principle of a consistent will is not grasped by any ancient writer as it is by Kant, who rightly made it absolutely fundamental. He formulated it as follows, calling it the basic law of the pure practical reason: "Act so that the maxim of thy will at every time might also be the principle of a universal legislation." This is the principle of consistency made emphatic. Sometimes he uses the formula: "Act from duty," in which "duty" means respect for law, that is, consistency. The famous opening sentence of the first section of his *Grundlegung zur Metaphysik der Sitten* shows how highly he values the Logical Law: "It is not possible to think of anything anywhere in the world, or even out of it, which could be regarded as good without limitation, with the single exception of a good will."

Not all writers see the absolutely fundamental character of this Law. Scholastic ethics, for instance, has made the essence of morality consist primarily "in relatione actus humani ad legem aeternam" ("in the relation of human activity to eternal law"); and only secondarily "in habitudine actus humani ad rectam rationem" ("in the attitude of human activity toward right reason"). Here right reason is made binding not for its own sake, but because of its relation to the eternal law.[2] There is full recognition of the supremacy of reason in the moral life, but it is a superhuman reason that is made the test of goodness. However, an ethics that is built on a rational interpretation of experience cannot start with the knowledge of superhuman and eternal laws; if it is to attain such knowledge, it must be at the end and not at the beginning of its investigation.

---

[2] Gury, CTM, 15 (cited from Saint Thomas). Note A. C. Knudson's criticism of the naïve argument that moral law implies a lawgiver, in DG, 229.

There have been writers who have seemed to ignore or even deny the Logical Law. Those who make consequences alone the test of goodness tend to emphasize the consistency of intention less than it deserves. Those who appeal to any principle of external or social authority as ultimate would seek to crush the inner logic of the will by force and compulsion. Nietzsche also has little use for the rational. Even a writer like Emerson has often been quoted as a foe of logic. "A foolish consistency," he said, "is the hobgoblin of little minds." But did he mean that all consistency is foolish? Is it not much truer to the spirit of Emerson to say that he meant the petty consistency which refuses to learn anything new or to change any opinion once adopted than that he meant the consistency of a sincere good will? In order to obey the Logical Law it is often necessary for us to criticize our own past; consistency with what we have been may mean inconsistency with reason. This is doubtless what Emerson meant. A similar analysis would show, I believe, that all writers, including Nietzsche,[3] who have seemed to deny the Logical Law have really presupposed it.

When a great man's life and thought is full of contradictions, as is sometimes the case, the intelligent critic does not say that the Logical Law is disproved; we cannot believe that the great man ought to have been contradictory; we can only say, "Here is the pathos and tragedy of life." This is illustrated by Paul Ernst's imaginary dialogue between Leo Tolstoy and a youth, in the cell in which Tolstoy died. The dialogue begins thus:

Youth: What, then, shall we do?
Tolstoy: What, then, shall we do? Can I answer the

---

[3] Nietzsche's doctrine of the "eternal recurrence" has striking affinity with the Kantian moral law.

question? All my life I have failed to answer it. I despise fiction and have written novels; I know that life with a wife and children subjugates the superior humanity in us by petty cares, superfluous efforts, and aimless chatter, and yet I did not leave my family until I began to die; I perceived that one who is richer than his brother is responsible for his brother's suffering, and yet I did not give my money to the poor. How can I answer the question, What, then, shall we do? You can answer that question only by your own doing.[4]

Perhaps even Tolstoy, with all his inconsistency, willed more logically than most of us who are conscious of no great problems.

6. THE LOGICAL LAW AS A PRINCIPLE OF SELF-RESPECT

In order to obey the Logical Law, it is necessary to respect one's own inner life. No one can control our will but ourselves; no one can determine whether we will to be consistent but ourselves. Others, more skilled in logic, may reveal to us inconsistencies of which we had not dreamed; and if we are able to understand their criticisms, we may profit by them. But the most skilled external logical analyst cannot tell whether I am intending to be consistent or not; he can tell only whether I have succeeded. The Logical Law, however, does not command success; it commands will. This implies that all persons, if they are to be moral in the sense of this Law, ought to respect themselves in the face of criticism. The good will is far more fundamental to character than is logical ability. But if one is to maintain self-respect, it can only be by sincere allegiance to the Logical Law.

This aspect of morality is formulated by Wilhelm Wundt, in what he calls "the individual norm of self-

---

[4] Ernst, EG, 61.

respect," as follows: "Think and act so that you never lose respect for yourself."[5]

At times it is psychologically difficult to maintain self-respect when we are morally entitled to it, in view of the fact mentioned by Urban that "we are often most ridiculous when we try to express that which is deepest in us."[6] Ethics, however, is not morals made easy, and obedience to the Logical Law will require the support of all the virtues which grow out of obedience to the entire System of Laws.

7. Violation of the Logical Law

As our discussion here and in Chapter II has presupposed, and as experience amply testifies, the Logical Law can be violated. We can intend to be inconsistent. Our affective consciousness, our impulses, instincts, and habits, social pressure, and our own indecisiveness, are tendencies which lead the will to vacillate and contradict itself unless it keeps attention firmly fixed on its purpose to conform to the Logical Law.

The Law is violated whenever, recognizing that the Law is true, we do not will to be consistent. Hence, unconscious or unintentional inconsistency does not violate it. As we have seen, Socrates believed that intentional inconsistency was impossible; but he was certainly wrong. If a student wishes to be educated, yet does not study, he violates the Law; he wills his education, and does not will it, at the same time. If a citizen wishes to be respected, yet does not pay his bills or offer any explanation to his creditors, he both wills and does

---

[5] Wundt, ETG, III, 152. Kant brings out the same point. He asks: "Has not everyone who is even moderately honorable discovered that he has abstained from an overwise harmless lie merely in order not to despise himself in secret in his own eyes?" KdpV (Reclam S), 123.

[6] Urban, IW, 391.

not will to be respected; he violates the Logical Law. In general, to will any end whatever without willing the best available means, or to will means which inevitably lead to an undesired end, are the typical cases of violation of this Law. But, as was brought out in the discussion of Emerson, changing one's mind is not a violation of the Law. The duty of consistent willing includes the duty of correcting our own past errors, as far as we know them to be errors, in the direction of a greater consistency.

SELECTED BIBLIOGRAPHY

The Logical Law is implied in the *Meditations* of Marcus Aurelius, especially Book IV; see Haines, MA, 66-97.

Kant is its chief exponent. Read the extract in Rand, CM, 539-564. Criticisms of Kant: Bowne, POE, 110-111; Drake, PC, 100-102; Mackenzie, MOE, 190-206; Paulsen, SOE, 350-355; etc. Kant's ethical writings are available in English in Abbott, KTE.

Emerson's essay on Self-Reliance, available in countless editions, is useful in this connection.

CHAPTER VI

2. THE LAW OF AUTONOMY

1. THE LAW OF AUTONOMY AND ITS PLACE IN THE SYSTEM

STATEMENT OF THE LAW OF AUTONOMY: *All persons ought to recognize themselves as obligated to choose in accordance with the ideals which they acknowledge.* Or: *Self-imposed ideals are imperative.*

Like the Logical Law, the Law of Autonomy is purely formal. It defines obligation solely in terms of the intent of the person in the act of choice. Yet, by the fact that it introduces the element of self-imposed or acknowledged ideals, it goes beyond the Logical Law, which prescribes only such consistency in intentions as would forbid both willing and not willing the same ends at the same time.

An ideal, simply defined, ordinarily means a plan of action or a type of experience which is approved.[1] To approve means to desire or to regard as good. To acknowledge means to accept as the best basis for choice. Hence, ideals may be approved without being acknowledged, and acknowledged without being actually chosen, and chosen without being critically examined.[2] Since the Law of Autonomy considers only the intent to acknowledge certain ideals, without a critical examina-

---

[1] For a fuller definition, see Brightman, POI, Chap. III.

[2] Ralph Barton Perry once wrote that "if the individual imposes his own law, he cannot disobey it; if he ceases to obey it, he no longer imposes it." (*Phil. Rev.*, 9(1900), 645.) But this is based on an oversimplified intellectualistic psychology; the profounder Pauline experience, "What I hate, that I do," comes nearer to the facts of ordinary life. We may impose and approve a law which we do not cease to approve when we disregard it in practice.

tion of whether they really ought to be acknowledged or not, it belongs among the Formal Laws; but because it turns attention from the mere will (the fact of choice) to the end and aim of choice (the value, action, or object chosen), it is on the way to the Axiological Laws. It may, then, be regarded as a Formal Law which is the link or transition between the Formal and the Axiological Laws. The delicately complicated nature of this relationship reveals the organic structure of the System of Laws; each Law is connected with all the others and needs the others for its completion.

2. Proof of the Law of Autonomy

If the Law of Autonomy is not true, then a person is not under obligation to choose in accordance with the ideals he acknowledges. Then he would have to choose either in accordance with ideals which he does not acknowledge or else in accordance with no ideals at all. In either case he would be rejecting the ideals which he does acknowledge, for human beings cannot help having ideals of some sort. It follows that whenever one's choice violates the Law of Autonomy, it also violates the Logical Law, for it leads to a self-contradictory attitude of the will to its ideals. The Law of Autonomy is further confirmed by the fact that all scientific and philosophical reasoning is dependent on it, since reason is a self-imposed ideal which every sane mind acknowledges. Therefore, the Law of Autonomy is true.

3. Its Basis in Experience and History

The Law of Autonomy is based on experiences of obligation and of law as embodied in ideals. If a person exists who has no experiences of ideals, he may be said to be nonmoral—incapable of moral experience and of intellectual life. But if any ideal whatever be acknowledged, whether the general ideal of reason or a specific ideal, such as ambition or industry, then the data for this Law are available. This is equally true, whether the ideals acknowledged by the person are socially approved or socially disapproved.

There is an experience which needs to be distinguished clearly from that of autonomy, namely, the experience commonly called "having one's own way." To have one's own way often means to do whatever one strongly desires to do, irrespective of ideals; whereas autonomy means that one's desires should be judged by one's ideals. No one can doubt that there is a conflict between our desires and our ideals; that is to say, between our desires when we are thoughtless and our desires when we are thoughtful. Autonomy refers to ideals; when we "have our own way," we may disregard the ideals which we acknowledge when we are thoughtful. The element of thoughtfulness is implied to some extent even in the lowest ideal because it is a *plan* of action, not an isolated act; a *type* of experience, not a single experience. The principle here involved later appears on a higher level in Law 8, The Law of Ideal Control (Chapter XII).

The Law of Autonomy finds a kind of empirical support (which, however, is not to be confused with logical proof) in the data of abnormal psychology. Rudolf Allers, for instance, has pointed out that lack of sincerity (*Unechtheit*) is the fundamental trait of all neurosis.[3] He mentions three types of *Unechtheit:* (1) Insincerity of experience (the double life); (2) discrepancy between one's nature and one's conduct; and (3) denial of one's own nature. Despite the fact that conflict may arise between the ethical and the psychoanalytic treatment of such types, it is sure that the need for sincerity and so for autonomy is deeply intrenched in our

---

[3] Allers, WSP, 279-281.

psychological being. Emerson stated an ideal rather than a fact, when he said, "No man can violate his nature." As surely as we have a moral nature, we violate it.

There is, however, at least one fact of fairly common experience that seems to count especially against the Law of Autonomy. That Law speaks of an obligation, or, as we commonly say, a duty; but to quote Bentham, "The word [duty] itself has in it something disagreeable and repulsive." In fact, he holds that it has grown out of the assumption of authority on the part of writers concerning the standard of morality. "Ought" is "an authoritative imposture." Not duty, but interest, is the principle he advocates; yet he says that examination will show the coincidence of duties with interests.[4] But after reflection on Bentham's experience, which is representative of the attitude of many, we find that it reduces to an objection to the *word* "duty" rather to duty itself, for he admits that duty coincides with interest, and asserts elsewhere that it is for pleasure and pain to point out what we *ought* to do.[5] His objection to the word is founded on the fact that so many writers try to prescribe duty to us. His criticism of duty as external prescription and authoritative imposture means that the basis of morality is within. Thus it is really a concealed appeal to the Law of Autonomy. This seems to be true of most persons who experience antipathy to duty. They are really experiencing a desire for autonomy—for self-imposed duties—as opposed to the duties which are mere commands of external authority.

The history of ethics shows that the principle of this Law has long been more or less clearly recognized. As far back as Homer's day, Telemachus said to the suitors:

---

[4] Bentham, DE, I, 9-11, 32.
[5] Bentham, PML, 1.

"But if ye deem this a likelier and a better thing, that one man's goods should perish without atonement, then waste as ye will." The Stoics distinguished between "what is in our power" and "what is not in our power" and taught that the wise man would be "independent of externals," that is, autonomous. Saint Thomas defined sin as "voluntarius recessus a lege Dei" ("a voluntary departure from the law of God"); but, although this makes sin voluntary, it is incompletely autonomous, unless the law of God be self-recognized and self-imposed by the sinner.

It was Immanuel Kant who first made the principle of autonomy clear-cut and fundamental. "The autonomy of the will," he wrote, "is the sole principle of all moral laws."[6] While he was one-sided in making it the sole principle, he was certainly right in making it an essential principle. His famous categorical imperative, developed in the *Fundamental Principles of the Metaphysic of Ethics,* is really a synthesis of the Logical Law and the Law of Autonomy. It runs: "Act only according to that maxim by which you can at the same time will that it shall become a universal law."

E. von Hartmann hardly exaggerated when he said that "the most significant advance which ever was made in the theory of ethical principles occurred through Kant's reform of ethics."[7] Wundt implies a similar judgment when he incorporates the Law of Autonomy into two of his fundamental "norms," as follows:

"Fulfill the duties which thou hast taken upon thyself, whether to thyself or to others.

"Thou shalt give thyself to the end which thou hast acknowledged as thine ideal task."[8]

---

[6] Kant, KdpV (Reclam S), 46. He often refers to it as a *Faktum,* a fact of pure reason, *ibid.,* 42, 59.

[7] Hartmann, GGP, 64.

[8] Wundt, ETG, III, 152, 158.

The same idea is suggested, though not stated, by Lipps. He holds that the ideal of personality is to be such a person that you can be loyal to yourself without violating your loyalty to moral law.[9] More recently Dünnhaupt has formulated it thus: "Determine thy duties and live for them."[10] The Law of Autonomy has been widely recognized as the only sound basis for education. Pestalozzi, for example, adopted it in the form: "The ethical will subjects itself only to the law which it gives to itself."[11]

In spite of the fact that Kant's contribution is fundamental and logically necessary, there has been a tendency among some writers to belittle Kant's achievement. In so far as the criticism of Kant asserts that his theory, as it stands, is not a complete account of the moral life, its justification will be considered later in this chapter. But it must be granted that most of the criticism is, to say the least, less thorough than Kant's own thinking. The sociological attack on Kant (Lévy-Bruhl), the charge that autonomy is egoistic (Dewey, Santayana), the confusion of autonomous duty with the duty of military discipline (Kleinsorgen and others), the view that an imperative necessarily implies an other who commands (Schlick), and the view that Kant's theory is no more than preaching (Drake), all fail to perceive the universal logical necessity in the Kantian principle of autonomy.

4. Spontaneous and Critical Conscience

The Law of Autonomy usually functions in experience through what is called the conscience. Our conscience tells us what ideals we approve and warns us when our

[9] Lipps, EGF, 155, 170.
[10] Dünnhaupt, SSRK, 16.
[11] *Cit.* P. Natorp, *Arch. f. syst. Phil.*, 1(1895), 290.

conduct deviates from those ideals, or commends us
when it conforms to them. The power of conscience lies
in the fact that it brings home to us what we already
believe, but have overlooked or have tried to overlook.
As the vehicle of the Law of Autonomy, conscience has
been held to be of absolute authority, akin to the voice
of God. "Conscience," says Romano Guardini, "is the
place where the eternal enters time. It is the birthplace
of history. . . . History means that through free
humanity something eternal comes to pass in time."[12]

But these and other lofty sentiments about conscience
cannot pass unchallenged. Conscience is not an un-
failing voice telling us definitely what ideals we are to
regard as imperative. Sometimes it does not speak
when we wish it would; sometimes it speaks in two ways
at once, partly reflecting our early training, and partly
our present opinions. Thus there arises the necessity of distinguishing between the emotional and the
critical conscience.

Conscience as it functions spontaneously is uncritical and often emotional ("pathological," as Kant called
it, using the word etymologically and not medically).
It is a strong feeling of obligation, either impelling or
inhibiting action. It reflects the past moral experience of the individual, especially the habits of feeling
which have come to him from his social environment.
Hence the spontaneous conscience usually embodies the
customs or standards of the person's family, church,
schools, and nation. In a general way, it may be said
that the teachings which are handed on from one gen-
eration to another and stamped into the conscience of
youth have the merit of having been tested by the
experience of the race. They have at least survival
value.

[12] Guardini, GGS, 30.

But to treat the utterances of the uncritical conscience as though they were commanded by the Law of
Autonomy, is equivalent to making either social tradition or individual emotion the last word in the moral
life. A conscience molded by the social environment
could not be perfect unless the environment were perfect. Furthermore, the demands of society often meet
with a violent emotional resistance, "the imp of the perverse"; and the social-feeling and the imp-feeling each
claims right on its side. Moreover, many of the strongest demands of the spontaneous conscience are "moral
illusions"; they are "rationalizations" of desire which
impel us to say "I ought" when the real psychological
truth is "I want."

The spontaneous conscience, therefore, needs rational
criticism. But it is a psychological fact that a ruth-
less disregard even of the most perverse spontaneous
conscience has evil effects in rendering the individual
less sensitive to moral situations. Spontaneous emotion, moreover, often has a positive moral value. The
intuitions of poets and prophets, untested by reason,
may be profound moral truths. Emotional conscience,
therefore, should never be violated without adequate
reason which sincerely satisfies the person. This is the
truer, since the spontaneous conscience of "an ordinarily well-brought-up young person" (to use J. S. Mill's
phrase) is usually right in typically familiar situations.
But it often gives unclear or wrong guidance in unusual
situations (as Drake points out). This is evidenced by
the conduct of the average man in war time, or of the
ordinary American traveler abroad.

How, then, shall we move from uncritical to critical
conscience? A complete answer can be given only after
a complete study of all the Laws; the ideal critical
conscience would be the conscience enlightened by the

entire System of Moral Laws. But even at this stage we can point out that a rigorous application of the Logical Law and the Law of Autonomy would do much toward the cultivation of a more critical conscience.

The word "critical," of course, does not mean fault-finding. It means evaluating, judging, wisely estimating. Criticism in the realm of conscience, as in other realms, involves definition, observation, analysis, and a relating of the subject matter criticized to one's view of experience and one's highest standards and ideals. Examination of the spontaneous conscience shows that it often contains contradictions. War conscience often contradicts peace conscience. Labor conscience contradicts capital conscience. Social conscience contradicts individual conscience. Moreover, when emotional conscience is right, it is so by chance and not for any good reason. The conclusion at which one arrives after elimination of violations of the Logical Law and the Law of Autonomy often leads to a change in moral practices. Even when the change is a perfectly clear improvement, on which intelligent observers agree with the person involved, it often happens that the uncritical conscience continues its ravages and makes the task of loyalty to the new insight subjectively difficult. But moral laws allow no exceptions on account of difficulty; impossibility is, of course, another matter, as will be seen later in connection with the discussion of the Law of the Best Possible.

5. VIRTUES AND CHARACTER

By a virtue is meant a relatively permanent attitude of will in fulfillment of obligation, the habit of a good will which obeys the Logical Law and the Law of Autonomy. The great classical discussion of virtue in Aristotle's *Nicomachean Ethics,* which is still the standard treatment of the theme, asserts the autonomous character of virtue. "The virtues," says Aristotle, "are acts of self-determination" (προαιρέσεις, "deliberate choices," 1106a), which enable us to judge character better than do men's deeds (1111b). They may, therefore, be regarded as the habitual application of the Law of Autonomy, while conscience is the index of its content. Virtue is steady obedience to rational conscience.

Nevertheless, a full treatment of the problems involved by the virtues would, on account of the systematic interrelations of the Moral Laws, involve anticipation of Laws which we have not yet discussed. Therefore a relatively brief statement of the virtues will suffice at this point, its purpose being to show their relation to the Law of Autonomy.

Let us consider six typical cardinal virtues, namely, temperance, courage, wisdom, justice (these four being Plato's table of virtues, also emphasized by Aristotle), benevolence, and veracity. Temperance, courage, and wisdom are primarily individual, and justice, veracity, and benevolence primarily social, although all six have a bearing both on the individual and on society.

Temperance is the self-control of the autonomous will. The ancients were wrong in confining the virtue of temperance to the control of our sensuous nature, as are those moderns who use the term solely in connection with the control of the appetite for intoxicants. The entire range of experience, without exception, is in need of temperance. The principle of this virtue is developed more fully in the Law of Ideal Control, which supplements the Formal by the Axiological Laws.

Courage is loyalty to the ideals acknowledged by the autonomous will in the face of difficulties and perils. Obviously, this individual virtue has great social significance. Lack of courage in the face of social criticism and opposition may mean the collapse of social progress. This virtue affords an excellent opportunity for the illustration of the famous doctrine of the mean. Aristotle views every virtue as the mean between the excess and the defect of some quality. Courage, he tells us, is the mean in the feelings of fear and confidence.[13] An excess of courage is too much confidence, overconfidence, or bravado, seeking danger for love of danger or display, where the will recognizes no obligatory ideals. A deficiency of courage is fear, cowardice, disloyalty to acknowledged ideals in the face of danger.

Wisdom involves loyalty to the Logical Law and to the ideal of reason, but goes further than this, for it involves also discrimination among values. It thus implies skill in regard to the Axiological Laws.

Justice has been defined in more different ways perhaps than any other virtue. This reflects the fact that men are not sure what a just order of society would be. Plato's masterpiece, the *Republic,* is devoted to an attempt to define justice.[14] Seth defines it very satisfactorily as the will so to act that none be hindered in their moral development by my action. If equal opportunity to all is thus the end of justice, the problems which it raises obviously carry us beyond the Formal Laws.

Benevolence is the positive counterpart of justice. It is the will so to act that others will be helped in their moral development by my action. This virtue of positive helpfulness or universal love, while taught by the Stoics and others, has come to its widespread recognition in the modern world chiefly through the influence of Christianity. In its practical applications it is

---

[13] Aristotle, *Nic. Eth.,* 1115a.
[14] It would be instructive to work out a history of the definitions of justice.

very important to have it closely associated with justice and wisdom if the intent to be helpful is not to be
self-defeating. The admonition of Jesus to be "wise as
serpents and harmless as doves" has often been forgotten by his too zealous followers who have sometimes
sought to force goodness on others to such an extent
as to violate the autonomy and the self-respect of those
whom they intended to benefit. No virtue is more
needed in the world than genuine love—good will, sincere and wisely directed benevolence; yet no virtue is
more in peril of being misapplied. Here again the
organic and systematic wholeness of the moral life
comes to clear expression. This virtue is the basis of
the Law of Altruism.

Veracity, the last virtue which we shall treat, is the
habitual will to communicate with others in undeviat-
ing consistency with what is believed to be the truth.
This virtue is sometimes taken to refer only to verbal
communication, and we often hear a person trium-
phantly boast, "There, I got out of that without lying,"
after he has succeeded in giving a false impression without using words that were literally untrue. Hence,
it is important to note that the word "communication"
in the definition refers to any form of conduct—words
spoken or left unspoken, deeds done or left undone—
with the intent of producing an impression on the mind
of others inconsistent with the truth which is the subject of the communication.[15]

The total life of virtue (or of its contrary, evil or
vice) produces an habitual attitude toward life, a tendency of the will to be loyal (or disloyal) to the Moral
Laws; and that typical habitual attitude is what we

---

[15] An interesting investigation of current estimates of virtues was
reported in President D. L. Marsh's Baccalaureate Address in 1927.
See *Bostonia*, July, 1927.

call character. We may say that our character is the attitude toward the virtues which we may usually be depended on to manifest in our choices. Obviously, it is an empirical fact that men sometimes act out of harmony with their character. If this were not so, Schopenhauer's view of the unchangeability of character would be true, but as it is, character is gradually changed by the repetition of occasional acts which are either above or below its customary level.

6. RESPONSIBILITY

Originally the conception of responsibility was purely social. As "response" implies, it means the fact that I may be called on to "answer" for what I have done; and I am "responsible" to the authority whom I have to answer. (*Cf.* the German *Verantwortlichkeit, antworten.*) This meaning survives in many current usages; we still speak of the responsible editor of a journal (it is required by law in Germany that the name of such a person be printed in every periodical), the responsibility of a subordinate to his superior, of the fact that elected representatives are responsible to the electorate, or of human responsibility to God. But here we have legal, social, and religious rather than ethical uses of the term. Moral responsibility, as a corollary of the Law of Autonomy, means that man is responsible to himself. The ideals which he recognizes and imposes on himself are ideals which he has no excuse for not obeying. If, however, he does disobey them, reason requires that he give an account to himself of what he has done, judge his conduct by his ideals, hold himself responsible. Such responsibility is moral maturity; until it has been achieved one may be said to be morally still an infant. Responsible persons are subjects of ethical conduct; others are only its objects, for they must be treated responsibly, even though they cannot treat themselves so.

This idea of responsibility has been expressed in a typically German sentence by Heinrich Barth, which reads: "Die Idee ist nicht der Nimbus des Menschen, sondern seine Wahrheit und seine Krisis."[16]   Paraphrased this means: The self-imposed moral ideal is not a halo which imparts a special sort of sainthood to man; it is simply the truth about man and at the same time man's own responsible self-condemnation. Barth's point is that responsibility should be treated frankly and realistically, not sentimentally.[17]

7. AUTONOMY AND HETERONOMY

Kant, to whom we owe the chief development of the principle of autonomy in ethics, has contrasted it with the opposed principle of heteronomy. His treatment of heteronomy, however, is not fully satisfactory, and we shall not follow his exposition literally.

Autonomy is a law given by the will to itself; heteronomy is a law given to the will by some external power. "External" does not necessarily mean external to the person; it means only external to the will. For instance, every instinct and emotion is heteronomous, as well as every request, command, law, or prescription originating from other persons, human or divine.

The problem of the relation between autonomous and heteronomous factors is a complicated and difficult one. At first sight it might seem to follow from the Law of Autonomy that all heteronomous laws are immoral. Yet, if this were true, moral social co-operation could never

---

[16] H. Barth, PPV, 156. Literally: "The ideal is not man's halo, but his truth and his condemnation."

[17] Heinrich Barth's distinguished brother, Karl Barth, uses this idea as a starting point for his famous "theology of crisis."

happen and the autonomous individual could never learn anything from anyone.

Closer examination shows that the principle of autonomy is really violated only when heteronomous commands are adopted as a rule of moral action without regard to the Logical Law or the Law of Autonomy. Cases in which superior force absolutely compels me to do or suffer what is contrary to my own ideals, although rarer than is commonly believed, do occur; but when they occur, the Law of Autonomy is not violated because the will does not consent to the violation of its ideals. The evil happens despite the utmost resistance of the will, and in such a case no act which I am compelled to perform, however shameful or harmful it may be in my judgment, is morally wrong, for it is not an act of my will; it is an act of the power that compels me. But when my will consents to a heteronomous suggestion from any source—desire, inclination, social environment—which is contrary to the ideals that I recognize, or even acts on such a suggestion without any consideration of whether it is contrary to those ideals or not, then the Law of Autonomy has suffered a violation.

Yet it by no means follows from the fact that heteronomous principles may be inconsistent with autonomous ideals that they must necessarily be so. Indeed, if human beings are at all alike, if they live in a common world, and if reason is in any sense a common possession of all "rational" beings (as the agreement in logic and mathematics indicates), then one would expect that the logical and autonomous judgments of one person would have some points of contact with those of another. Even heteronomy may have a rational origin.

For an ideal to be genuinely autonomous it is not necessary for the will to have created it out of its own inner consciousness, or even, as Kant thought, out of "pure reason." It is only necessary that the will shall consistently and sincerely acknowledge the ideal. A self-imposed ideal need not be a self-manufactured one. In order to be autonomous it is not in the least necessary for a person to be capable of the unique work of a moral genius in thinking of something that no one else ever thought of before. There are, it is true, persons who cannot endure being like others; the result is that they come to be like the most disagreeable and obstinate sort of others. A rational autonomy, however, will seek to become more rational, and will, as one means of attaining rationality, give consideration to heteronomous suggestions which are at all promising. Not only that, but the rational person will not wait for ideals either to emerge spontaneously within himself or to be suggested by others; the reason which dictates his autonomy will also lead him to seek light from heteronomous sources.

Aristotle must have been thinking of such matters once when he was reading Hesiod's *Works and Days;* and if he was human, as well as scientific, he must have smiled as he found the lines which he quoted in Book I of his *Ethics* (1095b) :

"Best of all men is the man who finds out the truth independently.
Capable also is he who heeds the good teaching of others.
But he who knows nothing himself and cannot learn from instruction,
He is an utterly useless member of human society."

8. Defects of Purely Formal Ethics

The discussion of conscience, of virtues, and of heteronomy has emphasized the place of reason in the moral life, a place which is fundamental, as the Logical

Law reveals. These discussions have also shown the truth that reason compels us to look beyond the Formal Laws for the full content of the moral life. The Law of Autonomy commands us to be loyal to self-imposed ideals, but it does not tell us how to proceed wisely in selecting ideals. It is imperative, then, to supplement the Formal Laws (laws of intention) by Axiological Laws (laws of value).

That this is necessary follows from the very nature of the will (to which the Formal Laws are restricted). Every will is a choice; and when we choose, we must choose something. Kant seemed to think (according to some of his utterances) that we could choose mere conformity to law. But actual life is not merely a rational form; it is made up of concrete values. The Aristotelian and the Epicurean types of ethical theory have dwelt more on the values to be chosen than they have on the law of choice; whereas Christian and Kantian ethics have emphasized the spirit, the intention or will, more than the thing done. A complete ethical theory must find ample place for both factors, and, if it is not to be self-contradictory, must formulate a consistent system of laws covering the entire range of moral experience.

The insufficiency of a purely formalistic ethics may be shown in numerous ways. Psychologically, as Simmel rightly points out, man is not a purely rational being, but a totality, which we analyze, for various scientific and practical purposes, into reason, sensibility, etc.[18] Hence, ethical theory must give more attention to the other sides of our nature than does strict formalism. Moreover, defects in autonomy as an exclusive principle have been pointed out. There is obvious obligation to be true to our ideals; but there is equally obvi-

---

[18] Simmel, LA, 198.

ous danger in being true to them when they are wrong.[19] Furthermore, there is a tendency in formalistic ethics to underestimate the value of a rich and many-sided life; at least, such a life is not commanded by the Formal Laws. H. Barth expresses this idea when he says that "the pure devotee of duty has to be satisfied with a minimum of the fullness of life."[20] Not until the Axiological Laws are developed, especially the Law of the Most Inclusive End, is this defect remedied. Again, the tendency of the Law of Autonomy may be to exaggerate the value of honesty at the expense of love; the autonomous individual may be ruthlessly honest and cruelly destitute of regard for others. From still another point of view, the formal character of the Laws we have been discussing renders it possible for one to observe them and still to fall under Goethe's condemnation:

"He calls it reason, but he makes it mean
    More beastly living than the beasts have seen."[21]

In other words, formalism does not give a method for guarding sufficiently against the rationalization of our desires.

These criticisms do not imply that Kant was misguided and that the Formal Laws are false. It remains true that those Laws ought to be obeyed in every moral situation, and a situation in which they are disobeyed is certainly wrong. The criticisms, however, indicate that the Formal Laws need supplementation by the Axiological Laws. Many writers, of whom W. G. Everett is a conspicuous representative, go so far as to subordinate the Formal Laws to the principle of value. As we have seen, the practice of obedience to the Logical

---

[19] See Lipps, EGF, 152-153.
[20] H. Barth, PPV, 114.
[21] "Er nennt's Vernunft und braucht's allein
    Um tierischer als jedes Tier zu sein." *Faust*, Part I.

Law and the Law of Autonomy produces character; and Everett regards character value merely as one among other values.[22]   It cannot be denied that character is a value, which truth is additional evidence for the systematic interrelation of all the Moral Laws. But the "character values," as Everett calls them, or the Formal Laws (according to our classification) stand in a peculiar relation to the other values. A person can be moral without experiencing æsthetic, or religious, or recreational values, for example; but his moral life has collapsed entirely if he lacks character values. They are the principles which sustain and unify the whole moral enterprise. They are absolutely necessary, and are the only specific values that can be said to be absolutely necessary to the moral life. Other *Laws,* as we shall see, are needed; but no other specific *values* stand on a level with them. It therefore obscures their uniquely essential status to co-ordinate them with other values. A distinction between the formal aspect and the value aspect of the moral life reveals its structure more adequately than does such a classification.

Having examined the Formal Laws and seen both their necessity and their insufficiency, we are ready for an investigation of the Axiological Laws.

Selected Bibliography

See the bibliography under Chapter V.

Kant's *Fundamental Principles of the Metaphysic of Ethics* (Abbott, KME) is particularly important for the Law of Autonomy.

Kleinsorgen, CE, is a German critique of Kant from Haeckel's standpoint. Liebert, KE, is the best brief recent survey of Kant's ethics in German.

Laurie, EER, XXIX, deals interestingly with "The Emotions of Reason."

---

[22] Everett, MV, Chap. VII.

CHAPTER VII

3. THE AXIOLOGICAL LAW

1. THE AXIOLOGICAL LAW AND ITS PLACE IN THE SYSTEM

STATEMENT of the Axiological Law: *All persons ought to choose values which are self-consistent, harmonious, and coherent, not values which are contradictory or incoherent with one another.*

This Law begins the second main group of Laws, which in Chapter IV (§ 3) were called, as a group, the Axiological Laws. The Formal Laws deal with the rational principles of choice; the Axiological Laws deal with the rational principles of the values chosen. The Formal Laws prescribe that I shall not entertain contradictory intentions; they command sincerity. The Axiological Laws prescribe that I shall not, however sincerely, seek for contradictory values; they command intelligence. Obedience to the Formal Laws is far from guaranteeing obedience to the Axiological. The latter demand a more objective and teleological point of view, more detailed empirical observation of value experience, and more intellectual work in their application. It is relatively easy for an individual to tell at a moment's notice whether he is or is not obeying the Logical Law and the Law of Autonomy. It is considerably more difficult for him to determine whether he is obeying the Axiological Laws, namely:

3. The Axiological Law.
4. The Law of Consequences.
5. The Law of the Best Possible.

125

6. The Law of Specification.
7. The Law of the Most Inclusive End.
8. The Law of Ideal Control.

It is plain, then, that the moral life, in conformity with these Laws, is a life of critical evaluation and intelligent construction. Moreover, it is the judgment of an authority like Troeltsch that "the main problems of ethics do not lie in the realm of subjective ethics [what we call the Formal Laws], which is relatively simple, but in that of objective ethics [our Axiological and Personalistic Laws], which is difficult and complicated."[1]

The problem of the Axiological Laws—indeed, of the whole System of Laws, but especially of this part of it—is to define the *summum bonum,* the "greatest good" of human life. To what conditions must our experience of value conform if it is to be truly and permanently valuable? This is the problem to which we now turn our attention.

2. Proof of the Axiological Law

The proof of the Axiological Law is similar to the proof of the Law of Autonomy. The Axiological Law rests on the fact that every normal human being chooses values. But if a chosen value—such as rational thought in a state of intoxication—is self-contradictory, it is impossible of realization; and if it is incoherent with other chosen values, it involves contradictory choices and hence is a violation of the Logical Law. Moreover, the choice of two contradictory values implies that one of the two will contradict an acknowledged ideal, so that the Law of Autonomy will also be violated. The Axiological Law is, therefore, true; and its proof has

[1] Troeltsch, RLRE, 624.

also demonstrated its interrelations with the other Laws.

3. Its Basis in Experience and History

A description of the experiences of value and of the relations of values to ideals was given in Chapter III (§ 4), and the reader would do well to refer to that material for a statement of the empirical basis of the Axiological Law. The outstanding facts may be summarized very simply. All men experience values (approved or desired or satisfactory situations); and the values which we naturally seek and which, so to speak, solicit our attention are in conflict with each other. We like health and we like overindulgence in foods and drinks which undermine health; we like educational success, social success, and economic success, yet the attainment of all three at the same time by the same person is sometimes impossible. My interests as a member of a political party or of a church or of the economic order may conflict with my interests as an autonomous moral person; yet I value the party and the church, as well as autonomy. The Axiological Law steps into this conflict with the rule of reason and asks the person to make a rational selection of values. Since we cannot have everything that we like because our likes are mutually exclusive and even destructive, we need to decide what values we shall pursue. The only alternative empirically is that forces other than our will shall decide for us, and that we shall become what the old Syrian essayist, Lucian, called "the plaything of the stronger force."

It should be noted further that the advance from the Formal to the Axiological Laws marks a psychological shift from "introversion" to "extraversion," as Jung calls it; or from a subjective to an objective interest.

The habit of thinking constantly about one's own motives tends to develop excessive introspection and morbid conscientiousness. The habit of acting for the achievement of objective values enables a person to forget himself in his work, and, if that work is itself reasonable (in conformity with the Axiological Law), it is a greater source of satisfaction than is either the direct pursuit of pleasure or overattention to conscience.

Allers has said that "only he is fully free from neurosis who is genuinely devoted to the tasks of living. . . . Only the saint is superior to neurosis."[2] Possibly Allers is somewhat optimistic, since not even saints have been free from neurotic tendencies. But the psychological truth on which Allers and the Axiological Law build is that self-development comes largely through self-forgetfulness in work. It is with this thought that Voltaire brought his *Candide* to an end; after his devastating satire on the optimism of Leibniz which regards this as the best of possible worlds, instead of surrendering to pessimism, Voltaire makes his hero settle down with the words, "We must cultivate the garden." The value of achievement and of wholesome work is abundantly verified in experience; and the misery of conflicting values is equally well attested. Dilthey has written of "the tragedy" of Leibniz's life, which shows how the conflict of values even on a high plane can affect one's development. He says: "The scientific work of Leibniz, the urge to make his knowledge available for life, and the plans for the improvement of civilization which he pursued, all stood mutually in each other's way."[3]

The conception of a rationally consistent end of human endeavor goes back at least as far as Plato's

---

[2] Allers, WSP, 282.
[3] Dilthey, GDG, 30.

Idea of the Good and its place in the hierarchy of Ideas.
It appears variously in Aristotle's descriptions of happiness, in Part V of Spinoza's *Ethics*, in Hegel's dialectic, in Sidgwick's rational hedonism, in Bosanquet's
ideal of coherence, in Royce's principle of "loyalty to
loyalty," in Sorley's conception of a system as distinguished from a scale of values, and, in fact, in all ethical
theories that are not purely formalistic. This ideal is
stated by Paul Natorp as follows: "The criterion of
the ethical is found in the complete, law-abiding self-
consistency of the ends of the individual subject and
also of all subjects capable of will, thought of as united
in a realm of ends."[4] More simply stated, it is, "Decide
to be reasonable," as Driesch puts it.[5] Experience and
history alike show that the Axiological Law is a normal
expression of human morality.

4. DERIVATION OF IDEAL VALUES FROM EMPIRICAL VALUES

The actual experiences which are desired or preferred
by any human being or society are called *empirical
values*. The experiences which ought to be desired or
preferred are called *ideal* or *rational values*. Empirical
values are objects of actual choice; ideal values are objects of a rational choice. Yet it is not to be supposed
that they fall into two separate and distinct classes, so
that no empirical values are ideal and no ideal values
are empirical. On the contrary, all ideal values either
must be found among or must grow out of the empirical
values. Even if they come from heaven, they drop upon
the place beneath.

There are, however, differences of opinion as to how
ideal values are derived from the empirical ones. It is

---

[4] Natorp, *Arch. f. syst. Phil.*, 2(1896), 235.
[5] Driesch, ST, 206.

sometimes held that the socially approved empirical values are the ideal ones. It is true that social approval implies testing by many experiences; and if a belief seems reasonable to me and to no one else, I am justified in entertaining some doubt about my judgment. But in many cases there is no social agreement about ideal value; and if social approval is essential, the lone, heroic reformer, persecuted by society, must always be wrong. The social theory, therefore, does not give satisfactory guidance, although it tells how some ideal values arise and sets up an ideal for a future society which may approve ideal values.

Others hold that biological usefulness is the criterion of ideal values. Such values as enable the organism to survive ("survival-values") and adjust to the environment prove their worth and hence they are the ideal values. This conception is in harmony with functional psychology, behaviorism, and certain aspects of pragmatism, as well as with one interpretation of the ethics of Nietzsche, who makes power the supreme value. But opposed to the biological theory is the fact that many of the values which we prize most highly, such as beauty, imagination, pure theoretical knowledge, and mystical experience, have no particular biological function. If the biological standard is to prevail, it must be at the cost of rejecting all values which do not prove biologically useful. This would mean an amputation of some of man's most highly prized experiences.

Other theories may be summarized under the head of idealistic. Instead of appealing to social approval or to biological survival, that is, instead of resting on one aspect of experience and making it binding, these theories appeal to the systematic view of experience as a whole. This is the position of most classical philosophy, and there seems to be no important reason for questioning its validity.[6] It rests on observation, criticism, and systematization of our total view of experience. It moves through analysis to synthesis and synopsis.[7] Within its limits, great variety is possible. Universal hedonism (utilitarianism), perfectionism, and the system of Personalistic Laws developed in the present volume, are all developed by the idealistic method and subject to its constant criticism.

While there is no logical objection to this method of deriving ideal values from empirical ones, it has its practical difficulties. "Idealistic system" is less definite than social approval or biological utility, and a complete view of the value experience as a systematic whole is extremely difficult to attain. Yet, with all its difficulties and vagueness, it has the advantage of pointing in the direction in which the moral development of humanity will always have to move as long as it remains rational.

Its application may be made clearer by one or two illustrations. Maternal affection is an instinctive, empirical value. Yet a mother may easily manifest it in a selfish or unenlightened way, which leads to serious consequences for the spoiled or too-sheltered child. Maternal love becomes an ideal value only when its impulses are tested by intelligent regard for the child's welfare, that is, by the contribution which the love makes to the present and future development of the child toward a useful and happy life. Thus the empirical value is tested by an idealistic system. Stealing is a very different type of illustration of the same principle. For the thief, stealing may be an empirical value; "stolen sweets are best." But stealing contradicts property rights, which the thief asserts for his own

---

[6] See Urban, IW, *passim*. *Cf*. also Chap. III of the present work.
[7] See Sorley, MVIG, Chap. X, and Brightman, ITP, Chap. I.

possessions, and violates respect for personality. It is an empirical value, but not an ideal one. Sometimes an empirical value—such as the pleasing increase in the circulation of blood in one's hands after clapping—may be ideally neutral as compared with the value of the music which one is applauding. Again, empirical disvalues, such as intense suffering, may be a source of ideal satisfaction if they are in the service of an ideal value, such as the advancement of world peace or the bringing of a better social order. It is clear that every empirical value should be tested by its relations to an idealistic system which conforms to the Axiological Law.

5. VALUES AS INTRINSIC

A distinction has commonly been made between intrinsic and instrumental values, ever since Aristotle pointed it out in the opening paragraphs of the *Nicomachean Ethics*. Intrinsic values are ends; instrumental values, means. The former are valued for their own sake, the latter for the sake of what they cause or lead to. M. Picard uses the term "immediate" as a synonym for intrinsic, and "contributory" as a synonym for instrumental. These terms certainly stand for a real fact of experience. We should regard practicing on a piano as utterly meaningless and valueless did it not lead to good playing; but good playing is valuable in itself. The mere possession of food or of wealth is intrinsically of no use; only as the food or wealth become instruments for the sustenance and the enjoyment of human life do we find intrinsic value through them. Since, then, the instrumental values are meaningless apart from the intrinsic, we shall treat the intrinsic values first.

The standard basis in recent American literature

for a "table" of the values is to be found in W. G. Everett's *Moral Values*.[8] His table is as follows:

    I. Economic Values.
   II. Bodily Values.
  III. Values of Recreation.
  IV. Associational Values.
   V. Character Values.
  VI. Æsthetic Values.
 VII. Intellectual Values.
VIII. Religious Values.

The first member of this table, the economic, we can postpone until our treatment of the instrumental values. Economic value is exchange value. It is exclusively instrumental, for its function is to lead to some possession which may either be consumed or enjoyed, that is, to an experience of intrinsic value. Economic goods as such are not intrinsic values. Even a painting when regarded from the economic point of view is not thought of as so much beauty but only as so many dollars. On the other hand, economic values exist only because we recognize and need intrinsic values.

The remaining seven may be regarded as a complete list of the intrinsic values of life, if each one be considered broadly enough. The commonest criticism on the score of completeness is that if values of recreation are recognized, then values of work should also be recognized.[9] But this additional category is not necessary; the whole task of achieving and maintaining the intrinsic values by means of the instrumental is work. Work is the normal functioning necessary to maintain value experience as a whole, and is present throughout the entire life of value. Recreation, while equally normal,

---

[8] Everett, MV, Chap. VII, The World of Values.

[9] Parker, for instance, speaks of technological value, or the interest in workmanship. See HV, Chap. XIII.

is not a universal trait of all achievement of value, but, rather, is a special aspect of value experience, an occasional mood or enjoyment, not a constant essential fact. Hence recreation is a special value, while work is a factor in all value.

Attempts have been made to group or classify these values. Urban, for instance, divides them into the organic (bodily, economic, recreational) and hyperorganic. The hyperorganic are (1) values of sociality (association and character) and (2) spiritual values (intellectual, æsthetic, religious).[10] This classification, while relatively valid, is subject to criticism. Not all recreation is organic; surely social and spiritual recreation also occurs. Not all character values are primarily social; inner sincerity and self-respect are predominantly individual. On the other hand, the intellectual and the religious values are at least as social as is character. My own earlier division[11] into lower and higher corresponded to Urban's organic and hyperorganic, save that I put associational values into the class of lower values. The reason was that association by itself, apart from goodness, truth, and beauty, is empty and worthless. But the same is true of other values. Religion without goodness or truth is impossible; and beauty expresses bodily and associational, as well as religious and intellectual values.

These considerations show the impossibility of a list of values arranged in ascending order. They confirm what Everett calls the "interpenetration" of the values, as well as Sorley's view that the values form a system rather than a scale. The Axiological Law suggests that

---

[10] Urban, FOE, 164. Parker divides the values into those of "real life" and those of imagination. See HV, table of contents. But the same values really appear in both realms and such separation is artificial.

[11] Brightman, ITP, Chap. **V.**

no single value can stand alone, and that the only strictly intrinsic value is the whole system of coherent values, or, stated more empirically, that the highest intrinsic value is the experience of a person whose values are harmonious.

This view of intrinsic value gives us some important clues. If the whole of value experience is that which gives value to the parts, then we can see why associational values seem so worthless by themselves and so supremely worthful when experienced in connection with other values. We also see why bodily health is commonly regarded as a lower intrinsic value than goodness, truth, and beauty; it is because in it the relations to the system of value as a whole are far less numerous and complex than they are in the case of most of the other values. At the same time the high instrumental value of bodily health justifies giving care of the body an important place in ethical science; some have said that it should have first place!

This last point leads to a further aspect of the system of values. Not only are the intrinsic values interrelated as respects their very nature and meaning (so that each is seriously mutilated if it does not include within itself something of the nature of the others), but they are also mutually instrumental to each other. For example: In order to experience religious value, I must have some intellectual values as an essential part of the religious experience. But also each is instrumental to the other; clear thinking about religion aids religion and causes it to become better, while religious experience raises problems which stimulate the intellectual life. Yet it is important to note that each of the major types of intrinsic value (health, recreation, association, beauty, reason, and religion) retains its rights as a distinctive point of view which cannot be wholly subordinated to others without loss. Art gives to and receives from other values; but if the uniqueness of the æsthetic point of view is not recognized, the spirit of beauty is impaired.

6. Values as Instrumental

Any condition, object, experience, or process which may serve as cause of an intrinsic value is an instrumental value. As has already been pointed out, every intrinsic value is also instrumental; it is more or less productive of other values.

There are, in addition, two types of value which are purely instrumental, namely, the natural and the economic. By natural instrumental values are meant all noneconomic aspects of the purely physical world which render the experience of intrinsic value possible. Our bodies, the air we breathe, the landscape, the sky—in short, all of the free goods of nature are natural instrumental values. While we often ascribe to these natural objects the intrinsic value of beauty, what we really mean is that these objects are capable of causing value experience in us; we do not mean that the physical fact of a tree is in itself beautiful if no person sees and enjoys it. We mean, rather, that the physical fact is capable of engendering satisfactory and harmonious experience in a conscious mind. The intrinsic value lies in that experience. The physical tree is an instrumental value.

Economic values are also purely instrumental. One who treats them as intrinsic is called by the significant name of miser, a wretched person—one who is willing to live in misery, destitute of the intrinsic values, in order to add to instrumental values which he does not treat as instruments. The right attitude toward economic values is perhaps the most pressing need of the world today. Yet it is not the task of the theoretical ethicist to solve the economic problems of society. That task belongs to the economist. But the economist must take from ethics the moral laws in accordance with which all worthy economic activity must go on, while the ethicist who is concerned with a practical problem must take from economics the facts and laws of the economic order. Much harm has been done by an attempt of the science of the intrinsic to dictate to the science of the instrumental, and vice versa.

Yet the distinction between intrinsic and instrumental, while very significant for division of labor among the sciences, as well as for the ethical evaluation of the true end of human action, is not absolute. It is subject to limitations from at least three points of view.

First, it should be noted that instrumental values are, from the standpoint of practical ethics, equally essential with intrinsic. We do not live for them, but we live by them. Without a sufficient natural and economic basis, the intrinsic values cannot be developed. What constitutes a sufficiency will vary greatly in different cases, but a sufficient physical and economic basis, however slender, is an absolutely necessary presupposition for the good life. It is, therefore, not ethical to despise economic goods, or sound health. On the contrary, their adequate development is a necessary part of the ethical life. They are bad only when they are not so developed as to be suitable means to the end of attaining intrinsic values.[12] It is therefore ethically imperative that instrumental and intrinsic values be viewed in their organic connections, as well as in their distinct functions.

---

[12] See the discussion of the violation of the Logical Law in Chap. V, § 7.

Secondly, it is a psychological fact that an end for which we are working is present more or less clearly in the consciousness of the intelligent person throughout the whole series of means or instrumental values which lead up to it. When the artist assembles his brushes and paints and canvas and begins blocking out his picture, the conception of the final appearance of his painting must be to some extent present in his mind, imparting significance to every act which he performs as a means to the end in view. No artist can rely wholly on his subconscious. An instrumental value can be instrumental only if, by anticipation, the intrinsic value to which it leads is already present in it. Even when this seems not to be true, and the end has not been at all clearly foreseen, the labor on the instruments of life acquires a new meaning as soon as we see that something has been accomplished. The inventor or the poet sees the value of his preliminary pains when the finished product—radio or poem—is achieved. It may be said, then, that the end does "justify" the means, provided the means actually lead to the end and do not conflict with it. The end-value radiates its beauty and worth back over the humble instruments which were necessary to achieve it.

Thirdly, the very nature of the Axiological Law shows that instrumental values must be considered in systematic relations with intrinsic values. The point just made about the end's justifying the means illustrates this. The intrinsic values cannot survive in refined academic leisure apart from the toil of life. They rest on a basis of physical reality and economic wealth; hence an ethical system of values must recognize that basis and prescribe systematic consistency and harmony between the instrumental and the intrinsic as well as within the intrinsic. Thus the Axiological Law points to the rule of reason in every value-producing activity as well as in the values that are produced.

7. THE PLACE OF PLEASURE IN VALUE

Historically, much confusion has been introduced into axiological theory by excessive overemphasis on, as well as by denial of, the place of pleasure in value experience. Pleasure is agreeable or satisfactory consciousness. The definition of pleasure seems to be identical with the definition of intrinsic value (at least of empirical, if not of ideal, value). Certain it is that there is no intrinsic value which can be regarded as valuable without some element of pleasurable feeling in the experience. Even Kant, whose thought is at the opposite pole from hedonism, says that "it is a part of duty to establish and to cultivate this feeling [of satisfaction in obeying the moral law], which really alone deserves to be called the moral feeling."[13]

But it is as great a mistake to make pleasure the whole of moral value, with Epicurus, as it is to exclude pleasure entirely from moral value, with Kant in his less amiable moments. Pleasure is one element in moral value, but intelligence is another. And intelligence does not merely take the form (as Bentham thought) of calculating how much pleasure or happiness we can get, but, rather, of determining what kind of happiness is morally worthy and what kind of life is worthy of happiness.

To say that the good is pleasure is to give very little information about it. It is almost as empty as it is to say that the good is consciousness. The good *is* consciousness, *is* pleasure; but the essential moral question is, What kind of consciousness or pleasure? And this question remains unanswered when the appeal is only

---

[13] Kant, KdpV (Reclam S), 55.

to the word "pleasure." This is all the truer, since, to paraphrase Fichte, the kind of pleasures you will enjoy depends on the kind of man you are. An honest, reasonable, thoughtful person will find some experiences disgusting or wearisome which less reasonable minds find delightful. On the other hand, the reasonable person has opened up to him new sources of pleasure on a higher level. Better still, the reasonable person is enabled to discriminate between higher and lower pleasures, and to perceive that rational structure is at least as essential to value as pleasurable consciousness. The good man judges his pleasures by his ideals, that is, by moral laws. He does not judge the moral laws exclusively by his pleasures. As Simmel remarks, it is a psychological fact that "an increase of the sum of earthly happiness does not satisfy our moral sense if it does not befall one who is worthy of it."[14]

Hence an approach to ethics from the standpoint of moral laws gives us more information about the structure of goodness and more basis for discrimination between good and evil than does hedonism. If, for instance, a person has undertaken to obey the Logical Law and he is told that pleasure is the essence of all value, he is not to be blamed if he sees no necessary connection between logical willing and pleasure. Yet if, for that reason, he were to seek pleasure regardless of the Logical Law, his life would become less satisfactory very soon; it would be a nest of self-canceling contradictions. If we set ourselves the task of obeying the Logical Law and the other Laws, we shall find life's highest pleasures; but if we set ourselves the task of finding pleasures, we are likely to lose them.[15]

There is a road through reason that leads to the high-

---

[14] Simmel, MW, I, 391.
[15] This fact is called the hedonistic paradox. See Everett, MV, 142.

est happiness. Apart from reason, there is no way of determining the highest happiness. But no road leads at all clearly through pleasure to reason. Hedonism overemphasizes one abstract aspect of value as formalism overemphasizes another. Perfectionism, Christian Ethics, and the System of Laws are related attempts to include the truth of both extremes in a synthesis.

The Viennese philosopher, Schlick, however, believes that he can refute antihedonistic theories of value by the question: "What are the absolute values to me? What happens if I do not care about them?"[16] If we identify the absolute values with the Moral Laws, there is a very simple answer to Schlick's question. If we disregard or violate the Moral Laws, the result is self-contradiction and chaos. Disobedience to the Laws is a violation of the conditions of integrity and rational living. The result is futility, failure to find the meaning and value of life. The man who thinks that he is superior to reason and to law is described by Herder as "a monster who wants to be everything at once" with the result that he "is nothing completely."[17] What are the "absolute values" to me? They are the conditions of sustained, connected, meaningful experience. What happens if I do not care about them? A life that contradicts itself.

SELECTED BIBLIOGRAPHY

Brightman, POI, Chap. IV; Drake, PC, Chap. XIV; Everett, MV, Chap. VII; Hobhouse, RG; Paton, GW; Parker, HV, Chap. XVII (an excellent and fresh analysis of moral values); Perry, ME (the whole theme of this book is essentially The Axiological Law); Royce, PL, Chap. III (here the Formal and the Axiological Laws tend to coalesce); Sharp, ETH, Chap. III; Simmel, MW, II, Chap. VII (in German); Sorley, MVIG, Chap. II (very able); Stapledon, MTE, Chaps. II and VII.

---

[16] Schlick, FE, 87.
[17] Herder, GG, 16.

CHAPTER VIII

4. THE LAW OF CONSEQUENCES

1. THE LAW OF CONSEQUENCES AND ITS PLACE IN THE SYSTEM

STATEMENT of the Law of Consequences: *All persons ought to consider and, on the whole, approve the foreseeable consequences of each of their choices.* Stated otherwise: *Choose with a view to the long run, not merely to the present act.* (In the fuller statement, the phrase "on the whole" is necessary, for some bad consequences may follow good choices, although the predominant tendency of the consequences may be good.)

This Law is necessary in view of the fact that experience is an ongoing process, a "stream of consciousness" (James), and the System of Laws is therefore no set of timeless abstractions, but, rather, a body of principles for the guidance of the ongoing of experience. The Law of Consequences brings out more clearly this aspect than do the other Laws. On the other hand, the Law of Consequences depends on the rest of the System for its real significance, for we cannot tell whether we ought to "approve" consequences unless we have some intelligible standard for our approval or disapproval. That standard is found in the other Axiological Laws, as well as in the Formal and the Personalistic. It is evident, then, that the Law of Consequences both implies and is implied by the rest of the Moral Laws. The popular tendency to treat consideration of consequences as the sole ethical standard is thus refuted, while the moral importance of consequences is fully recognized.

142

2. Proof of the Law of Consequences

The proof of this Law rests on the fact that every end or value chosen, as well as every act of choice, becomes a cause of further effects. To will a cause is, therefore, equivalent to causing these further effects. In so far as these effects are foreseen, we will them when we will their cause. In proportion as we are intelligent, and desire to know what we are doing, we shall extend our knowledge of the effects of our choice from those now actually foreseen to all those which we can foresee with improved methods of investigation. Without such foresight we cannot tell what effect our act will have on the future conformity of our experience to moral law. It is a fact of experience that to value a cause is not necessarily to value its effects; one may value the possession of an automobile without valuing the economic consequences of ownership, or one may value the right of franchise without valuing the judgment of the electorate in the exercise of that right. But to will a cause the foreseeable effects of which one does not on the whole rationally approve (that is, approve as in harmony with moral law) is to violate both the Law of Autonomy and the Axiological Law. We choose the present act in accordance with self-imposed ideals, while at the same time choosing consequences which violate them. Or we choose harmonious values in an act and at the same time choose consequences which contradict them. Therefore consistent obedience to the other Laws necessitates obedience to the Law of Consequences.

From a practical point of view control of consequences by choices is rendered doubly necessary by the fact that unexpected consequences play so large a part in human life. Few foresaw the economic depression that followed 1929. Unforeseen consequences of human

action create situations which any rational being would
wish to avoid if he could. The obligation to cultivate
control through foresight and anticipation of all possible consequences is therefore very great.

3. Its Basis in Experience and History

Experience not only affords a constant illustration
of the law of cause and effect, but also serves to confirm
the basic moral insights of the race by the desirable
consequences of moral conduct. The physical, biological, psychological, and social sciences provide methods
for the discovery of the consequences of many human
acts. This scientific light on consequences greatly increases the range of moral responsibility. Sanitation
and hygiene are striking examples of this fact, as are
the contributions of the science of economics to our
knowledge of the causes of human weal and woe.

The essential principle of the Law of Consequences
has been recognized by many moralists. The scholastics,
for instance, laid down the maxim: "Qui est causa
causae, est causa causati" ("He who is cause of a cause
is the cause of that which is caused by it"). The scholastic distinction between willing "actually" and "vir-
tually" is also relevant; the former occurs when the will
here and now is directed explicitly toward any object,
while the latter occurs in those acts "which flow . . .
from an actual will as a cause."[1]

But the chief insistence on the Law of Consequences
has come historically from the hedonists, notably from
Bentham. As he says, "The ends of morality will be on
all occasions best served by the habit of comparing the
consequences of action."[2] He elaborated the Law of
Consequences in his doctrine of the elements or dimen-

---

[1] Gury, CTM, 4, 3.
[2] Bentham, DE, II, 77.

sions of value (which for him meant pleasure or pain).
These elements are:

1. Its intensity.
2. Its duration.
3. Its certainty or uncertainty.
4. Its propinquity or remoteness.
5. Its fecundity, or the chance it has of being followed
   by sensations of the *same* kind.
6. Its purity, or the chance it has of *not* being followed
   by sensations of the opposite kind.
7. Its extent; that is, the number of persons to whom it
   extends, or (in other words) who are affected by it.[3]

These elements all refer to consequences save the first
named, intensity, and they are all without exception
quantitative principles, not laws of structure or of quality. They enable Bentham to build up his famous hedonistic calculus, whereby he assigns a numerical pleasure
and pain value to each one of these elements in every
moral act, so that he finds his duty by summing up the
values on each side and subtracting.[4]   If pleasure is
greater, the act is good; if pain is greater, it is bad. The
purely quantitative, hedonistic standard, while fasci-
nating, is an obvious oversimplification.   Nevertheless,
Bentham deserves great credit both for attaching so
much importance to consequences and also for working
out the detailed elements which need consideration. He
thus made a real contribution to the development of
ethics as a science, for his elements, with minor changes
in wording (for "pleasure and pain" and "sensations"
read: "experiences of value"), can be and should be in-
corporated into any system of scientific ethics, unless it
can be shown that we ought not to consider the consequences of our acts (see § 4).

The Law of Consequences is sometimes present in an

---

[3] Bentham, PML, 29-30.
[4] Bentham, PML, 31.

unintended form in writers who think that they are rejecting it. Nietzsche's Superman is scornful of consequences; yet in *Thus Spake Zarathustra*, Nietzsche teaches that we should abandon the ideal of *Nächsten-liebe* (love of neighbor—the nearest) for that of *Fern-stenliebe* (love of the furthest). He means that, instead of satisfying ourselves with doing what present humanity desires, we should fix our gaze on the possibilities of the distant future and live for them. In other words, we should consider the most remote consequences of our acts instead of confining our attention to immediate consequences. In this, all idealists agree, and it is, for practical purposes, what they mean by "the eternal values."

The poet Schiller has another reason for considering consequences. Only thought about the future lifts us above the deadly sameness of ordinary existence:

> "Man has to think of the dawn of the morrow,
>   Hope for its happiness, fear for its sorrow,
>   If he would carry the load of today,
>   Treading its weary monotonous way."[5]

4. INDIFFERENCE TO CONSEQUENCES

There is, however, one fact that stands out in apparent conflict with the Law of Consequences, namely, the frequent teaching and practice of indifference to consequences on the part of some of the best members of the human race. We must at the start recognize that consequences, in so far as they are not my actual present choice, are not in themselves my moral experience. Scholastics, with their accustomed clarity, have seen this and have laid down the maxim: *"Per se* actus externus nul-

---

[5] Etwas fürchten und hoffen und sorgen
  Muss der Mensch für den kommenden Morgen,
  Dass er die Schwere des Daseins ertrage
  Und das ermüdende Gleichmaass der Tage.

lam moralitatem addit actui interno" (*"In itself* an external act adds no morality to an internal act").[6] That is, if I have sincerely willed an act, my morality is no greater if I am able to carry it out physically and no less if I am not. The actual consequences, even the immediate consequences, are morally indifferent if my will is good. This seems like a return to purely formal ethics, and an abandonment of the principle of the Axiological Laws; but such is not the case, for everything turns on our definition of what constitutes *moralitas,* or a good will. According to the Formal Laws a good will should be self-consistent; according to the Axiological Laws it should also aim at consistent values. It should, then, strive for intelligent achievement. But the axiological (or teleological) principle does not cancel the truth of the formal; although the will aims at objective values, the essence of a moral act is the will or choice. We have, therefore, to admit that the scholastic maxim is correct and that it is consistent with the Axiological Laws.

James Martineau carries the disregard for consequences to an extreme when he says:

"Instead of measuring the worth of goodness by the scale of its external benefits, our rule requires that we attach no moral value to these benefits, except as signs and exponents of the goodness whence they spring; and graduate our approval by the purity of the source, not by the magnitude of the result."[7]

If "goodness" and "the purity of the source" be extended to cover the most intelligent and conscientious consideration of consequences of which the agent is capable, even Martineau's statement is consistent with the Law of Consequences.

[6] Gury, CTM, 16.
[7] Martineau, TET, II, 25.

But there remains a practical, if not a theoretical, difficulty. The best judgment of the race at times, and the popular judgment much more often, approves a certain reckless disregard of consequences. "Take no thought for the morrow." "Leave the dead to bury their dead." This recklessness in right doing is embodied in the saying, "Fiat justitia pereat mundus" ("Let justice be done though the world perish"), and in the lines of Horace, which the young Fichte took as a motto to write in his school books:

> "Si fractus illabatur orbis,
> Impavidum ferient ruinae."

("If the world collapses, the ruins will fall on one who is unterrified.") Eduard von Hartmann defines the ethical as a refusal to regard consequences. It is approval or disapproval which involves "disinterested evaluations of human action without any reflection on its consequences for us or for our kind (or even for the doers)."[8]

If we now consider these utterances carefully, we find that there is usually more recognition of consequences than appears. The same Jesus who advised against taking thought for the morrow also taught that the wheat and tares should grow together until the harvest, and thus implied that the ultimate consequences were significant. When Kant interprets the "Fiat justitia pereat mundus," he takes it to mean, "Let justice prevail, though all the rogues perish."[9] He thus betrays an interest in different consequences for rogues and for good men. The radical statement of Hartmann, however, goes too far. To act in total disregard of consequences is to "go it blind"; and blindness, whether

---

[8] Hartmann, PSB, 106.
[9] See the Rosenkranz edition of Kant, Vol. VII, 281.

voluntary or involuntary, is not better than sight. One can, it is true, understand what might lead to such a statement. It may be regarded as a violent protest against letting any nonmoral consideration determine our acts; to deviate from the right on account of fear of punishment or hope of reward is certainly wrong. The good life demands great courage in the face of obstacles. But nothing justifies a good man in being voluntarily ignorant of the obstacles he is going to face or of the results he is going to achieve.

It must then be made clear that the Law of Consequences is not a dictate of prudent cowardice. When Socrates chose to drink the hemlock rather than to escape from prison and thus evade obedience to the laws of Athens, he seemed to be defying consequences; but he was really considering them most intelligently, for he sincerely preferred death to life in violation of his country's laws. Likewise Spinoza, when he chose to remain a grinder of lenses rather than to accept a call to a professorship of philosophy in Heidelberg, did not disregard consequences; on the contrary, he considered that lenses with freedom were more valuable consequences than a professorship with restrictions. The eleventh chapter of Hebrews is a classic study in the Law of Consequences.

It must be granted that there is a noble recklessness and an ignoble recklessness. The only noble recklessness considers consequences and weighs them carefully, but is willing to risk all for the highest ideals. Ignoble recklessness may take the form of a blind disregard of results; or it may be a ruthlessness which calculates consequences and makes everything bend to an evil issue. Such ruthlessness Schlick rightly makes the chief trait of the egoist.[10]

---

[10] Schlick, FE, 55.

5. Consequences: Objective and Subjective

Discussion of consequences has been rendered unclear by some authors on account of their failure to take into account the whole range of consequences. Consequences are both objective and subjective. In ethical theory, "objective" refers to the end or content of the moral act, while "subjective" refers to its intent or form. Every choice that we make has consequences of both sorts; it achieves a series of ends (values and disvalues, goods and evils); it also has its effect on the will and the character.

Hedonism has exerted a confusing influence on the study of this problem for at least two reasons: It has tended to assume that any and all consideration of consequences must be hedonistic, and it has also tended (as Bowne often remarked) to underestimate the significance of the inner, subjective consequences. A very different evaluation of the two types of consequences is implied by the question, "What shall it profit a man, if he shall gain the whole world, and lose his own soul?" It is necessary, if we are to choose intelligently, for us to consider the whole range of consequences in the light of our standards of value.

It should also be noted that there is often a great discrepancy between objective and subjective consequences. Very extensive and satisfactory objective ends may be secured at the cost of subjective self-respect; whereas a high degree of subjective value may lead to meager or even bad objective results. The Law of Consequences would naturally be best satisfied by a maximum achievement in both fields; and intelligence ought to be directed toward this dual, objective-subjective rightness both of the act and of its consequences. Yet only subjective rightness is morally indispensable.

6. THE MORAL OBLIGATION TO USE SCIENTIFIC KNOWLEDGE

A corollary of the Law of Consequences—as is already implied in § 3—is the moral obligation to be intelligent and especially to be sufficiently well informed in the field of the various sciences to know and to control the normal consequences of action. Even ordinary observation, without technical science, if carefully made, will enable one to avoid many serious errors. But for constructive morality on a large scale, whether individual or social, scientific knowledge and method are essential. One of the great contributions of Professor John Dewey to modern culture is his insistence on the moral utility of science. In this connection, Bernard Bosanquet's essay, "We Are Not Hard Enough on Stupidity," is stimulating.[11] Every good man will share the sentiments of poor Queen Louise of Prussia, who exclaimed, "Ich hasse entsetzlich die Dummheit" ("I hate stupidity frightfully"). Without intelligent, scientific knowledge—and also, we may add, without a certain amount of essential philosophical reflection—consequences can neither be foreseen nor estimated.

7. TYPICAL PRACTICAL PROBLEMS

Up to this point relatively few practical problems have been discussed. There are three reasons for this: First, we are primarily concerned with theoretical and not with practical ethics in this study; secondly, on account of the System of Laws which we are developing, fruitful consideration of concrete practical problems cannot occur until the System as a whole has taken shape; and, thirdly, it is far more useful for the reader to make his own autonomous applications than to find

[11] Bosanquet, SSE, Chap. IX.

ready-made solutions in a book, for ethics consists of moral laws rather than a moral code—of principles rather than precepts. Nevertheless the theoretical treatment itself is in danger of being unclear if its application to concrete cases is not considered; and the obvious end and aim of studying theoretical ethics is to control actual experience by moral norms. Hence we shall now present a few test cases which naturally arise in connection with the Law of Consequences.

One group of instances may be discussed under the question, Am I responsible for acts which I do not perform? Popular opinion usually attaches .more moral responsibility to positive action of my own than to any event which occurs without such action. Yet there certainly are events which occur as a consequence of my attitude for which I am just as responsible as though I had caused the event directly. Let us take the case of a gang leader who orders a member of his gang to kill an offending rival. In this case the person who does the killing is, of course, responsible; but, if we may speak of degrees of responsibility, he is less responsible than the one who gave the order, for the intent to kill originated with the latter and the consequence was first foreseen and approved by him. We may be helped in understanding such cases by the scholastic definition of moral cause in terms of *jubens*—ordering. He who orders a murder is moral cause of the murder. The old maxim, "What I do through another, I do myself," is valid.

But there are cases of responsibility for acts which I do not perform other than those of acts which I order done in my behalf. Observation shows that inaction is just as fruitful a source of consequences as is action.[12] Certainly, intentional inaction is a moral situation.

[12] So Simmel, MW, I, 37.

If two friends who are crossing the street are about to be run down by an automobile unless they hurry, and one observes the danger, while the other does not, the one who observes may run and save himself without warning the other. But if he does so intentionally and the other is killed, the one who refrained from warning his friend is as responsible for his death as though he had killed him himself. He is, it is true, less responsible than the gangster who orders a murder; but if he grasped the situation and deliberately left his friend unwarned, the Law of Consequences is his inexorable judge.

Another illustration of the same principle is silence. "Silence gives consent" is an ancient rule; "Qui tacet, consentire videtur."[13] A volume could be written on the ethics of silence. There is wise and responsible silence which keeps confidences. There is weak and cowardly silence which may result in false inferences either regarding the one who is silent or regarding persons or causes which are assailed, when the silent one fails to say the words which would save a reputation or defend a principle. Inaction and silence, then, when intentional, are subject to moral judgment both because of their voluntary character and also because they have consequences in many cases as certain as those of action.

Still another aspect of this problem is brought out by reflection on the unintended consequences of our choices. Consequences ensue with equal necessity whether they are intended or unintended, once the cause has been set in motion. I perform the act, and am plainly responsible for its intended consequences. But I am also responsible for unintended consequences beyond the range of the act itself, if I can foresee them. A person starts a bowlder rolling down a mountainside, "for the fun of it." The

---

[13] Gury, CTM, 3. Regula 43 juris.

picnic party five hundred feet below is just as effectively destroyed whether the person's intent was purely recreational or murderous. It is therefore one's duty to foresee, as far as possible, the events which will probably follow on his act, even though he does not directly cause, much less will, them. This obviously widens the range of responsibility far beyond what is conventionally recognized.

Another group of practical problems centers about the mixed consequences of human action. Few, if any, acts are both fecund and pure in Bentham's sense: that is, sure to be followed by experience of the same kind and sure not to be followed by experiences of the opposite kind. Almost every choice, however good, has some undesirable consequences; and almost every choice, however bad, has some desirable consequences. Careful analysis of the probabilities in some cases shows that, whatever is done, there will be evil consequences; and perhaps, whatever is done, the evil will outweigh the good. It then becomes the duty of the good man to choose between evils, and to select the less evil of two courses, both of which are predominantly evil. It is conceivable that a nation facing the possibility of a war might have to decide for or against a declaration of war on this basis; although the probability that peace will involve greater evils than war is, under modern conditions, almost infinitesimal.

The last practical problem which we shall mention in this connection is whether mankind can survive without its vices. Reformers have assumed that the use of alcohol and of other narcotics, prostitution, economic greed, and war, for example, are vices which can be eradicated, and without which this would be a better world. Realistic opponents of reform have argued either that these vices cannot be eradicated, or that, if they could be, mankind could not endure existence, and would invent new vices to take the place of the old ones, or new ways of gratifying the old ones. They also argue that such vices are an economic necessity. This is, of course, a question that can be practically settled only by the experience of the distant future, but it suggests a lesson for reformers to learn from their opponents. More intelligent consideration should be given by reformers to the probable bad consequences of a reform. If mankind is to survive either with or without its vices, the foes of those vices need to make a more comprehensive application of the Law of Consequences than they have usually done. Abraham Lincoln is an excellent example of a reformer who gave due weight to that Law.

These practical problems constitute a natural transition from the Law of Consequences to the Law of the Best Possible; for we see clearly that the nature of the consequences of human action is such as to prevent a perfect attainment of values. We have to be satisfied with the best possible.

SELECTED BIBLIOGRAPHY

Bentham, his works and discussions of his view, *passim;* Bowne, POE, Chap. II; Everett, MV, Chap. III.

CHAPTER IX

5. THE LAW OF THE BEST POSSIBLE

1. THE LAW OF THE BEST POSSIBLE AND ITS PLACE IN THE SYSTEM

STATEMENT of the Law of the Best Possible: *All persons ought to will the best possible values in every situation; hence, if possible, to improve every situation.*

This Law stands in a paradoxical relation to all of the other Laws in the System, for it both heightens and moderates their effect by its emphasis on the best.

It plainly heightens their effect. For instance, the Law of Autonomy, in the light of this Law, not merely commands allegiance to self-imposed ideals, but also commands that we select the best from among such ideals. From the standpoint of the constant search for the best this Law means constant improvement, wherever improvement is possible, and so it might be called the Melioristic Law. Since the best is attainable in many cases only by a positive control of situations and the production of values which would not exist if we did not will them, it may be called the Law of Creativity. As Melioristic Law and Law of Creativity it adds new force to the Axiological Law, for that Law now means not merely a consistent organization of the values actually given in individual and social life, but it means a critical selection, improvement, and creation of values.

Yet at the same time the Law of the Best Possible moderates the effect of the other Laws. It makes clear that our duty is not some Utopian ideal, the building of an imaginary castle in Spain, or the realization of any unattainable absolute. Our duty is within the limits of what we can do.   Since those limits vary greatly for different individuals, and since a just estimate of the limits of possible achievement is difficult to arrive at, the Law of the Best Possible cautions us not to be too severe in our judgments on our own success or the success of others in obeying the Moral Laws.   A person who knows the surrounding country does not drink the water of a river which, although clear, is polluted.   A stranger sees the clear water, drinks it, is taken ill, and perhaps dies.   The person who knew of the pollution of the water obeyed the Law of Consequences and survived. Shall we say that the one who drank in ignorance was morally blameworthy for failing to investigate?   The Law of the Best Possible requires that we determine the extent of the sincere and unsophisticated innocence of the victim before we hold him morally responsible; it is possible that he was a resident of the slums and had never seen a river in the open country before.   Thus this Law may be called the Law of Tolerance or the Law of Mercy.

While these two effects of the Law—that of heightening and that of moderating the others—are very different from each other, they are not contradictory.   There is no contradiction in saying that the moral law demands the best, but no more than the best; and that both energy and mercy toward ourselves and toward others can be combined.   It is the ability to unite differences in a harmonious whole that develops a strong and well-balanced character.   This Law, then, makes an important contribution to the systematic wholeness of the moral life and to the organic relations of the Laws.

2. Proof of the Law of the Best Possible

If the Law of the Best Possible were not true, it would be right to will a value which one's best judgment regards as less valuable under the circumstances than some other attainable value. The self would then be in the position of both preferring and not preferring the greater value, which would violate the Logical Law and the Law of Autonomy.

The attentive reader may suspect that we have proved too much. It may appear from our proof that the moral person is always obligated to choose the best; in which case he has to ask what the best is. If he were to reply that he regards art, or love, or religion, as the best thing in life, would not the proof of this Law, which prescribes the best at all times, imply that every act of choice should be devoted exclusively to the realization of the one best value? It would be impossible to endure the monotony of a life devoted exclusively to one single value, and no human being has ever done it or seriously tried to do it. But it is not necessary to interpret the Law thus. Life is not a series of separate and distinct value-atoms; as the Axiological Law and the entire System of Laws show, the values are interrelated in an organic whole. The term, "the Best," therefore, does not refer to any single value; it refers to the application of the whole system of values in conformity with Moral Laws. It is obviously impossible, however, to bring the whole content of this system to expression in any single act, or, indeed, in any finite time. It is an ideal for inexhaustible realization. Yet there still remains the question of what "the best possible" can mean in any definite moral situation, if it refers to so vast an ideal. It must be pointed out that the full definite meaning cannot be evident until we have studied all the Laws. Meanwhile, special attention should be called to the phrase, "under the circumstances," which appeared in the proof. It points ahead to the Law of Specification. That Law will show, more clearly than does the Law of the Best Possible by itself, that the "best" is not the whole System of Laws, but, rather, a concrete act in a concrete situation which is most consistent with the System as a whole. If this be taken into account, it will be seen that the proof does not prove too much.

3. Its Basis in Experience and History

The Law of the Best Possible grows especially out of two aspects of our experience; the fact that we do actually prefer certain values to others, and the further fact that we tend to relate these preferences to each other in a more or less connected system. These two factors are elements in what were discussed in Chapter III as experiences of value and experiences of law. This Law, of course, like all the Laws, includes also the experiences of obligation; but experiences of *preference* and of *systematic connection* are the chief data in the present instance. The concept of a "best possible" derives its meaning from the fact that we find some ends to be better than others. We usually prefer health to illness, harmony to discordant noise, kindness to unkindness. Yet each of these preferences is set in relation to our whole system of preferences, so that, on account of our judgment in the light of that whole, we sometimes prefer illness to health, if the illness is a necessary result of doing a duty or achieving an end which we value more than life. The ideal of a "best possible" is the outcome of a series of such experiences—moral experiments in the laboratory of living—seen as a connected whole, organized and criticized. Obviously, this ideal is never, and in the nature of the case never could be, completed. Experience is a moving process, new values often arise, and new insights are achieved. That no more can be demanded than what is possible follows from the very function of ideals, which is to control experience. An ideal or moral law which could not function to control experience would be an ideal that contradicted its own purpose.

The Law of the Best Possible, more clearly than some of the other Laws, rests also on the experience of free choice. Utitz calls attention to the fact that there are muscles which, if they respond to stimulus at all, do so with their entire strength, according to the "all or nothing" law. But this is usually not true of character. When a person is confronted with a situation, sometimes he responds with the full force of his whole and best character, and sometimes he doesn't, although there are persons who tend to respond completely much more frequently than do others.[1] Numerous factors condition the degree of completeness in the response; but one of them is usually the "free" effort or choice of will. Some persons when playing a game or doing a piece of work never force themselves to do their best possible until the last minutes of play, or the last few hours before the work must be completed. Others habitually hold themselves up to the "best possible" from start to finish. The Law of the Best Possible, building on these observed differences, calls on all to follow the example of the last-named group.

The history of ethics shows that the principle involved in the Law of the Best Possible has long been recognized. Aristotle's doctrine of the mean[2] implies a recognition both of "bestness" and of "possibility," for it holds that virtue is a mean between excess and defect; that is, it is the best among a series of possible acts. In modern times Rousseau, at the outset of *Le contrat social,* raises the question whether there can be a just and sure principle, "if we take men as they are

---

[1] Utitz, CH, 220.
[2] Aristotle, *Nic. Eth.*, Bk. II, 1103b-1104a.

and laws as they can be." He seeks, obviously, the best within the limits of the possible. Kant and all formalists in ethics agree that the moral law commands nothing which cannot be done, and that the categorical command of morality always can be obeyed.[3] The right is the best and the best is possible. Simmel brings in a related factor when he speaks of the *probability* of fulfillment as a value-element in ethical demands.[4]

The so-called phenomenologists, notably Max Scheler, under the influence of Brentano and Husserl, find that value-experience contains "evident" (what we call self-evident) distinctions, which reveal that value a is higher than value b.[5] While Scheler has done much to stimulate interest in ethics, and his emphasis on our perception of distinctions is empirically a sound starting point for a theory of the best possible, nevertheless there is in his thought too much confidence in the finality of a value distinction which is once perceived and too little insight into the unity and wholeness of the system of values and laws by which every intuition must be judged.

If we turn to a writer of the opposite type, one who denies the very possibility of theoretical ethics, like Lévy-Bruhl, we find that even he believes that the "amelioration of a given social state is possible . . . by means of a social and rational art."[6] Thus, while he denies theoretical ethics on the one hand, on the other he asserts the validity of an ideal of improvement. This implies a best possible.

---

[3] See art. "Können" in Eisler, KL, and Kant, KdpV (Reclam S), 52. So P. Natorp, *Arch. f. syst. Phil.*, 2(1896), 237, who says, "If I declare it ought to be, I presuppose that it can be." Sorley, MVIG, expresses the same view.

[4] Simmel, MW, II, 1.

[5] Max Scheler, *Jahrb. der Phil.*, 2(1914), 93.

[6] Lévy-Bruhl, MSM, 274.

Recent statements which embody the Law come from Laird and Urban. Laird has said that "what a man ought to do" is synonymous with "the best thing the man in question can do." In going on to add that this is not necessarily "what will have the best consequences,"[7] he implies what we have found to be the organic and systematic character of the Laws, so that no single Law alone—especially not the Law of Consequences—is a safe guide to right action. Urban also formulates a basic maxim of value which is equivalent to our Law of the Best Possible, namely, "The better ought to be chosen rather than the worse"—a principle of the maximization of value.[8] There is no question about the historical and contemporary recognition of this Law.

4. THE PROBLEM OF THE IMPOSSIBLE IDEAL

In spite of the almost trite and obvious validity of the Law of the Best Possible in any rational and just ethics, an objection to it will occur to anyone who takes ideals at all seriously. It is well enough to say tolerantly that we need not do better than we can; yet no thoughtful and right-minded observer of human life can repress the conviction that things ought to be better than they can be. We have to admit that the truly ideal state of affairs cannot be brought to pass. The Law of the Best Possible, therefore, seems like an offensive compromise, a surrender of the claims of the impossible ideal. If we could not find the value of X in a difficult quadratic equation, we should insult intelligence were we to proclaim that the "best we could do" was right, even if the value we obtained was evidently not the

---

[7] John Laird, *Mind*, 38(1929), 273, 274.
[8] Urban, IW, 342. See also the less forceful formula of E. B. Andrews, "The good is worthy to be chosen," in Everett, MV, 259, n.

correct value of X. If a pianist tries to play a selection and fails to keep time or to interpret the composer's intention adequately, we do not say that the selection was well played because the pianist was doing the best possible for him under his limitations.

The problem of the impossible ideal is thus no simple one, and it seems to refute the Law which we have proved by logic, by experience, and by history. However, a more careful analysis shows that the refutation is only apparent. The judgments that the solution of the quadratic was wrong and that the playing was bad were not moral judgments in spite of the use of moral terminology—"wrong" and "bad." The former was a mathematical and the latter an æsthetic judgment, and a reference to the will does not enter into such judgments. But the very essence of a moral situation is its voluntary character, the fact that it is chosen by the will; hence the moral verdict would be that the persons who were bad mathematically and æsthetically were good morally.

Is it, then, sufficient in the moral realm to do our best? A problem persists. Surely we ought to be reasonable, and just as surely we cannot be perfectly reasonable. As Tillich says, "What ought to be realized goes absolutely beyond what is realized."[9] Religion has held before the moral life the ideal of a *lex aeterna* in the will of God.[10] Theodor Lessing expresses the difficulty sharply in the words: "What ought to be is always and under all circumstances relatively impossible." The philosopher Geulincx had said, "Ubi nihil vales, ibi nihil velis" ("Where you have no power, there you have no will"), which is equivalent to a negative statement of the Law of the Best Possible. But Lessing asks whether

[9] Tillich, SW, 146.
[10] Gury, CTM, 15.

Dante's love for Beatrice was then wrong.[11] It was surely an unattainable ideal!

The imperative validity of a beauty, a love, and a reason that can never be completely fulfilled in finite time is essential to the moral life, and the Law of the Best Possible must not be allowed to obscure it. But there is no ultimate contradiction between the Impossible Ideal and the Law of the Best Possible. All life should be moving in the direction indicated by these impossible ideals with which practical men are so often impatient. In fact, we cannot know that any act of ours is the best possible for us unless we have an ideal of something still better than what we are by which to measure our attainments and our relative progress. This is one secret of the power of the paradoxical saying of Jesus: "Ye shall therefore be perfect, as your heavenly Father is perfect." Moreover—and this is the vital point—every real moral achievement in our experience enlarges our powers to some extent, and, as we grow, the best that we could do today is surpassed by the best of tomorrow. Thus at every stage of life the Impossible Ideal should be the goal at which we are aiming; yet our failure to reach it, after doing our best, is neither a ground for moral self-condemnation nor yet for ceasing to move toward that ideal. These truths show again that no law stands alone, and that the Law of the Best Possible will need further supplementation, especially by the Law of Ideal Control and by the Law of the Ideal of Personality.[12]

5. "THE WILL TO BELIEVE" AND THE BEST POSSIBLE

In his most famous essay, William James has dis-

---

[11] Lessing, SWA, 52, 49, 50.

[12] With the discussion in the text, the author's treatment of the "ought-to-be-yet-cannot-be" ideals should be compared (POI, Chap. III).

cussed "The Will to Believe." Using James's own language, the will to believe means that "our passional nature not only lawfully may, but must, decide an option between propositions, whenever it is a genuine option that cannot by its nature be decided on intellectual grounds."[13] James applied this principle to matters of various kinds, including religious belief, and most critics have been inclined to the opinion that he was wrong in the free play he gave to desire in that realm. But substantially all are agreed that he was right in the moral field. As James says, "The question of having moral beliefs at all or not having them is decided by our will,"[14] which is plainly a statement of the Law of Autonomy.

But James's thesis has a peculiar application to the Law of the Best Possible. How are we to determine the limits of what is possible to us? We have found that the Law is a law of tolerance; may it lead us to tolerate our own weakness to such an extent that we come to follow the line of least resistance and call *it* "the best possible"? Or are we to define the possibilities of human nature within the Marxian limits of physical work and bodily enjoyment as the highest values?[15] In answering such questions, James's will to believe has a real significance. "There are," he says, "cases where a fact cannot come at all unless a preliminary faith exists in its coming. . . . Faith in a fact can help create the fact. . . ."[16] In moral matters, James would say, truth is to some extent dependent on our personal action. What is possible depends on what we believe to be possible. He who has strong desire and great confidence

[13] James, WB, 1-31, esp. 11.
[14] *Op. cit.*, 22-23.
[15] See Fabricius, AG, 35.
[16] James, WB, 25.

can make the "impossible" actual. The biography of great men is full of instances of such accomplishment. Nietzsche's doctrine of the Superman—the *Ubermensch* —is an idealized picture of a being who wills most powerfully the highest possibilities. The writings of Carlyle convey a similar message.

Yet a just estimate of human morals must avoid extremes, as we have learned from Aristotle. While few people ever rise to the full heights of their possibilities, it must be recognized that some, and usually the most conscientious, accomplish less than they should because they undertake too much. Setting too high a standard of responsibility generates complexes, worry, and breakdown as surely as setting too low a standard generates moral laxity and lack of control. Moreover, the limits of one's strength vary greatly under different conditions. "At one moment I am actually and completely strong, at another weak."[17] The state of one's nervous system affects the threshold of responsibility.[18] One needs a high degree of sincerity combined with sound judgment to appraise fairly the limits of the best possible. Given a realistic knowledge of human nature which avoids fantastic extremes, the will to believe may well inspire the individual and society to attain values that appear impossible. The unification of the will of a nation in war time shows what can be achieved through social excitement, as the careers of reformers and founders of religions show what determined loyalty to an unpopular ideal can lead to.

6. The Best Possible Veracity

As we had occasion to note in Chapter VI (§ 5), veracity is one of the cardinal virtues. The Law of the

[17] Simmel, LA, 209.
[18] See Hartmann, GGP, 216.

Best Possible affords a good opportunity to examine the application of this virtue.

That it is a virtue is clear from our previous discussion. Disregard of veracity produces both individual and social chaos and contradiction. Without truthfulness we cannot depend on others for the co-operative realization of values. Yet the Law of the Best Possible raises some problems in connection with veracity. In the first place, if it is our duty always to will the best possible values, this duty applies to the communication of truth as well as to other matters. This means that we ought to exercise a certain amount of discrimination in the truth that we tell. Even Kant admits this, although grudgingly. "It is true that I think a great deal with the clearest conviction and to my great satisfaction which I shall never have the courage to utter, but never shall I utter anything that I do not think."[19] Yet, on this basis, it would be possible for a person always to tell the truth, but always to select truths of so low an order of value that he violates the whole tenor of the Axiological Laws. One who feels called on to earn a reputation for veracity by consistently telling the truth about his dislikes, or about the worthless experiences he has had, or about his reasons for doubt and despair, is not discriminatingly truthful. He has violated the Law of the Best Possible. The truth should be told; but it should be significant truth. This does not mean that only pleasant truths should be uttered; on the contrary, courage requires that all sides should be faced. Indeed, it is just as wrong to confine oneself to pleasant truth as it is to unpleasant; the result is sickish and self-destructive. Hence the Law of the Best Possible prescribes the use of balanced judgment in the telling of truth. The fact that a statement is true does

---

[19] See *Kantstudien,* 7(1902), 121.

not mean that it is always right to utter it, although adults who hold themselves to this rule in "polite society" are sometimes secretly grateful to children who blurt out the suppressed truth.

We have said that a true statement is not always right. A more difficult problem arises when we ask, Is a false statement always wrong?[20] Or, to put it more accurately, is it always wrong to intend to give an impression contrary to the essential truth, either by words or by silence, by action or by inaction?—for we can lie or tell the truth in all of those ways.

If we were to depend on the Logical Law alone, we should hold, with Kant and Fichte, that a lie is always wrong, for it is always a logical contradiction of what is known to be true. We should not lie to save a life or a whole civilization. On the other hand, if we were to rely on the Law of Consequences alone, we should be inclined to justify every lie that leads to desirable consequences. We should then lie, not only to save life, but to save feelings, to save money, and, in short, to save trouble. The Law of Consequences is, however, a somewhat treacherous friend to the liar, for the trouble saved by a lie often leads to further and much worse trouble. But, even so, the Law of Consequences needs supplementation by other Laws, especially by the Law of the Best Possible. That Law differs from both the Logical Law and the Law of Consequences by containing within itself a clearer reference to the System of Laws as a whole than they do. If, then, we seek guidance from that Law, we are not confining ourselves to one Law alone, as in the two former illustrations, but are confronting the whole range of moral obligation.

Does the Law of the Best Possible forbid falsehood

---

[20] An authoritative and exhaustive treatment of lying is found in Lipmann and Plaut, LU.

as rigorously as does the Logical Law, does it allow it as freely as does the Law of Consequences, or is it a mean between the extremes? It is certainly not an exact mean, for it points much more in the direction of rigor than in that of laxity. If we seek the best possible, we shall see that very few values, if any, compare with that of truth. Veracity is so essential to good living that it is worth a great deal of trouble and money and injured feelings to preserve it. The lightness with which truth is treated by many people is one of the reasons for believing that civilization is on the downgrade. Without truthfulness, justice cannot be done, contracts are meaningless, science is impossible.

Nevertheless, many moralists hold that to make an absolute rule that a lie should never be told under any circumstances is to sacrifice all other virtues and values to veracity. There are some circumstances where any possible words or deeds will give a false impression, in which case the best possible is the least evil lie. There are occasionally instances of a clear choice between telling the truth and saving a life. In a court of justice the decision should be in favor of truth. But the case of the patient whose life might be saved by a lie, or that of a crowded assembly which may be induced to leave a building peaceably if lied to but which would fall into a panic if told of the fire that had started, is different. Here the responsible person has to decide whether the best possible for him is to depart from veracity or to be the cause of the probable death of innocent people. While there is greater practical difficulty in deciding one's duty on this principle than on the basis of Kantian rigorism which prohibits all lies, it is fairer to the interests of life as a whole.

Summarizing, we may say that the Law of the Best Possible indicates veracity to be the general rule of the good man, but allows him to lie in cases in which veracity would cause the loss of values even more precious than the communication of truth.

Selected Bibliography

The Law of the Best Possible is formulated by Bradley in ES, 157. Two excellent essays on it have been written by John Laird, namely, "Concerning Right," in *Mind*, 38(1929), 273-292, and "On Doing One's Best," in *Jour. Phil. Studies*, 6(1931), 56-71. A valuable but difficult treatment of the background of the Law is found in Urban, IW, Chap. X.

On the special problem of veracity, the following are useful. Lipmann and Plaut, LU (the standard German authority); Abbott, KTE, 361-365 (for Kant's view); Calkins, GMG, 110-118 (modern Kantian); Drake, PC, 244-254, Sharp, ETH, 286-293, and Sidgwick, ME, 295-311 (all three hedonistic); Bowne, POE, 221-226, Paulsen, SOE, 664-712, and Seth, SEP, 226-229 (all close to the point of view of the present chapter).

CHAPTER X

6. THE LAW OF SPECIFICATION

1. THE LAW OF SPECIFICATION AND ITS PLACE IN THE SYSTEM

STATEMENT of the Law of Specification: *All persons ought, in any given situation, to develop the value or values specifically relevant to that situation.*

The Law of Specification stands in· close relation to the Law of the Best Possible. How can the best possible be determined without a study of the situation in which it is to be realized? But the Law of the Best Possible, like all the preceding Laws, has its chief interest in the universal rather than the particular. The problem of the relation of the universal and the particular is one which has occupied the minds of thinkers from Plato and Aristotle down through the Middle Ages, from Continental Rationalists and British Empiricists to Kant and Hegel, and modern idealists and realists alike. It would lead us far afield to go into that problem in detail in our present study.[1] Suffice it to say that the moral life is a special instance of the relation of the universal and the particular. The particular person in particular acts obeys universal laws. The particular and individual element plays a much larger part in the moral life than in the physical sciences; the individual person has a unique value which no physical thing has. Hence a place should be found in the System of Moral Laws for this individual element. The Personalistic Laws will do this for the individual moral person. The Law of Specification does it for the situation which he confronts. It points out that we always deal with a concrete, empir-

---

[1] Brightman, ITP, Chap. V.

171

ical situation of a particular kind, with its own specific experiences of value.

Thus the Law of Specification serves as a balance to the Law of the Best Possible. The latter points us to the ideal of perfection—to what we called "the Impossible Ideal." The former points us to the actual conditions in which we are living. Thus the Law of Specification gives body and substance to all the other Laws, as well as to the Law of the Best Possible. Moreover, it checks any tendency in the Laws toward abstraction by calling attention to the concrete variety of experience. Because it recognizes that every situation has a value, and in some cases a unique and irreplaceable value of its own, it may be called a Law of Pluralism.[2] It lays stress on the fact that the actual values of life are many and diverse, as the Axiological Law laid stress on the fact that true value must be a harmonious system. Since the latter Law points to the unity of value, it may be called a Law of Monism. But there is no contradiction between the pluralism and the monism, in the light of the System of Moral Laws. A varied content is bound together by unified laws in every science, and in every personality. Yet it is easy to forget the claims of the plurality while defending the unity, as ascetics have done, or to forget the claims of the unity while defending the plurality, as æsthetes have done.

It is clear, then, that the Law of Specification has a unique and essential place in the System.

2. PROOF OF THE LAW OF SPECIFICATION

Every situation is a problem. It may contain contradictions within itself, or violate our ideals, or demand action. In some way every situation drives us

---

[2] See Sterling P. Lamprecht, "The Need for a Pluralistic Emphasis in Ethics." *Jour. Phil.*, 17(1920), 561-572.

beyond itself for a full understanding of its meaning. Yet the Law of Specification deals with "the value or values specifically relevant" to a situation. This expression means the value which will best solve the problem raised by the situation while also conserving as well as possible the value given in it. If a person chooses any value, no matter how excellent it may be in itself, which needlessly fails to solve the specific problem or to conserve the unique value of the situation, there would then be a simultaneous violation of at least three of the other Moral Laws. The Axiological Law would be violated, for there would be no adequate attempt to aim at a rational system of values; the Law of Consequences would be violated, for consequences would be ignored; and the Law of the Best Possible would be violated, for no attempt would be made to seek the best solution of the problem raised by the situation. To disregard the Law of Specification is voluntarily to leave a concrete problem unsolved. The result of one unsolved problem is more unsolved problems. Only conformity to the Law's demands promises a rational life. Therefore, the Law of Specification is valid.

3. Its Basis in Experience and History

The whole structure of experience speaks for the Law of Specification. All experience without exception takes place in time, and no event can be literally repeated. Similar events can, of course, occur at a time later than that of the original event; but, however similar these later events may be in other respects, they necessarily differ as to the time at which they occur. Furthermore, at no two moments in time is the total situation in which a moral choice occurs the same. The person who performs the moral act has changed in some respects, both consciously and unconsciously; the physical environment is to some extent different; the social environment even more obviously and significantly so. In the case of a physical experiment, these differences are relatively far less important than in a moral situation, since physical science is concerned with matter and energy which it assumes to remain constant during changes; but in the moral life the essential subject matter is the personal will, and it is in process of growth and development in its whole nature. Hence the uniqueness of every moment of experience, the so-called "irreversibility of time"[3]—the fact that time can move only into the future, but not into the past—imparts a specific and individual character to every moment of our experience. Each present is, to some extent, unique and irreplaceable; hence it merits unique attention. This could be carried to absurd extremes if one were to attach absolute uniqueness to every fleeting instant. The uniqueness is relative and not absolute, while the values of life are not to be found in fleeting instants, but in active processes which build up a whole, such as the appreciation of a poem or the planning of a journey. Each such concrete value-whole, however, is relatively unique, and its special contribution to life, its special circumstances and consequences are therefore worthy of the most intelligent and careful consideration we can give them.

In the history of ethics the same motives of utility which have led hedonists to emphasize the Law of Consequences have also led them to a high evaluation of the specific situation. Aristippus the Cyrenaic (Fourth Century B. C.), the first great hedonist, taught that we are sure only of the present and that present pleasure is

---

[3] See B. W. Van Riper's article, "On Cosmic Reversibility," in *Phil. Rev.*, 26(1917), 361.

therefore worth more than possible future pleasure. The obvious consequence of such a view, carried to extremes of indulgence, is to destroy the possibility of future pleasure; but it well shows the intense hedonistic interest in the present situation. Surely a proper evaluation of what we have is better than an other-worldly rejection of all present values in behalf of a future beyond the grave. As the Law of Consequences taught us due regard for the future, so the Law of Specification teaches due regard for the present; and we owe both in large measure to the hedonists.

At least two other streams of ethical thought move in the direction of the Law of Specification, namely, the social interest in a person's calling and the pragmatic interest in the concrete and particular situation.

The social interest in one's calling has a classical expression in F. H. Bradley's essay in his *Ethical Studies* on "My Station and its Duties." The same thought is expressed in the *Berufsethik* (ethics of one's calling) of German moral theory. Sometimes the "calling" refers to one's occupation, trade, or profession, and then the Law of Specification points toward the special duties of the physician, the cobbler, the bond salesman, the journalist, or the lawyer, duties which are to some extent embodied in codes,[4] but these are usually more noble in their intent than specific in their application. Sometimes the term "calling" has a religious coloring, and then one submits to the circumstances "to which God has called him." Sometimes it is even closer to the Law of Specification, and one's station or calling means the actual situation, whatever it is, in which we find ourselves, and the specific duties which attach to it. But this whole point of view, however interpreted, is in danger of taking the present status as something final,

_____
[4] See Taeusch, PBE, and Heermance, CE.

and may be used in defense of an almost fatalistic sub-
mission to an existing social order or a caste system of
either Oriental or Occidental type. Such a view is far
from being implied by the Law of Specification, which
is no glorification of the *status quo.*

Another tendency of ethical thought toward a recognition of the Law of Specification is found, as we said,
in the pragmatists. Dewey has done much to call attention to the concrete moral situation and its practical
and social implications and consequences.[5] He has gone
too far, probably, in questioning the validity of general
principles. But he has performed a great service in
showing that valid generalizations must grow up out of
and apply to concrete and specific experiences. In this
connection we should consider not only the technical
pragmatists, but also the so-called philosophers of
"life," those who, like Bergson, Simmel, and Guardini,
seek to escape from deadening formulae and abstractions into the fullness of experience.[6] Guardini, for
example, makes the grasping and the interpreting of the
situation the chief work of conscience. He defines
the situation as "a structure of men, circumstances,
and events in which I participate," and holds that
every situation (as we have already pointed out)
is *einmalig* (unique).[7]

It was historically necessary (in the sense of being
imperatively needed) that this interest in the concrete
and particular should come to expression in ethical
theory; for too much moral science had been in terms
of abstract virtues and goods, without sufficient relation either to the individual's conscience and circum-

---

[5] See Dewey and Tufts, ETH, on "The Moral Situation."
[6] Rickert, PL, gives a lively and sometimes unfair, but always
entertaining, picture of this movement in various phases.
[7] Guardini, GGS, 33-34, 21-22, 31.

stances or to the social situation. Formalists addressed the conscience without adequately considering the rest of the situation. Perfectionists and hedonists alike have inclined to study concepts like "the good," "value," and "pleasure," without recognizing the moral importance of the specific guise which these abstractions assume in concrete experience. E. B. Andrews's formula, "The good is worthy to be chosen," true as it is, is typical of an ethical theory which leaves out of account the specific obligations arising from specific situations; a circumstance all the more surprising in view of the moral energy and insight of Doctor Andrews. The Law of Specification is theoretically essential as a corrective of too abstract maxims and practically essential as a guide to present obligations. But even so great a thinker as Kant was not aware of its significance. British and American thought has here supplied a needed empirical corrective.

4. "INDEPENDENCE OF EXTERNALS"

The Law of Specification is firmly established in accordance with the foregoing considerations. But it must be granted that there is one side of moral experience to which it fails to do justice. Precisely as in our investigation of the Law of Consequences it appeared that the good man is indifferent to many consequences, instead of calculating them carefully,[8] so now it seems that the goodness of the good man does not arise from or depend on the particular situation in which he finds himself. The good man may almost be defined as he who rises above circumstance and who is true to his ideal no matter what the situation may be.

This is illustrated by the Stoic doctrine of "inde-

---

[8] See Chapter VIII, § 4.

pendence of externals." The Stoic wise man distinguishes between the things that are in his power and
the things that are not in his power.[9] The former are
the domain of will and moral life. The latter fall outside both of will and of character, and the part of the
wise man is to be independent of everything that is
external to his will. He should not be moved by any
change or loss or circumstance beyond his control,
whether it be his own suffering and deprivations or the
sufferings and death of his loved ones. It is from this
doctrine of "independence of externals" that the popular meaning of the adjective "stoical" is derived, in
the sense of "indifferent to pain or pleasure."

The same independence of externals is sometimes
manifested in a different way by the concentration of
the artist. Ernst tells of a Chinese artist who, when
asked by the Emperor for his secret, replied: "I collected
my mind to bring it to absolute rest. After three days
I had forgotten every reward that I could gain. After
five days I had forgotten all reputation I could gain.
After seven days I had forgotten my limbs and my
form." Then he went to the forest and saw the trees,
and finally when he perceived the right tree he said,
"My heaven-born nature and the heaven-born nature of
the tree came together."[10]

Now, do the Stoic sage and the Chinese artist afford
a refutation of the Law of Specification? By no means.
On the contrary, each presupposes that we should examine the situation carefully and deal with it discriminatingly. We must distinguish what is and what is
not in our power. We must, the Chinese teaches us,
meet every demand in the situation which the goal of
disciplined æsthetic creation imposes on us. The union

---

[9] See the writings of Epictetus and Marcus Aurelius, *passim.*
[10] Ernst, EG, 12.

of the artist's heaven-born nature with the heaven-born
nature of the tree is an ideally perfect instance of conformity to the Law of Specification. Stoic and Chinese
alike neglect practical aspects of the Law which are
relevant in the everyday work of life, but they do not
contradict or disprove the Law. Rather, they presuppose it.

5. Local and Universal Loyalties

As was shown earlier in the chapter, most of the previous Moral Laws (and most other types of law, especially natural) are interested in the universal, whereas
the Law of Specification is interested in the particular.
This difference among the Laws reflects a very real problem in practical life, namely, that of the relation between local and universal loyalties, which will appear
in a more definite and personal form in the treatment
of the Law of Individualism and the Law of Altruism.

If we follow the Law of Specification rigorously,
without considering the other Laws, we shall be more
concerned about local than about universal loyalties; in
fact, we may sacrifice the latter to the former. But
needlessly to sacrifice the local to the universal is just
as serious an error as is the reverse process; and it is
a significant fact that most of the great men of history
who are regarded as morally superior are characterized
by a strong sense of local loyalty, that is, of loyalty to
the specific situation in which they are living and the
specific aim of their life. Patriotism has often been the
refuge of scoundrels, but great and good patriots
abundantly illustrate the principle of local loyalty. In
fact, the greater their insight into universal ideals, the
more devotedly have they labored to realize those ideals
in their own country. Likewise religious leaders have
obeyed the Law of Specification. Jesus was conscious

of having been sent to "the lost sheep of the house of Israel." Martin Luther once said, "I am born for my Germans, and I will serve them."[11] This consciousness of local loyalty has been brought to theoretical expression by Wundt in his norm, "Diene der Gemeinschaft, der du angehörst"[12] ("Serve the community to which thou dost belong"), and by Royce in his essay on provincialism.[13]

But it is essential that the ideal of local pride always be co-ordinated with the ideal of universal loyalty, unless the Law of Specification is to override and destroy the rest of the System of Moral Laws. John Wesley's "The world is my parish" should be taken in connection with Luther's Germans. When local loyalty becomes exclusiveness, when patriotism becomes provincialism, when devotion to specific causes or classes of society produces twenty-seven different political parties in Germany ("splinter-parties," as they are called), then the Law of Specification is plainly in need of correction by the larger perspectives of the Axiological Law and the Law of the Best Possible.

In the light of this insight we may say that race pride is right, but race prejudice wrong; institutional devotion is right, but blind subordination to institutions is wrong; in short, that loyalty is right, but fanaticism is wrong. The principle here at stake is developed in an original manner by Josiah Royce in his theory of "loyalty to loyalty."[14]

6. THE SITUATION AND THE WILL

In the presence of any specific situation, after an attempt has been made to give full weight to the principle

---

11 Cited by Treitschke, DL, 13.
12 Wundt, ETG, III, 155.
13 Royce, RQP, Chap. II.
14 Royce, PL, *passim*.

of the Law of Specification, different types of individuals will react differently. The passive type will submit to the situation, will accept it, will adjust to it as well as possible.[15] The active type will rebel against the actual situation in the interests of the ideal, and will at once propose some plan of reform or improvement. In the presence of an evil, the passive type, at its best, will ask, How can I endure this bravely? The active type will ask, What can be done to remedy this? To a certain extent, this difference in type among individuals is an ultimate psychological fact, and it is unjust to regard either type as wholly wrong. A good man may be of either type, just as one good man may differ from another in temperament or in heredity. Both types exercise their wills: the passive, in order to adjust his attitude to the situation, and the active, in order to adjust the situation to his attitude. The merit of the passive type is its respect for fact and for the personalities of others. The merit of the active type is its interest in improving social conditions. Each individual, as a morally autonomous person, needs to study his own type and discover how, in accordance with the Law of Specification, he may achieve the best kind of life of which he is capable.

These reflections raise the whole question of the relation between the given situation and the will of the individual. Experience shows that situations are capable of a certain amount of control. Only further experience and the progress of scientific knowledge, can determine the degree of control that may ultimately be achieved. But at any stage of scientific knowledge certain types of control are available. Within a given situation, voluntary attention may, to a large extent, con-

---

[15] A reference to "types" implies no hard and fast classification. Most persons combine both types.

trol both the aspects of the situation which are selected for consideration and also (although less easily) the attitude to be assumed toward the situation; the latter, however, is usually more a product of previous habits than is the former. Moreover, situations are not merely "given." We are often able to select the situations in which we shall be, especially if we are economically independent. But freedom of movement, and so of effective choice of situations corresponding to one's interests and ideals, is much restricted in the case of the great masses of people who are so dependent on others economically that their time and energy are not free for the development of their own lives. The effective control of situations rests, then, to a very large extent, on an economic basis. When persons of the active type find themselves economically unfree, the results individually and socially are likely to breed unrest and even revolution, unless society co-operatively sets about the task of creating more just conditions. Here again the study of one Law shows the imperative need of considering all of the Laws and the whole range of moral experience.

SELECTED BIBLIOGRAPHY

The chief treatments of this Law are: Bradley, ES, Essay V on "My Station and Its Duties"; Dewey and Tufts, ETH, Chap. X on "The Moral Situation"; and Royce, RQP, Chap. II on "Provincialism."

See also: Laing, SMP, Chap. VI on "The Unity of the Good"; and Sterling P. Lamprecht, "The Need for a Pluralistic Emphasis in Ethics," *Jour. Phil.*, 17 (1920), 561-572.

CHAPTER XI

7. THE LAW OF THE MOST INCLUSIVE END

1. THE LAW OF THE MOST INCLUSIVE END AND ITS PLACE IN THE SYSTEM

STATEMENT of the Law of the Most Inclusive End: *All persons ought to choose a coherent life in which the widest possible range of value is realized.*

If the Law of Specification was a principle of moral pluralism, and the Axiological one of moral monism, the Law of the Most Inclusive End is a synthesis of the two, with a pluralism of content and a monism of form. Its content is pluralistic because a "most inclusive" end contains the utmost variety possible. Yet its form is monistic because it contemplates the realization of this variety in a unitary whole, a coherent life.

While thus related to the previous Laws, this Law also introduces a new principle, namely, that of a life plan. Other Laws have, it is true, applied to life as a whole (although the Law of Specification emphasized the present situation of life); but they have been confined to prescribing obedience to consistent principles of subjective willing and of objective valuing. The Axiological Law, for example, did no more than to indicate that values ought to be coherent. The Law of the Most Inclusive End goes much further and specifies both that a coherent life—a plan for growth and development— is the aim of the good man and also that such a life should include the greatest variety compatible with that plan. It is thus a Law of complexity and of synthesis. A fuller discussion of the idea of a life plan will be found later in this chapter, but its complete definition must be postponed until the treatment of the Law of the Ideal of Personality.

In spite of the contrast with the Law of Specification, to which attention has just been called, there is also a certain affinity with it. The Law of the Most Inclusive End plainly implies (even if it does not state specifically) that the life plan of one individual may and probably will differ from that of another, just as the Law of Specification implies that situations differ. With all the common ideals that bind reasonable men together, each individual differs to some extent in endowments and opportunities from every other, and the most inclusive end for one will be a different combination of values—a different specialization and development—from the most inclusive end for another. This brings an element of individual imaginative and æsthetic creation into the building of a life plan. It would be nothing short of cultural and moral calamity if the growth of social standardization should crush out this side of life.

It is evident from what has just been said that the Law of the Most Inclusive End contains an anticipation of the Law of Individualism. It implies the uniqueness of each individual life and raises problems which only the Personalistic Laws of Individualism, Altruism, and the Ideal of Personality will solve. The limit to the Law of the Most Inclusive End is fixed by the Law of the Best Possible.

2. Proof of the Law of the Most Inclusive End

If the Law of the Most Inclusive End were not valid, the Law of Autonomy would be violated, for some acknowledged ideals would be left voluntarily unrealized; the Axiological Law would be violated, for there would not be the fullest coherent harmony of values;

and the Law of Specification would be violated, for the characteristic values of some situations would be lost. Hence the Law of the Most Inclusive End is true.

3. Its Basis in Experience and History

The fact of the variety of interests in human life, on which this Law rests for its empirical basis, is well established by biology (laws of heredity, variation, genes, etc.) and psychology (both general and individual). Each individual has a wider variety of possibilities than he can ever realize, and there are great differences among individuals. The development of this variety must be either autonomous or heteronomous; that is, it must either be guided from within by intelligence or controlled from without by whatever influences happen to play upon the individual. If the control is chiefly heteronomous, it often happens that the most significant possibilities of one's life are choked out by circumstances. However, it is a fact that an intelligent, trained observer may understand a person's capacities better than that person does himself, and experience shows the wisdom of seeking good advice. The voluntary following of advice acknowledged to be good is autonomous, not heteronomous. Thus the individual aspect of the Law of the Most Inclusive End[1] is compatible with many types of social co-operation, and even is built on social data.

The variety which the present Law indicates has a further empirical basis in the intense psychological dislike which every normal person has for monotony. External monotony can be endured when the inner life is richly furnished. Inner monotony and lack of spiritual resources drive millions to seek variety in almost any sort of amusement "for a change." Life is at least

---

[1] Everett, MV, 221, etc., speaks of "the more inclusive interest."

tolerable on either basis.   But where there is both inner
and outer monotony, the human being is driven to dis-
traction.   The practice of the pursuit of the most inclusive end is the only guarantee against monotony, for
it furnishes the mind with resources of its own, even
when the environment is barren.

The notion of a life plan also is a natural outgrowth
of the empirical situation.   There are relatively permanent tendencies in every life, whether we call them
instincts, sentiments, dispositions, habits, purposes, or
conditioned reflexes.   There are also factors in the individual and in his environment which tend to interfere
with those tendencies.   They also tend to interfere with
each other.   Thus, man is an end-realizing organism in
need of regulation; and the present Law is one of the
principles of regulation.   James's conception of the
self as "a fighter for ends,"[2] and MacDougall's purposive psychology, as well as the *Gestalt* psychology,[3] are
further evidence of the importance of purpose and
wholeness in life and point in the direction of a life
purpose or *Gestalt*.

The principle of the Most Inclusive End has a long
history.   It was already implied in Plato's Idea of the
Good, which unified the whole variety and meaning of
life.[4]   The hedonists' desire for as much pleasure as
possible, while based on a narrow theory of value, points
plainly in the direction of this Law.   It is true that the
Law has been ignored or even denied by some.   The
Cynics and some of the Stoics, by overemphasis on the
principle of independence of externals, tended to reduce
the wants of life to a minimum in order to be sure of
their satisfaction.   Reason alone was recognized as a

[2] James, POP, I, 141.
[3] See Koehler, GP.
[4] Consult Lodge, PTE, esp. Chap. XXI.

value by the famous Cynic, Diogenes, and he desired no participation in social values, and asked no favor of Alexander the Great, other than that the ruler should step out of his sunshine. Even in the intellectually far superior ethics of Kant, no provision is made for the richness and variety with which the Law of the Most Inclusive End is concerned.

On the other hand, the whole development of perfectionism,[5] is an assertion of this Law. The perfectionists have taught that all the normal powers of life should come to harmonious expression (Aristotle, Paulsen, Bowne, Everett), and that reason dictates not merely individual but also social development, and the extension of life by participation in the values of social institutions (Hegel). All who have advocated perfection in the sense of the largest possible development of life (Green, Steinthal) or self-realization (Wright), or even "the will to power" (Nietzsche), have been concerned with the essential aim of the Law of the Most Inclusive End. The Law is formulated by Everett as follows: "The less inclusive must always be subordinated to the more inclusive interest."[6] This he calls a recognized law. It is axiomatic for perfectionists.

4. EITHER-OR AND BOTH-AND

There are some persons who see every situation in life as a clear choice between black and white, good and evil; they are the either-or type. The ancient Stoics, and many Christians, have regarded humanity as wholly divided into saints and sinners. You are either a saint or a sinner. In any given situation either you do right or you do wrong. Such is the rigorous and undiscriminating either-or view.

---

[5] See Chap. I.
[6] Everett, MV, 220-221.

Others, however, pride themselves on being broad-minded and liberal. To use a popular slogan, they will "try anything once." Their favorite doggerel is the motto:

> "There is so much good in the worst of us,
> And so much bad in the best of us,
> That it hardly behooves any of us
> To find much fault with the rest of us."

This type, which may be called the both-and, believes that all experience is worth having and that we should not exclude anything on the ground of its being bad. It holds that everyone is both saint and sinner and that every act has something good about it.

The either-or type is based on an exaggeration of the truth that there are moral distinctions, and that, by virtue of the Law of the Best Possible, every human being is either aiming to do his best or is not so aiming. The both-and type is based on an exaggeration of the truth that there is a great variety of value, and that, by virtue of the Law of Specification, we ought to seek the value in every situation. But the Law of the Most Inclusive End furnishes a corrective to both exaggerations. It shows that the either-or type is unreasonable in demanding that we either accept or reject entire every possibility that presents itself to us. Life is not so simple as that. It is not, for example, a clear-cut choice between sensualism and idealism, as Wagner depicts it in *Tannhäuser*. The Law of the Most Inclusive End is closer to Robert Browning's theory of the mutual helpfulness and interrelatedness of flesh and spirit. It is unreasonable to demand of human beings a choice between a life of devotion to pleasure and a life of devotion to goodness. The values of bodily enjoyment are real values, and so are the higher ideals of morality.

Indeed, exclusive devotion to any one value is self-destructive. Any value ceases to be a value if pursued exclusive of all others. The Law of the Most Inclusive End shows that the either-or type needs correction at this point and that we should learn from the both-and.

But at the same time it is wrong and impossible to carry out the both-and principle completely. There can be no Law of an all-inclusive end. It is an absurd and self-refuting idea. One cannot both do what one knows to be wrong and also have the approval of an intelligent conscience. One cannot enjoy the pleasures of complete idleness and the pleasures of a disciplined mind in the same lifetime. Further, as Messer and others have pointed out, there is a psychological law of diminishing returns, whereby "as the range of the value-consciousness increases, the intensity and immediacy of the experience diminishes."[7] Any attempt, then, to carry both-and too far in the direction of all-inclusiveness is corrected to some extent by nature (although not soon enough for the best moral results). Excess surfeits. There are limits to our capacity for value-experience. Hence the Law of the Most Inclusive End is at once a synthesis of the truth in the either-or and both-and types and a correction of their errors.

This solution may be criticized as being a compromise. But those who urge this criticism are disguised partisans of either-or. Such persons cannot endure the thought of compromise. Yet compromise is only another name for a fair and impartial adjustment of all the factors in a situation. Just as a group can work together only if each individual in the group is willing to give up some of his preferences in the interest of the group, and as nations can co-operate only by making mutual concessions, so the various values in human

---

[7] Messer, WP, 17.

nature can live together in peace and prosperity only when each one is willing to be limited for the welfare of the whole personality.[8]

5. Culture and "Americanism"

The Law of the Most Inclusive End is fittingly embodied in the life of a man or woman whom we call truly cultured. Such a person has deep insight into life. He is gifted with intelligent appreciation of wide fields of value, generously selected from art, music, science, literature, religion, philosophy, history, commerce, and the drama. He is well-poised, independent, and brave. In short, he is truly civilized.[9]

The number of genuinely cultured persons is much smaller than the potent social and economic restrictions on access to the sources of culture would render necessary. Economic success and social opportunity are by no means a guarantee of cultural attainments. On the contrary, there is often a more sincere and intelligent desire for culture among the relatively poor than among the wealthy. Free public libraries are often more effectively used than expensive private libraries; and it is a commonplace of observation that the best judges of music sit in the cheapest seats at concerts and operas.

In this connection, Americans would do well to reflect on European criticisms of America. The United States is, of course, the wealthiest country in the world, and it has profited enormously from its participation in the War and in the Peace. If economic wealth alone were a guarantee of culture, America would undoubtedly be the most cultured nation of the world. Even if Boston has been called the modern Athens and Chicago

---

[8] See Perry, ME, Chap. I, for an able development of this idea.

[9] Consult the series of essays by Matthew Arnold entitled *Culture and Anarchy.*

rivals Greater Boston as an educational center, Europe
has yet to be convinced of the existence of a genuine culture in the United States. Contemporary European
books and journals abound in allusions to America as
the "Dollar-land," the land of money-chasing madness,
the materialistic-behavioristic-pragmatic country without philosophy, art, or real religion. Such a country
exhibits "Americanism." A recent German writer has
said that America is well informed in technical, political, and economic matters, but that "in religious, philosophical, literary, artistic, and cultural matters in
general, the Americans have little worth mentioning to
offer to us." Another writer says that "he who wished
to live in America had to regard the instinct of con-
quest as the sole instinct of his life," and that therefore
"work became the supreme principle of American religion and philosophy."[10] This is all obviously indicative
of the opinion that America is exclusively practical and
neglects the higher intrinsic values. An American need
not discuss the justice of these criticisms. One does not
quarrel about culture. The point of our discussion is
that the individual or the nation that conforms to the
Law of the Most Inclusive End most adequately attains
the highest cultural level, and that economic success is
no guarantee of such conformity.

6. The Life Plan

We found that a new factor in the Law of the Most
Inclusive End, which had not appeared in previous
Laws, was the concept of the life plan. This concept
may be taken either too rigidly or too loosely. If taken

---

[10] Both quotations are from *Die Auslese*, 4(1930), December. The
first is from Professor A. Hanhart, in the "Sonderbeilage," p. 2.
The second is from an article by Theodor Lüddecke in the *Revista
de Occidente*, Madrid, March, 1930, summarized pp. 753-755 of *Die
Auslese*.

too rigidly, it would mean that the good man must from the dawn of his autonomous moral consciousness be guided by a definite conception of what he wants to become. If taken too loosely, it would mean that it is enough to plan to be "good" and to guide one's life by a general conformity to moral laws. Neither extreme is favorable to a normal moral development. What is needed is, again, an Aristotelian mean between the extremes (or an Hegelian synthesis of them). The actual life plan should be rigid enough to be reasonably definite, but loose enough to be susceptible to frequent revision and correction. The extent to which the future can be foreseen and planned for varies greatly with individuals and with circumstances.

The Law of the Best Possible is here the guiding principle for the application of the Law of the Most Inclusive End. The most evil attitude to assume in this connection is doubtless that of deliberately forming a life plan which one knows to be wrong; yet the attitude of refusing to look ahead and try to make any plan at all is almost as bad. The person who assumes the former attitude aggressively has the virtue of activity and may find out that he is wrong; whereas he who assumes the latter attitude is manifesting the absence of virtue and is not likely to find out anything about his capacities. He resembles a scientist who declines either to perform an experiment or to profit by the experiments of others. The formulation of a life plan is the construction of an hypothesis to be tested by the experiments of daily life. After all, the ultimate aim of physical science is the control of experience through experiment, and not mere knowledge of natural laws, interesting as that is. Above all, what Kant called the primacy of the practical reason over the speculative, that is, the fact that theoretical knowledge is always dependent for its function in life on the purposes of the moral will, must be recognized as a basis for a very practical interest in the application of the life plan. Aristotle, wiser as usual than many moderns, remarked that "we do not study virtue in order to know what it is, but in order to become good."[11] A life plan, then, must be a life function; in order to be an ethical principle it must work pragmatically. A plan of action is futile unless it is fulfilled in action. This, and not what the European critics call "Americanism," is the moral truth of pragmatism.

SELECTED BIBLIOGRAPHY

There are few specific treatments of this Law.

Everett, MV, 219-224, is basic; see also Perry, ME, Chap. I, and his GTV, Chap. XXI, III, on "The Standard of Inclusiveness," 645-658.

---

[11] Aristotle, *Nic. Eth.*, Bk. II, 1103b.

CHAPTER XII

8. THE LAW OF IDEAL CONTROL

1. THE LAW OF IDEAL CONTROL AND ITS PLACE IN THE SYSTEM

STATEMENT of the Law of Ideal Control: *All persons ought to control their empirical values by ideal values.*

This Law brings the Axiological Laws to their completion. It performs for the ends willed the same function that the Law of Autonomy performed for the will itself and that the Law of the Ideal of Personality will perform for the whole personality, namely, that of making explicit the control of life by ideals. In the Law of Autonomy the point was that the ideals, to be imperative, need to be acknowledged by the will; in the Law of Ideal Control it is that ideals, which conform to the Axiological Laws (ideal *values*), ought to function in the organization of the actually experienced empirical values; in the Law of the Ideal of Personality it is that these ideals should be unified and made concrete in an ideal of what human personality should be. We have here three stages of increasing rationality and concreteness in our thought of the ideal.

The Law of Ideal Control does not add a new principle to the System in the same sense in which the other Laws do; rather, its function is that of unification and systematization. Just as the implications of the Law of Autonomy enabled us to distinguish between the spontaneous and the critical conscience, so the implications of the Law of Ideal Control enable us to distinguish between empirical values (value-claims) and ideal values (real values), or, as Schwarz puts it, between

Wertschein (value-seeming) and *Wertsein* (value-being).[1]

2. Proof of the Law of Ideal Control

If the Law of Ideal Control were not true, the empirical conflict of values would be left uncontrolled. The tendency of this unrestrained conflict would be to destroy gradually all capacity for definite value-experience and thus to destroy the value-experience as a whole. This would cause a violation of all of the Axiological Laws.

The foregoing proof shows that this Law is a unification of the preceding Laws.

3. Its Basis in Experience and History

Referring back to Chapter III on the Data of Ethics, we find there in the discussion of the psychology of value and of law the chief empirical foundations for the Law of Ideal Control. We experience value, and we interpret it rationally. These are given facts, and the formulation of those facts in the present Law is perhaps the very heart of the System of Moral Laws.

That morality means control has been recognized by the wisdom of the ages; μηδὲν ἄγαν ("nothing in excess"), said the ancient Greek. Even Aristippus, the vivid hedonist, laid down the rule of ἔχω, οὐκ ἔχομαι ("I possess, I am not possessed"), which meant that he saw the need of keeping his pleasures under his control. Aristotle quotes a saying of the Pythagoreans to the effect that "the evil belongs to the unlimited, the good to the limited,"[2] which embodies the same idea. Self-control, self-guidance, and self-discipline are moral fundamentals.

---

[1] Schwarz, ETH, 7.
[2] Aristotle, *Nic. Eth.*, Bk. II, 1106b.

But Hartmann rightly pointed out in modern times that, while self-control is an essential condition of morality, it must not be confused with morality itself.[3] A person may be self-controlled in order to attain ends that are consciously wrong and are not "ideal values" in the true sense at all. This same point was doubtless in Wundt's mind when he formulated his "subjective humane norm": "Feel thyself as an instrument in the service of the moral ideal."[4]

In general, hedonists, while recognizing the need of controlling pleasures so as to secure the maximum pleasure in the long run, are averse to acknowledging that one specific pleasure is inherently more "ideal" than another, although John Stuart Mill admitted qualitative differences among pleasures. But it is interesting to find Bentham, the arch-hedonist who grants only quantitative distinctions in pleasure, saying that "that is pleasure which a man's judgment, aided by his memory, recommends and recognizes to his feelings *as* pleasure."[5] That is, even Bentham unconsciously appeals to the principle of ideal control by judgment within the very most elementary pleasure experience.

A present-day hedonist, Schlick, continues the standard hedonistic tradition in his theory that we cannot prove norms to be justified. Ethics, he holds, simply "finds the acknowledgment of them to be a fact of human nature."[6] This means that we cannot distinguish true from false ideals by any trustworthy standard. The only basis of ideal control is that we do treat some norms as ideal values to which we subordinate the empirical values, but that we have no justification for

---

[3] Hartmann, PSB, 424.
[4] Wundt, ETG, III, 158.
[5] Bentham, DE, I, 29.
[6] Schlick, FE, 13.

so doing. The *fact* that we acknowledge certain norms is ultimate. This is a refusal to distinguish between the descriptive and the normative study of value-experience. But the principle of reason, applied in the spirit of all the Axiological Laws, would seem to furnish a means of proving norms to be justified in spite of Schlick's assertion to the contrary; and his theory is at worst no denial that we do acknowledge ideals as controlling factors.

The control of empirical by ideal values, then, may be said to be very generally held, save for certain exceptions which will be discussed in the following section.

4. NATURE AND CONVENTION

There has been a tendency which has emerged frequently in history that may be called the revolt of the empirical values against the ideal values, or the revolt of nature against convention. The Greek Sophists made a distinction between what was true by nature (φύσει) and what was true by convention (νόμῳ). That there is some truth in what they had in mind is not to be denied. It is related to the distinction between fact and theory, and to that between instinctive tendencies and traditional tabus and inhibitions. Nevertheless, it is extremely difficult to define. In a certain sense, everything a living being does is natural; that is, it is a fact of nature, and the most "unnatural" behavior, as we call it, is really a natural process. The distinction between "nature" and "convention," therefore, is a distinction within nature. "Convention" is just as hard to define as is nature. Does it mean all traditional standards? Does it mean whatever men agree on? Does it mean whatever life becomes as a result of critical thought?

When the Sophists rebelled against convention, some few of them meant the restraints of moral standards;

when Rousseau rebelled, he meant the artificialities of civilization; when the extreme psychoanalyst rebels, and expresses his suppressed desires, he means both what the Sophists meant and what Rousseau meant. The vague and confused feeling of the age for nature as opposed to convention was illustrated by the vogue, before the World War, of Pastor Charles Wagner's cult of "the simple life"; by the Youth Movement (especially in Germany), as a protest against the congested conditions and hectic pleasures of the great cities, and a return to outdoor life, simpler amusements, and more wholesome living; and also by the uncritical revolt against all standards of morality which often expresses itself in unrestrained conduct and unthinking obedience to impulse.

Here, then, is a problem of practical as well as theoretical significance. In order to approach it more intelligently, let us break it up into separate questions.

First, we may ask whether a separation between nature and convention is legitimate. We have already touched on this, pointing out that the distinction is certainly no absolute one, since "convention" itself is a phenomenon of human nature, as well as are our instinctive desires. Convention, as the term was used by the Sophists, meant human opinion, human thought. It is certainly legitimate to make a distinction between conduct into which our opinions and thoughts enter as determining factors and conduct which is not guided by such intelligence as we possess, but is purely spontaneous, impulsive, or instinctive. Taking the separation between nature and convention in this sense, it is of great importance to the moral life to understand it. Strangely enough, some regard nature, even in this sense, as obviously superior to convention, while others —the idealists, the rationalists, and the overwhelming majority of moral reformers—regard rational "convention," or almost any purposive guidance, as obviously superior to uncontrolled "nature."

The question then takes the form: Is "convention" legitimate? We can now see that this is equivalent to asking: Is control of our instinctive and impulsive behavior by conscious purpose desirable? In this general form, the question must be answered in the affirmative, as is evident from the discussion of the Law of Consequences in Chapter VIII. If we go ahead blindly, trusting nature to guide us aright without any forethought or intelligent selection from among the possibilities of conduct, we cannot hope to survive as well as the lower animals which live a "natural" life without reason. Our nature is more delicate and complicated than theirs, both physically and psychologically, and is more in need of attention.

The cult of nature, then, is obviously an exaggeration. As a protest against unintelligent conventions, against a guidance of life by standards which crush or distort it, against the dishonest artificialities of civilization, it is a wholesome tendency. But we do not reach the heart of the problem until we face the question in yet another form: Is control of nature by ideal values harmful? Something, although not much, can be said for an affirmative answer to this question. A too rigid "Puritanical" repression of natural desires by rigorous discipline in some instances produces a reaction in which nature rebels and a distorted life results. The psychoanalytic casebooks are full of such instances. Nevertheless, Freud himself recognizes the need of control,[7] and it is utterly illogical to argue that because unwise control leads to disaster, therefore no control is prefer-

---

[7] "Culture must be built up on coercion and instinctual renunciation." Freud, FOI, 11.

able. Absence of control by ideal purposes is even surer
to lead to disaster than is the most fanatical rigorism.

The question is sometimes raised whether *grandeur
d'âme,* the creativity of great artists, and the full development of genius may not be hindered by ideal control.
It is true that the great man, who sees through to the
core of human nature, may reject many points in the
current code of the society in which he lives. But the
student of ethical theory has learned to distinguish
between conformity to a social code and loyalty to self-
imposed ideals. The genius may be excused for violations of a code if they result from devotion to his ideals
and those ideals embody his best self. This is, however,
far from implying that moral law would excuse a genius
or anyone else for a voluntary violation of his own
ideals. Shelley is a conspicuous instance of a genius
who violated a code in obedience to his own standards,
but who held himself conscientiously to those standards.
It was he who spoke of the need of a "fence of reason,"
which is just what is meant by the Law of Ideal Control. A similar instance is Goethe; and his famous saying, "In der Beschränkung zeigt sich erst der Meister"
("The master shows himself by his self-limitation"), is
another putting of the same Law. No great literature
or art, and no great living, has ever been produced without control. The attempt to abolish all norms and restraints is self-defeating.

The problem of "nature" *vs.* "convention" thus becomes the problem of unrestrained life in accordance
with instinct as opposed to life in accordance with reason. This, in turn, is the question whether it is better
for certain mechanisms within the self to control the
whole self without its consent, or for the self as a unity
to consider each of its interests and mechanisms in the
light of its total purpose. The peril of too much ration-

alism and idealism is not to be compared with the peril
of blind and irrational living. It is safe to say that the
international behavior of the modern state has largely
been a series of violations of the Law of Ideal Control.

5. A Principle of Criticism and Growth

In practice it has often happened that the advocate
of the Law of Ideal Control has tended to become dog-
matic and fixed in his ideas. This was not true of the
great idealists, Socrates and Plato; but it has been
true of some of their followers.

It is therefore desirable to make clear that the tendency in question, far from being a result of the Law
of Ideal Control, is really a violation of it. Taken
seriously, the Law is a principle of criticism—including
self-criticism—and growth. For every ideal actually
applied to life generates a value-experience which is, of
course, an empirical value, however high its level may
be. Every such value is, in turn, subject matter for
ideal control. In other words, all of the ideals which
have hitherto entered into my life should daily be confronted by the standards of the highest insight I have
yet been able to attain. This necessarily will mean that
I shall have to revise or even reject today some of the
standards which seemed final even as recently as four
or five years ago. Ideal control is thus a process of
never-ending growth.

Lipps has well stated the implications of this fact.
He says: "[I am] morally obligated to change my conviction, to be untrue to myself in my willing, to break
a promise, a contract, an oath, if they have an immoral
content, or I recognize their content as immoral."[8] This
is indeed a radical position and has serious implications
for the relations between civil law and moral law, but

[8] Lipps, EGF, 153.

it is the only possible one for a person who desires to take his moral life honestly.

6. The Power of Rational Ideals

It is common to say that our culture and morality are but a thin veneer which disappears as soon as a crisis arises. The behavior of men in war time and even in the world of ordinary business relations tends to make it easy to accept this cynical estimate of human nature. Ideals seem weak and ineffectual in the presence of the titanic forces of life. President Henry Churchill King embodied this thought in his book, *The Seeming Unreality of the Spiritual Life*.

Many idealists have moods of profound depression, just as mystics know what is meant by "the dark night of the soul." Fichte, in such a mood, wrote that only a few men are evil and violent, "for the majority of men lack the strength to be really bad; as a rule they are merely stupid and ignorant, cowardly, lazy, and mean."[9] Sincere and able men, like Feuerbach and Karl Marx, have made their fundamental view of human nature rest on the belief that not reason, but the physical man, was "the measure of all things."[10] Illustrations of the tendency to regard rational ideals as powerless could easily be multiplied from literature, history, and life.

Yet this tendency, strong as it is, has been opposed by an even stronger one in the life of the benefactors of the human race—philosophers, saints, scientists, poets, reformers, inventors, and many of the greatest statesmen and industrialists. This has been the tendency to believe that devotion to ideals not merely makes life worth living, but is the most potent force in human history. The great influence of Aristotle over the human

[9] Cited by Treitschke, DL, 41.
[10] See Hartmann, ES, 72.

mind, from Greek days down to the present, is due partly to the range and quality of his powers of ideal interpretation, but perhaps even more to his devotion to truth, which he himself expresses thus: "It might perchance seem better, yes, to be our duty, in order to save the truth, to destroy even our own opinions, especially as we are philosophers. For, though we love both, yet it is a holy duty to prefer truth."[11] Even a military realist, like Napoleon, "always found in the moral forces of the life of nations the most dangerous foes to his world-empire and he persecuted the 'ideologues' with his wildest hatred."[12] The fear which the possessors of power have in the presence of ideals sincerely held is illustrated by the death sentences passed on Socrates and Jesus, to mention only the most conspicuous instances; or by the fanatical persecution of pacifists in war time by the government of the United States. These facts are indubitable proof of the power of ideals. Perhaps one secret of this fear lies in the fact that a person genuinely committed to ideal control is rendered only the more energetic by the presence of obstacles. As William James once remarked, ethical conduct is in the direction of greatest resistance. The continued moral energy of the race despite the utmost discouragements and disillusionments is testimony to the power of ideal control.

SELECTED BIBLIOGRAPHY

Treatments of the virtue of temperance in almost every textbook of ethics bear on the subject of this chapter.

Also: Brightman, POI, Chap. III; Otto, TAI; Fung, CSLI; Shafer, CAN.

---

[11] Aristotle, *Nic. Eth.*, Bk. I, 1096a.
[12] Treitschke, DL, 81.

CHAPTER XIII

9. THE LAW OF INDIVIDUALISM

1. The Law of Individualism and its Place in the System

Statement of the Law of Individualism: *Each person ought to realize in his own experience the maximum value of which he is capable in harmony with moral law.*

With the Law of Individualism we have reached the third and last main division of the System of Moral Laws, namely, the Personalistic Laws. While, as is evident from the very nature of the subject matter of ethics, all ethical laws must apply to personality in some sense, the Laws previously considered have all dealt with some special aspect or part of personality, one of its interests, or a set of interests. The Formal Laws dealt solely with the will as a subjective fact. The Axiological Laws dealt with the values which the will ought to choose. The Personalistic Laws are more comprehensive; they deal with the personality as a concrete whole. The Law of Individualism, for instance, deals with the person's obligation to himself, as a total personality; the Law of Altruism deals with the mutual obligations of persons in their interrelation; while the Law of the Ideal of Personality deals with the standards by which each person and group of persons ought both to estimate and to guide its development.

In the present arrangement the Law of Individualism comes first among the Personalistic Laws. This is based on the view that the individual person is the moral unit. To say this does not mean that "the individual" is an isolated atom, independent of social factors. Such a view is, of course, absurd.[1] Individuals are bearers of biological heredity, which connects them with others, and they are profoundly influenced by the behavior, the opinions, the feelings, and the wills of the countless other individuals to which we give the name of society. But it should not be forgotten that society consists of individuals. The statement that society affects the individual or that society is responsible for the sufferings of the individual merely means that individuals affect each other on a large scale. There is no "society" or "social mind" apart from the individuals constituting the society. Within the individual mind, it is true, some processes are primarily concerned with the private affairs of the person, while others are concerned with social relations. On the one hand, the individual may face his own problems in solitude; he may assert his will or indulge his personal feelings. On the other hand, he may be subjected to influences from others. The coming of one other person into his solitude at once affects his mental processes. The presence of many others, especially if they are an excitable mob, may result in the crowding out of rational will from his mind and the dominance of low-grade emotions similar to those which are felt by others in the mob. But the so-called crowd mind or mob mind is merely the presence of similar mental processes in a large number of individuals who have ceased to consult their own

---

[1] A man like Kierkegaard could go to the most radical extremes in revolting against the emphasis on the membership of the individual in a larger whole. He wrote: "Influenced as I was by Hegel and everything modern, without sufficient maturity to appreciate greatness, I couldn't help pointing out in my Dissertation, as an imperfection in Socrates, that he had no eye for totality, but looked only at the individuals. Hegelian fool that I was, just this very thing is the great proof how great a moralist Socrates was!" Cited in Dollinger, SK, 149.

best judgment because of their excited desire to co-
operate with others in the mob.

Since, then, the individual is the real unit in all social
situations, the Law of Individualism is naturally the
first of the Laws of Personality to be considered.
Whether obligation to oneself is or is not the basis of
obligation to others is a matter for later consideration;
but certainly a self is the only being capable of a moral
act or a moral obligation. "Society" has no obligations; but every member of society, in all his acts, has
obligations.

2. Proof of the Law of Individualism

Since values exist only in individual selves, if they
are to be realized at all, and if the Moral Laws are to
be obeyed at all, it must be by the efforts of individual
selves. Such efforts would have to be directed toward
the realization of moral value either in other selves or
in the individual. But if all effort were directed toward
the realization of value in others, no individual would
be able to exercise control over the values realized in
his own life; this would violate the Law of Autonomy
and the Law of Ideal Control, and would therefore destroy the basis for sustained social effort. Moreover, if
the value realized in the individual be not the maximum
of which he is capable under the conditions of his life,
the Law of the Best Possible is violated. Hence the
Law of Individualism is true.

3. Its Basis in Experience and History

The Law of Individualism grows partly out of the
experienced fact that all possibility of conformity to
Formal Laws is individual, because will is always the
act of an individual; and also out of the fact that all
value is the experience of an individual. This latter

statement is true, whatever be the objective basis of value. We may hold that value is always due to a physical stimulus of some sort; or to some sort of behavior; or to the perception of a unique quality in things; or to a Platonic Idea; or to social tradition or co-operation; or to the will of God; or to the organic unity of the universe. All of these views are held in various forms and combinations at the present time. But, as far as the immediate experience of value is concerned, one fact remains the same whatever be the ultimate origin and interpretation of our value-experience, namely, that the *realization* of value, its actual functioning in experience, occurs in the consciousness of individuals.[2]

From another point of view, we find a basis for the Law of Individualism in the tendency to self-preservation which is naturally strong in all human beings, unless it is broken by unbearable experiences. In fact some, like Feuerbach, actually identify the will with "the love of life, the impulse to self-preservation and happiness."[3]

Equally significant is the experienced fact of the unity of the self. To be an individual is to be a unity. Our moral problems and our moral goals both arise from the fact that each one of us is an individual with conflicting tendencies in his nature, yet, in all the conflict, experiencing at the same time an imperative need for self-consistency. The moral individual is the one who grasps his complex experience as a whole and guides it toward the best of which it is capable. No one can understand any act performed by himself or anyone else unless he considers the whole personality which is expressed in the act. "He who cannot grasp the individual as a whole," says a German philosopher, "is

---

[2] See Schuppe, ERP, Part II, esp. p. 109.
[3] Feuerbach, *Werke*, X, 230.

incapable of grasping anything about the individual in any absolute way."[4]

The obligation to realize value in one's own person has been very widely recognized. Kleinsorgen, an interesting unconventional monist who follows Haeckel, has stated the ethical norm in terms of "the principle of self-preservation, the will for life and progress."[5] This will be recognized as a rather vague statement of the Law of Individualism. Kleinsorgen mentions as defenders of this principle the Stoics, the Epicureans, Rousseau, Lamettrie, Helvétius, Holbach, Frederick II, Hobbes, Locke, and Spinoza. He might well have added both Christ, with his lofty valuation of the individual soul ("be ye therefore perfect"), and Nietzsche, the chief modern opponent of Christ, with his doctrine of "the will to power."

In one of his early writings, Schelling expresses the principle of individualism in quaint language: "Be! in the highest sense of the word; cease to be yourself an appearance; strive to become a Being in Yourself! This is the highest demand of all practical philosophy."[6] The duty to oneself is regarded as axiomatic by Sidgwick, who taught that "one's own happiness is a self-evident obligation."[7] William Stern, the distinguished psychologist and personalist, made the Law of Individualism the fundamental principle of ethics, in the following form: "Act as far as possible in accordance with the impulse to the preservation of the psychical or spiritual in its different forms, repelling all forces that tend to destroy it."[8] Schwarz makes the "Law of the Ethics of Personal Value" one of two fundamental laws of

---

[4] Simmel, LA, 201.
[5] Kleinsorgen, CE, 48 and 50.
[6] Schelling, *Werke*, I, 171.
[7] Sidgwick, ME, 379.
[8] Stern, KGE, 422.

ethics; it runs: "Choice of one's own personal value stands above regard for one's own particular states."[9] Schwarz's point in this law is a double one: First, that we have an obligation to ourself, and, secondly, that the obligation to the whole self stands above the satisfaction of any single experience.

Without multiplying further evidence, it may be asserted that the Law of Individualism is well grounded in the history of ethical thought.

4. DENIAL OF THE LAW OF INDIVIDUALISM

No ideal that has ever been held has gone unchallenged. It is well that this is so; for humanity can have confidence only in ideals which have been tested and criticized and have been proved true as a result of this process.

The Law of Individualism, for example, has been doubted both practically and theoretically. Practically, it has been doubted by the attitude of irresponsibility. Theoretically, it has been doubted partly on the ground that the universal is believed to be superior to the individual, and partly on the ground that the social is believed to be superior to the individual. Let us consider these objections somewhat in detail.

The irresponsible person says: Why should I be obligated to be different from what I am? I am what I am, and that's enough. Why should I be assailed with laws about maximum value? It is not difficult for human nature to become very enthusiastic about this idea, and to welcome an extreme type of what William James called a moral holiday. But if a person assumes this

---

[9] Schwarz, SL, vi. Simmel, as we have seen, likewise emphasizes the total personality, but in his essay on "The Individual Law" he dwells also on the place of each act as a pulse-beat in life. Simmel, LA, 196.

point of view, it is well that he should become clearly conscious of what he is doing. Not only is he opposing progress and the betterment of humanity, but he is also repudiating reason. He is saying that, even when he acknowledges that an attainable value is better than what he now possesses, he prefers his present state to the effort of improving it. Thus his attitude toward the possible maximum value is that of both approving it and not approving it. Irresponsible moral laziness is, therefore, the contradiction of reason itself. However comfortable it may be to enjoy the easy, but inferior present, in preference to the attainable and superior, although difficult, future, the rejection of reason and responsibility which it involves leads in the end to very uncomfortable results. He who rejects reason cannot justly appeal to reason. He who is irrationally irresponsible has no right to expect just or fair treatment from others, much less to demand it. In the end, rejection of the Law of Individualism, fully carried out, would make one an outcast from the human race. The practical rejection of the Law turns out to be self-refuting.

From the theoretical standpoint, we repeat, the Law of Individualism has been criticized in the interests of the universality of moral law. Moral law, it is said, is "overindividual"; that is, it is universal, common to all, not confined to any one individual, but over and above all individuals. Now, the Law of Individualism proclaims a special duty that the individual has toward himself as distinguished from all others. Moreover, in so far as the Law of Individualism prescribes the duty to seek one's own happiness—a duty which Sidgwick regarded as self-evident—it is not recognized by Kant as an obligation at all. Obligation appertains, according to him, only to the universal categorical imperative of the practical reason, but not to the admonition to seek our own happiness. The latter, "the general principle of self-love," as Kant calls it, is a natural tendency of everyone and does not need to be commanded by the moral law.

To the first of these two objections, namely, that the Law of Individualism lacks universality because it is confined to the individual, it may be replied that a moral law is universal not because it commands everyone to deal with the same situation or subject matter, but because it commands everyone to act in accordance with the same principle. In this case, the subject matter (the individual) is different for every person; but the principle is the same for all: Respect and develop yourself! Kant's objection is likewise insufficiently grounded. In the first place, he confines morality to the Formal Laws and does not recognize the Axiological Laws. Our whole study thus far has shown the incompleteness of this view. Moreover, Kant's belief that all men naturally seek their own happiness is not true in any sense that will satisfy the demands of morality. Men may naturally seek happiness, but they do not do so thoughtfully and intelligently; they need to be told by their intelligence to seek for "maximum value," as our Law says. And the Law which commands this is a universal principle, even though it has particular values or concrete happiness as its subject matter. Hence the principle of universality is not at odds with the Law of Individualism.

A final theoretical objection to the Law of Individualism was raised from the social point of view. Many seem to regard it as almost self-evident that the moral life is dependent on social relations and that therefore all moral obligations are essentially social. Two great philosophers, Hegel and Schopenhauer, who are in most respects at swords' points, agree in rejecting the Law of Individualism, although for reasons that are totally different.

While Hegel makes the Absolute a spiritual personality,[10] he does not entertain much respect for the individual human personality. The moral value of human life he finds in social relations and social loyalties; devotion to social institutions, especially the state, is the highest ethical ideal. Despite Hegel's insights into the nature of the mind and his keen eye for the rich meaning of experience, his interest in society led him to neglect the individual.[11] Schopenhauer, on the other hand, had no interest whatever in social institutions; but his pessimism led him to a feeling of compassion for others. We are all caught in the same trap, hence we should pity one another. This feeling of pity is the essential moral experience. It is absolutely free from selfishness. In fact, says Schopenhauer (in his book on *Die Grundlage der Ethik*), "the absence of all egoistic motivation is the criterion of an act of moral value."[12] Now, if Schopenhauer's major premise, that pity is the only moral motive, be correct, his conclusion must be correct. But pity is certainly not the only moral motive. It would have no force if there were no values. The desire to be reasonable and to attain positive values is the basic moral motive, as the Formal and Axiological Laws have shown. If this be true, then "egoistic" motivation, in the sense of a desire to attain values in my own person, is one of the corner stones of morality. If the individual does not achieve value, society will not achieve value.

---

[10] See Seth, HP, 150, 153, 159.

[11] See the brief, but vigorous, article by M. Rubinstein, "Das Wertsystem Hegels und die entwertete Persönlichkeit," *Kantstudien*, 15(1910), 263-269.

[12] Discussed by Dilthey, GW, II, 37.

Therefore, the attack on the Law of Individualism from the social point of view may be said to have failed. A keen observer has remarked that an altruistic act may, in some cases, be "easy virtue"; that is, an escape from the harder task of facing one's inner problems and solving them honestly.[13] The fundamental obligation to make one's own personal life the best that it can be remains unshaken by these attacks.

5. Egoism, Independence, and Individualism

The confusion of ordinary thought is indicated by the fact that words like "egoism" and "selfishness" have a predominantly evil meaning, while such terms as "independence" and "individualism" are on the whole good in their connotation, although all four have much in common. Of the four, perhaps selfishness is commonly regarded as the worst. It usually means such regard for oneself as violates or overrides one's obligations to others; in other words, it is independence, individualism, or egoism, which disregards moral laws. The word "egoism" has a peculiar fate. Popularly it is commonly identified with selfishness; but scientifically it is very often used by ethicists to mean a proper interest in self, or any interest in self (whether proper or improper morally), just as "altruism" is used to mean either a proper interest in others or any regard for them whether "good" or "bad." There is even some difference in the coloring of the terms "independence" and "individualism," as used by different people. Some imply that independence and individualism are wholesome; indeed, a large part of the aim of education is to develop independent powers of taste and judgment. On the other hand, those who value institutions above indi-

---

[13] Marie Louise Enckendorff, quoted by Gertrud Kühl-Claassen, *Arch. sys. Phil.*, 16(1910), 101.

viduals look with suspicion on every sign of individualism and regard the individualist as antisocial and as an
obstinate being unwilling to profit by the experience of
others or to co-operate with them.

The proof and discussion of the Law of Individualism
have shown that a certain amount of "egoism," that is,
of interest in the development of value in one's own experience, is not only allowable but is even obligatory.
The principle of the System of Moral Laws enables us to
define, in a general way, the point at which obligatory
egoism becomes immoral selfishness. It is the point at
which interest in the experiencing of values in one's own
person leads one to disregard any of the other Moral
Laws, or when interest in present personal satisfaction
outweighs interest in the wholeness of the moral life.
Selfishness, therefore, is, of course, bad when the regard
for others prescribed by the Law of Altruism, is abandoned in the interests of the self; but it is also bad in
many cases in which affectionate regard for others is
combined with violation of other Laws, such as the Law
of Consequences, the Law of the Best Possible, or the
Law of the Most Inclusive End. Not only does this
follow from the arguments of ethical science, but, in
the long run, the psychological consequence of selfishness is usually, as Hartmann said, that "he who tries to
live only for his own comfort and pleasure becomes dis-
gusted with life."[14] But the altruistic critic of egoism
needs to remember that he who fails to live for the realization of the highest values in his own person and to
develop them independently is of little social use, save
as a cog in a machine or a pawn in a game. And the
machine is run, the game is played, by those who are
concerned, for weal or for woe, with both individual
and social values.

---

[14] Hartmann, PSB, 592.

6. The Problem of Loneliness

Out of the experience of being an individual there arises the problem of loneliness. This problem does not exist in like degree for all. Whether one experiences loneliness or not is in considerable measure a matter of one's psychological type, education, environment, and economic success (which Aristotle regarded as essential to happiness). In individuals who are all of about the same level psychologically, where all conform to the same group standards fairly well and are engaged in congenial activities, loneliness is less likely to arise than in persons who differ from those around them either in their tastes and capacities or in their ideals. Indeed, loneliness is much commoner than one would expect. Famous men and women, who are living in the enjoyment of power and in the midst of admiring friends, are often very lonely because they are not understood, and because they find so few trustworthy persons. The theme of the loneliness of significant persons runs through Paul Ernst's recent book of beautiful philosophical dialogues, *Erdachte Gespräche*,[15] which we have frequently quoted. Even the most independent individualist like Nietzsche is at heart lonely. His doctrine of the Superman is in part an outgrowth of his loneliness, a "compensation" for his failure to find congenial companions among men as they are. "I want comrades," he said, "but living ones and not corpses!"

This fact has ethical implications. Shall we say that loneliness is an evil or a good, or "mixed" (as Plato might say)? Unless it is the effect of a bad will, it is not morally bad in itself. But our chosen attitude toward it may be very significant morally. First of all, we should note the values in solitude. Unless a person

---

[15] See Ernst, EG, 59 *et passim*.

is capable of experiencing and enduring a certain amount of loneliness, he is lacking in courage and independence. In fact, if we do not wish to be overwhelmed by the social environment in which we find ourselves, we shall welcome opportunities for solitude in which we can possess our soul in peace and consider our personal problems and purposes apart from the constant pressure of conflicting social demands. Nevertheless the advantages of solitude should not conceal from us the inner pain of loneliness, a pain which would become unendurable to the point of madness if the loneliness were absolute. Even when it is not absolute, it is a crisis of the soul. It may result in the development either of great cynicism or of great love. The former obviously tends to make the loneliness more complete, while the latter overcomes it in accordance with the wisdom of the ages as taught by Plato and Buddha, as well as by Marcus Aurelius and Christ.

7. SUICIDE

The extreme practical denial of the Law of Individualism is suicide—the voluntary refusal to continue willing, the choice to choose no more values.[16] The suicide chooses not to be an individual.

The argument against its moral justification under any circumstances is very strong. Suicide is always a violation of the Law of Individualism, and is usually also an act of selfishness, a refusal to face obligations owed to others or to continue life under hard circumstances in order to help others. The suicide eliminates himself, but he generally leaves a legacy of problems and unhappiness behind him. Moreover, the act of suicide is very often cowardly; it is due to fear of life and

---

[16] For statistics and other information, see the article "Suicide" in *Enc. Brit.*

its difficulties. Furthermore, it is presumptuous; it assumes that the suicide knows that there is no hope whatever for him. The person involved is rarely in a frame of mind capable of a fair weighing of evidence, and it is a safe rule to take persistent inclination to suicide as a sign of impulsive and unbalanced judgment. Even the pessimists, who have denied the value of life or have held that evil outweighs good, have refused to approve suicide.[17]

Traditional Christian (scholastic) ethics has rigidly condemned suicide (and private duels) ; and the Roman Church has refused the suicide the right of Christian burial. But it is noteworthy that capital punishment and war have not been equally condemned.[18] This raises the question whether it is clear that the taking of one's own life is inherently and absolutely worse than the taking of the life of others. The greater evil of suicide is not self-evident. It must be granted that there is some weighty opinion in favor of the right to commit suicide under certain conditions. The Stoics, perhaps the noblest ancient moralists, affirmed this right, as does a long-standing and still-respected Japanese tradition.

It is almost universally held that there are circumstances when it is right to take the life of another, although it is by no means clear that either war or capital punishment merits the favor extended to them by traditional ethics. Yet if a desperado attacks my wife and children in my presence and is about to kill them, I may have to choose between being responsible for their death and being responsible for his. In such a case, there would be few good men who would hesitate as

[17] So, for example, Schopenhauer and Hartmann. See Hartmann's essay, "Does Pessimism Lead to Suicide?" in GGP, 204-239.
[18] Gury, CTM, 184, 186, 191, 192.

to their choice. Now, if it is ever right to take the life of another, can we argue that it is never right to take one's own life? The religious argument that it is wrong for the individual to take the life that God has given, if it be treated absolutely, is applicable with at least equal cogency against war and capital punishment and even against the case of the desperado. It is not uniquely true of suicide. Nor does religion forbid all control of life.

In fact, it will probably have to be granted that there are conceivable circumstances in which suicide is justifiable, but that they are such as to occur very seldom in the course of history. Theoretically stated, the case could be described as follows: A violation of the Law of Individualism (such as suicide) would be justifiable only when refraining from such violation would result in a violation of the System of Laws as a whole. If it is perfectly clear that the other Laws command suicide, the Law of Individualism will have to yield. But Simmel states the loftiness of the conditions which must prevail, when he says: "I think that the ethical justification of suicide is not at all to be based on the amount of suffering which the subject has to undergo; but solely on the absolute absence of any obligations to other subjects."[19] Yet even this overlooks the positive nature of moral law. One needs to consider not merely the absence of social obligation but also the presence of positive duty. If suicide is to be justified, it must be on the basis of moral ideals which can be served by suicide alone. It is a paradoxical fact that most actual suicides are not justified by any such standard; and that when a person is high-minded enough to test his right to suicide by this standard, he is usually too high-minded to avail himself of it.

---

[19] Simmel, MW, I, 188.

8. SELF-RESPECT

The Law of Individualism may be called a principle of self-respect, along with the Law of Autonomy. Self-respect is such an appreciation of the value of one's own personal life as results in loyalty to the highest ideals and in a feeling of shame if one violates them to any extent. The essence of self-respect is that it is in no way dependent on social approval. It is the independent individualism of the good man.

Unfortunately, in practice self-respect often becomes confused with other principles which are much less praiseworthy. Self-respect may be identified with a sense of personal honor; but the sense of honor, as actually felt by many people, is largely a matter of social convention. If a guest at a banquet of state is seated less near to the host or hostess than one is entitled to sit by virtue of rank, this is taken as an affront to one's honor. Gambling debts are "debts of honor." A duel is called "an affair of honor." Such conventional honor becomes an exaggerated etiquette which has no relation to self-respect nor to moral value, but only to petty pride. Unfortunately, this kind of honor means more to many persons than does their self-respect.[20]

Sometimes an excessive concern for one's personal values develops into a most unfortunate egocentric sensitiveness. Allers has pointed out that neurotic cases are characteristically marked by "egocentricity."[21] The excitable responses of types lacking the power to inhibit any stimulus which even remotely reflects on their excellence or infringes on their rights is a matter of observation in daily life. It is, therefore, of great practical importance to guard against excesses of self-respect.

---

[20] The false feeling of honor is discussed by Simmel, MW, I, 190.
[21] "Die Ichzentriertheit der Neurose," Allers, WSP, 284.

9. The Limits of Individualism

In a system of laws, every law is limited in its scope by the other laws. This we have found throughout our investigation of ethical science, and especially in connection with the problems of veracity and of suicide. It is true that the Law of Individualism is so phrased as to take account of that limitation. It mentions "the maximum value of which he is capable in harmony with moral laws." However, the emphasis is on the obligation to realize maximum value in one's own experience.

Now, moral experience compels us to recognize that situations arise not infrequently in which there is a very marked limitation of the obligation, and even of the right, to realize a wide range of values in one's own person. The Law of the Best Possible imposes on everyone the duty of a discriminating selection, and a rejection of many values which one would greatly enjoy if one could have them. The rigorous discipline which is necessary to attain excellence in any field entails the forfeiture of excellence in most other fields.

There are two types of situation in which the limits of individualism are most acutely felt. One is that of a social relationship, usually close kinship or marriage, in which the destinies of two or more persons are inseparably intertwined, and in which a mutual responsibility could not be honorably denied. Under such conditions, when they are complicated by poverty or illness or old age, there often arises a situation in which it is impossible for both A and B to achieve a great degree of value. If son A, for example, goes to college, daughter B must be deprived of an education, or of happiness, or of health; and *vice versa*. In such a case, someone must sacrifice; but who? If each is ideally moral, each will feel the problem with equal keenness, and probably each

will be the one who desires to make the sacrifice. But
often each is not ideally moral. A may be the one whom
an impartial observer would judge to be worthy of the
greater opportunity; yet precisely A is probably, just
for this reason, the one with the keener conscience. Yet
if unselfish A sacrifices his individuality to the demands
of selfish B, it is not at all clear that the sum of human
value is increased. If the decision is made in the light
of all of the Laws—especially the Law of Consequences,
the Law of the Best Possible, and the Law of Altruism
—it will not be made solely in the interests of either
one or even of both of the parties concerned. It will be
made partly in the interests of the social consequences
of the alternatives, that is, the probable consequences to
the welfare of the greater number of people. Hence an
objective and reasonable moral person may occasionally
find himself in a situation where he will judge that he
ought to limit his own development for the sake of
someone else; or, in the far more difficult and responsible situation, where he will judge that he ought to
develop himself at the cost of the development of someone else. Such decisions should, of course, be arrived
at by mutual and objective discussion. Where temperament makes that impossible, the moral person has a
double responsibility to decide fairly.

A second type of situation where there is a limitation
of the Law of Individualism is that in which one is
convinced that the maximum value of which he is capable is to die for others. The supreme historical illustration of this is, of course, the death of Christ. But it is
far from the only illustration. History, biography, literature, and legend abound in instances. Arnold von
Winkelried gathering the hostile lances together to his
breast to "make way for liberty," Giordano Bruno
burned at the stake for his philosophical teachings, and

countless heroes who have faced death for their ideals, prove that the Law of Individualism can sometimes be fulfilled only by the voluntary self-sacrifice of the individual.

This problem of the limits of individualism leads us naturally on to a consideration of the next Law, the Law of Altruism, which is the correlative of the Law of Individualism.

SELECTED BIBLIOGRAPHY

Abundant material on individualism is easily accessible. Among the best treatments are Bowne, POE, 247-260; Dewey and Tufts, ETH, 363-398; Everett, MV, 225-249; Fite, MP (throughout a philosophy of individualism); Paulsen, SOE, 243-248, 368-373, 379-399. See also Hastings, ERE, VII, art. "Individualism," and XI, art. "Self-Sacrifice."

Among German treatments, note Simmel, MW, I, 85-212. Valuable articles: Ernst Horneffer, "Der moderne Individualismus," *Kantstudien*, 23(1919), 406-425; and Herman Schmalenbach, "Individualität und Individualismus," *Kantstudien*, 24(1920), 365-388.

CHAPTER XIV

10. THE LAW OF ALTRUISM

1. The Law of Altruism and its Place in the System

STATEMENT of the Law of Altruism: *Each person ought to respect all other persons as ends in themselves, and, as far as possible, to co-operate with others in the production and enjoyment of shared values.*

This statement is in need of some explanation. The first part of it means that each grants to all the right to fulfill the obligation which the Law of Individualism imposes on each. The second part, "to co-operate with others in the production of shared values," adds the concept, derived from experience, that many values are possible only through deliberate co-operation. The Law, as it stands, leaves open the question whether all values are "shared" values, that is, occur only in a co-operative experience. In fact, this question is so many-sided and ambiguous that a definite answer to it is not possible. However, even if it were answered affirmatively, it would not affect the validity of the Law of Individualism; for the obligation to realize maximum values in our own experience is not dependent on whether those values are primarily individual or primarily social in their reference. In any case the responsibility for their realization is personal.

The Law of Altruism is the second of the Personalistic Laws. It points out the extremely important fact that the principles and values involved in most of the other Laws are social in their reference and are capable of being realized fully only by social co-operation. So important is altruism that many would make it the sole principle of ethical life. But the System of Moral Laws implies a truth which is often overlooked, namely, that altruism is as empty and aimless as mere formalism or mere individualism unless social activity is guided by principles (Formal Laws) and aims at values (Axiological Laws) which are more than the mere fact of social interaction. Mere altruistic regard for others is empty by itself, just as associational values are meaningless by themselves.[1] While the content and aims of moral life are developed in social situations, they are no more exclusively social than is mathematics or physics. Mathematics has social validity not because it is socially approved, but because it can be rationally demonstrated. Physics is socially approved not because it is a useful convention, but because it is experimentally verifiable. Likewise ethics is socially accepted (in theory, if not in practice) not merely because it is a basis for co-operation, but because it is a rational interpretation of the facts of moral experience. Hence altruism could not be made the sole ethical principle unless altruistic experiences were the sole moral experiences. But the experiences on which the Logical Law, the Law of Autonomy, the Law of Specification, and the Law of Individualism are founded—to mention only unambiguous instances—are not primarily altruistic in their reference. They plainly have to do with the peculiar problem and situation of the individual.

Yet when one denies that altruism is the sole principle of a system of ethics, one is far from denying that it is an essential principle. In fact, it is only by virtue of its not being the sole principle that it can be a rationally binding one. This fact is well illustrated by an incident in the history of the Latin version of the

---

[1] See Chap. VII of *Moral Laws*.

New Testament. The familiar reading of the Golden Rule runs: "All things therefore whatsoever ye would that men should do unto you, even so do ye also unto them; for this is the law and the prophets" (Matthew 7:12). Taken by itself, in separation from the "system," that is, the total effect of the teachings of Jesus, this would mean that if you desire indulgence in narcotic drugs, you should give those drugs to others. Share your desires with others, however evil your desires may be! One of the early translators of the Gospels into Latin accordingly translated the "all things" not by *omnia,* but by *omnia bona* ("all good things"). This modification served to connect the Golden Rule with the conception of the good which Jesus had taught in his other sayings, and shows clearly the necessity of relating the Law of Altruism to the System of Laws.

2. PROOF OF THE LAW OF ALTRUISM

The Law of Altruism follows from an impartial generalization of the Law of Individualism; for, if each person ought to respect himself as a realizer of value, then each person ought to respect all others as realizers of value and so as ends in themselves. Further, no person can attain the end of the Law of Individualism with regard to the important class of shared values unless he co-operates with others in producing and enjoying them. The individual who refuses to acknowledge and obey the Law of Altruism implies that others need not treat him as a realizer of value. But this would prevent successful obedience to the Law of Individualism. Moreover, the discussion of the Axiological Law has shown that associational values are experienced as real values, so that the Law of Altruism could not be denied without denying the Axiological Law. The Law of the Most Inclusive End would also be violated, for an end from which altruism was excluded would be narrower than an end which included it. Therefore the Law of Altruism is true.

3. Its Basis in Experience and History

The tendency to altruism is very widespread in the whole system of animate nature, increasing as life becomes more complex. It was Sutherland's thesis in *The Origin and Growth of the Moral Instinct* that the phenomena of altruism—the whole range of benevolent conduct—were an outgrowth of the maternal instinct. Be that as it may, the fact of the interest of the individual in others, "consciousness of kind" (as Giddings calls it), the gregarious tendency, the instincts connected with sex, and the necessity of co-operation for mutual defense and securing of adequate food and shelter, are some of the facts which furnish empirical foundation for the Law of Altruism. No elaborate proof is needed to establish the truth that human beings actually take an interest in each other and find value in social relations.

The same truth has been almost universally made one of the foundation pillars of the moral thinking of the race. It is true that it was not central in the Aristotelian type.[2] Despite the social and political interest of Plato and Aristotle, the virtue of benevolence did not figure conspicuously in their thinking. It was even less prominent in the Epicurean type. But it was central in the Christian type (including the Hebrew, the Buddhistic, and the Confucian) and very conspicuous in the Kantian, as we shall see.

Under the influence of Christian teaching, *caritas*, charity or love, was added by the scholastics to the

---

[2] The reader may refer to the discussion of the four types of ethical theory in Chap. II.

Greek cardinal virtues as one of the theological virtues.[3] In most modern ethical theories the influence of the Christian maxim, "Love thy neighbor as thyself," has been felt. It is fashionable among certain historians to underestimate the influence of Jesus, and it is easy to point out the unchristian and unethical characteristics of modern civilization. But at least in the history of ethics definite traces of the altruistic teachings of Jesus are evident on every side.

The most important type of ethical theory to receive its classic formulation in modern times, the Kantian, is evidence of this.[4] Kant regarded his Categorical Imperative as a theoretical statement of the Golden Rule, and the following formula brings out clearly the altruistic intent of Kant's ethics:

Act so as to treat humanity, both in thine own person and in that of every other, always as an end and never merely as means.[5]

Kant also teaches that to seek the happiness of others is part of our moral obligation, so that he recognizes both elements in the Law of Altruism—respect for others and shared values (although not emphasizing the social aspect of value-experience). Moreover, Kantian reason is universal and social.

Likewise, if we turn to the modern hedonists, in contrast with the ancient ones, we find among them a general agreement on the altruistic principle. They argue that if pleasure be a good, another's pleasure is just as good as mine, so that the aim of the moral man should be "the greatest good of the greatest number" (Bentham, J. S. Mill). There is, however, a real psycholog-

---

[3] Gury, CTM, 106.

[4] For Kant's opinion of Christian ethics, see the article "Christentum," in Eisler, KL, 78-81.

[5] Kant, GMS, 120.

ical difference between my own experience of a given pleasure and my causing another to experience that same pleasure. Hence Sidgwick formulates his axiom of Rational Benevolence as follows: "That the individual shall have a regard for the happiness of another equal to the regard he has for his own." While this statement does not do full justice to the experience of shared value, it expresses the altruistic intent of the Golden Rule very clearly.

Wundt gives as one of his "norms" the principle: "Regard thy neighbor as thyself,"[6] which is identical with one form of the Golden Rule save for one word. It is noteworthy that the teachings of Wundt, the hedonists, and Kant, all agree with Jesus in deriving altruism from individualism, regard for others from self-respect; "whatsoever ye would that men should do unto you," or "as thyself" is made the norm of our attitude toward others.[7]

Some, however, insist on the absolute priority of altruism. Schwarz is an example of such. He speaks of *Fremdwertmoral* (an almost untranslatable expression, which may be paraphrased as "the ethics of objective values"). The fundamental law of this aspect of ethics runs: "The willing of religious, co-operative, social, and ideal objective values stands above the willing of the values of one's own personality."[8] Schwarz's law may be taken as a formulation of the Law of the Most Inclusive End. But he probably means more than that Law contemplates. He seems to assert that an altruistic act always stands above an individualistic one; but this is far from certain in all cases. A flat statement of that sort is subject to criticism from the standpoint of

---

[6] Wundt, ETG, III, 153.

[7] This is also emphasized by Kleinsorgen, CE, 72-73.

[8] Schwarz, SL, vii.

the whole System of Laws. Schwarz is typical of numerous too ardent supporters of altruism.

4. The Reason for Altruism : Different Theories

We have just seen that many derive the duty of altruism from the duty of individualism. This view is adopted in the exposition and proof of the Law of Altruism in the present chapter. It is implied in Schiller's striking phrase that "hatred of our fellow beings is prolonged suicide," as well as in the German proverb, "Wenn die Rose selbst sich schmückt, schmückt sie auch den Garten."[9] Yet the simple question, Why ought I to respect and help others? has elicited a wide variety of answers. Not all agree with the answer just referred to, namely, Because each individual is an intrinsic value and because the association of valuable beings is itself a value.

The aim of the present section is to give a compact and critical picture of some of the varied opinions about the ground for altruism. Martineau reported "the general consensus of modern English opinion" as assigning a purely social origin to moral consciousness.[10] A similar view is held by the contemporary Austrian philosopher, Schlick, who thinks that the meaning of the word "good" is determined by the opinion of human society.[11] However, if social standards are accepted as authoritative, and altruism is regarded as right merely because it is social, it is hard to see on what basis human society arrives at just social opinions or how a society could improve intelligently.

Intuitionists hold that the mind perceives the axiomatic certainty of the duty of altruism, just as we

---

[9] "If the rose adorns herself, she adorns the garden too."
[10] Martineau, TET, II, 27.
[11] Schlick, FE, 70. So also Simmel, MW, I, 17.

perceive the certainty that time is constantly elapsing; and they add that neither perception is in need of proof. But it is easier to have moral intuitions than to convince others of their truth; and if any reasons for a supposed intuition can be found, they should be.

Perfectionists hold that the aim of life is the development of the widest possible range of value. They thus base ethical theory on one principle, the Law of the Most Inclusive End. Starting from this basis, it follows that the individual cannot be perfected alone; his powers can come to their fulfillment only in co-operation with others. The egoistic individual is always a case of arrested development. Only he who works with and for others finds the fullest life. "Strive ever for completeness," said Schiller, "and if thou canst not thyself become a whole, join a whole as a serviceable member."[12]

Finally, it may be noted that the "overindividual," and so social, character of the moral life follows from the very notion of moral law. Moral laws are principles which refer to "all persons" (or "each person"), as the statements of the various Laws show, and thus are ties which bind humanity together by virtue of common experience and common reason.

5. THE PROBLEM OF SENTIMENTALISM

History seems to show that man cannot appreciate any truth without exaggerating it. Altruism, for instance, turns very easily into sentimental sympathy. In sentimentalism, feeling predominates to such an extent over thought and effective action that the intent of the Law of Altruism is frustrated; for sentimentalism does not lead to co-operation with others in the produc-

---

[12] Cited by Schwarz, SL, 377. Similar ideas are frequent in Bosanquet.

tion and enjoyment of shared values. When Christ says "thou shalt love," he is not to be taken as commanding his disciples to feel a sentimental affection. Kant rightly points out that not "pathological" (emotional, sensuous) love is commanded, but the practical love of a loyal will.[13] In a normal human being such a practical love will generate appropriate emotion, and for the social effectiveness of an act of altruistic kindness the presence of such emotion and the absence of emotional reluctance or coldness is extremely desirable. The culture of the emotional life is both an individualistic and an altruistic obligation. Nevertheless, Kant's point remains true; the will is the center of the moral life, and emotions are not good or bad in themselves but they derive their moral quality from the will that they express. Far more evil doubtless results from uncontrolled emotion than from unemotional will. In fact, the latter is a state of which few, if any, are capable.

There is danger in any emotional indulgence the limits of which are not confined within "the fence of reason." That such a "fence" need not destroy the emotional enjoyment is indicated by the fact that a game played under definite rules is enjoyable; while without rules no game is possible. The joys of cheating, such as they are, do not equal the joys of fair play. Even legitimate emotional expression has its limits. In his youth, Lessing wrote a couplet on the German proverb, "Geteilter Schmerz ist halber Schmerz" ("Shared pain is half pain"), which may be translated as follows:

What is the use when a friend weeps in pity for me?
His tears only double the pain of my first misery![14]

---

[13] See Kant, KdpV (Reclam S), 116.
[14] Was nutzt mir's, dass ein Freund mit mir gefällig weine?
Nichts, als dass ich in ihm mir zwiefach elend scheine.
                                        Cited by Treitschke, DL, 132.

Perhaps Lessing's rebellion against sentimental sympathy went too far, but some will understand what he meant. In other cases the danger of sentimentalism is perfectly clear. What surgeon wishes the presence of a mother when her child is being operated on? Not many average mothers can control emotion under such circumstances. There are many mothers whose sentimentalism makes them unwilling to permit their child to submit to a much-needed operation at all. Their sentimental fear of the operation is greater than their confidence in the law of cause and effect.

Sentimental abandon to the shared pleasure of the moment in the relations of the sexes is one of the chief practical obstacles to genuine thoughtful altruism, when it violates both the respect for personality and the production of true values, as it so often does. Recent statistics from Austria report that, while births in 1928 were 1.6 per cent less than in the previous year, the number of children with unmarried mothers increased 1.2 per cent. Of all Austrian children born in 1928, 26 per cent were illegitimate.[15] The effect of such a situation on the stability of the family and on personal responsibility is immeasurable. The conditions in Austria are illustrative of what happens whenever sentimentalism prevails over wisdom. Not much observation is needed to reveal the power of the emotional side of man's nature, the social damage which arises when it is uncontrolled, and the social benefit which comes from its moral control. The issue of sentimentalism *versus* emotional culture must be faced by everyone who seeks to conform to the Law of Altruism.

6. ALTRUISM AND IMPARTIALITY

Closely connected with the problem just discussed is

---

[15] Innsbrucker *Neueste Zeitung*, No. 189, 1930, pp. 5 and 6.

that of the relation between altruism and impartiality. The typical altruist easily tends to be a partisan of the group toward which his altruism is especially directed, and to be influenced by the desires of those whom he is trying to aid, even when he knows that the fulfillment of these desires would not be to the best interests of those concerned. The situation is rendered complicated by the natural tendency of people to prefer what they themselves desire above what someone else thinks is good for them. The person who aims to be of genuine altruistic service needs to achieve a high degree of fair-mindedness. If he is merely to oppose his own desires to the desires of those toward whom he is supposed to be behaving altruistically, he has no moral right to regard his desires as more worthy than theirs. On the other hand, it is equally unreasonable to seek to give others whatever they want, irrespective of one's own wants or judgment. When a social end is to be attained, the best possible end can be defined only by thought that is at once co-operative and impartial.

Society is conscious of the fact that co-operation on a low level is easier to attain than on a high level, and that genuine impartiality is rarely desired in any particular situation. In order to protect itself against its own acknowledged weaknesses, society has devised institutions to safeguard impartiality. Law, and especially constitutional law, is such a safeguard. Constitutions are framed with the best interests of all in mind. They are purposely made difficult to amend in order to protect the impartiality of the constitution against the desires of those who prefer their private interests to the public good. The judiciary is another similar safeguard. The American Bar Association has adopted a code for judges, Article 14 of which, "On Independence," declares that the judge should not be influenced by partisan desires, public demands, considerations of his personal popularity or fame, and that he should not fear unjust criticism. This position of a judge, as a bulwark of impartiality against the demands of popular preju- dice, is perhaps contrary to what extreme democracy would approve, but is essential to the preservation of social values and to social self-control. The most au- tonomous individual, if he is rational, has a sincere and deep-seated will that society shall not suffer from his acts. Thus the setting up of organs of impartiality is one of the greatest achievements of a society of auton- omous individuals.

7. FREE AND NECESSARY ASSOCIATION

Special problems, and varying degrees of responsi- bility, arise from the fact that some of the moral individual's relations to his fellows are necessary and some are free. Every person has necessary relations to his parents and family and the state. The necessary relations to the state become especially acute in the case of those who have no citizenship in any state, like many former Russian subjects who are unwilling to give allegiance to the Soviet Republic. Such persons stand in a unique relation to the state in the territory of which they happen to reside, as well as to Russia. The renunciation of citizenship, then, does not imply a de- nial of the necessity of relationship to a state.

In addition to the fundamentally necessary types of association, there are many forms of free association. One may choose groups with which one is to be re- lated; educational institutions (above the "compulsory" grades), charitable organizations, churches, clubs, and the like, are forms of free association.

The two types of association raise various ethical problems. One has no choice of parents or fatherland, whereas one can choose the free associations into which one will enter; but the obligations of the Law of Altruism—to respect persons and to achieve shared values—are alike in both cases. It is the task of practical ethics to consider detailed applications of these principles.

8. THE COMMUNITY

The individualistic basis of altruism, which has been mentioned in previous discussions, is perfectly consistent with co-operative interdependence of individuals in community life. But the theoretical consistency of the two does not imply practical consistency. There is a conflict between the realization of values which satisfy the personal interests of the individual and the achievement of the most valuable forms of community life.

Theories which gloss over this conflict do not penetrate to the heart of the moral problem. "Biological ethics," says Kleinsorgen, "demands no sacrifice for the common good, but an incorporation in it."[16] This is a mere phrase! It is refuted by the experience of many sons and daughters who have to choose between leaving home and sacrificing their own development by remaining with their parents who need or demand their presence, by cases in which the community requires participation in war, and by the self-abnegation of those who devote their lives to advocacy of an unpopular reform. It is too true that "the fate of the individuals who have made world history has been no happy one."[17] Bentham, with all his warm social interest, also failed, with many other English moralists and economists, to grasp the essential problem when he asked: "How should the happiness of all be obtained to the greatest extent, but by the obtainment by every one for himself of the greatest

[16] Kleinsorgen, CE, 74.
[17] Schlick, FE, 93.

possible portion?"[18] It ought to be clear that the answer to this rhetorical question is not what Bentham intended, but, rather, Not merely by the obtainment of the greatest possible portion of individual happiness for each one, but also by the development of the highest degree of devotion to the common good, often at the cost of personal happiness.

Kleinsorgen and Bentham err by their overemphasis on individualism, and Bentham, in particular, by an atomistic theory of society. But it is equally possible to gloss over the conflicts by an overemphasis on altruism, as in the excessively organic ethics of Hegel, in which individuals count only as they live in and for institutions and in which humanity as a whole, rather than the individuals, is the subject of moral life. Thus individual responsibility almost vanishes.

The direction in which an ethical theory, grounded in autonomous individualism, points is not toward an optimistic denial of the problem, nor toward a rigid demand that the individual always conform to the community desires, but toward the development of a morally tolerant community attitude, based on a recognition of the principle that all social organization is for the purpose of the enrichment and freedom of the members of the society. The genuinely "conscientious" objector to community standards should be respected by the community and treated on an entirely different basis from the mere "slacker." If it be said that society cannot go into the question of the motives of individuals, it may be replied that society already does that very thing. Society assumes that the motives of Friends are good, and excuses them from certain social demands in war time; it also distinguishes among various degrees of murder on the basis of motive. The same

---

[18] Bentham, DE, I, 16.

principle would give drama, art, and literature a greater freedom from unjust censorship than sometimes obtains.

But it is still true that the community has a right to protect itself; and there will remain a large number of cases in which the ethically justified conscientious objector will have to be restrained or punished by the equally ethically justified agent of the community. There may be a conflict of duties, which will last until a new insight modifies the clashing opinions. Till then, the innocent will suffer.

The conflict of which we are speaking comes to extreme expression in a rebellion. The welfare of the community based on the Law of Altruism makes such claims on the individual that rebellion against government is ethically justified only in the most extreme cases. Scholastic ethics has taught the right of disobeying human authority in those things which are evidently contrary to the law of God, but has denied that it was ever right to rebel.[19] Saint Thomas held that the remedy, in case of misgovernment, is to have recourse to God. But the scholastic denial of the right of rebellion rested largely on the theory of the divine right of kings, which is not held by modern ethics. It would seem, then, that the right of rebellion must be recognized as morally well grounded when a government has shown itself to be hopelessly and incurably unjust. For the American government to deny the right of rebellion is for it to deny the basis of its own existence, since the American Revolution was a rebellion. Yet no government can safely adopt as a policy the recognition of that right. Hence practical government must deny it, leaving to theoretical ethics the more consistent and

---

[19] "Numquam obediendum esse auctoritati humanae in iis, quae evidenter contra legem die sunt. . . . Numquam omnino licitum est rebellare." Gury, CTM, 183-184.

more dangerous truth. As Kant ironically remarked in his essay on Eternal Peace, "the possession of power inevitably destroys the free judgment of reason."

9. APPLICATIONS OF ALTRUISM

The two fields in which the Law of Altruism is at the present time most in need of application are the economic and the international.

For theoretical ethics to attempt to pronounce on the detailed solution of economic problems would be foolish, doubly so at a time in history when the economists themselves are at a loss and when the outcome of great economic experiments, such as those in Russia and Italy, is still in doubt. But it is the part of theoretical ethics to point out the fact that man in his economic capacity is just as subject to moral law as he is in any other capacity, and that, in particular, the Law of Altruism ought to control economic relations. It is evident that the principle of respect for others as ends in themselves means that profit alone cannot be the motive of industry and that even the creation of favorable working conditions, wages, and hours, by the employer does not fulfill the moral law adequately. Respect for the personality of the laborer demands that he be given a larger voice in the decision of questions that vitally concern him (industrial democracy), and that the problem of continuous employment for all who are capable of working be solved. To this end, it is essential that more co-operative intelligence be used in the kind of business enterprises that are started, that overcrowded fields be thinned out, and that real needs be met. Whatever may be the advantages of free competition in business, they are more than outweighed by its inhumanity to the individual.

As regards international affairs, there can be no doubt

from the standpoint of ethical science that the relations
of states to each other ought to be governed by the
same moral laws as guide the conduct of the good
individual. The extraordinarily complicated nature of
the problem, due to the many interests at stake, the
nature of representative government, the power of
tradition and of fear, and the mistakes of the past,
renders it extremely difficult in many cases to determine what the right international policy is. But
when it is once recognized that moral standards ought
to prevail in these relations, there will have been
achieved a great advance in the "imponderables," as
Bismarck called the moral forces of life.

That this is not yet recognized is plain. Hermann
Cohen, the Marburg neo-Kantian, once said: "As soon
as the concept of the nation becomes independent and
absolute, so soon it becomes barbaric." He thus pro-
claimed the principle that nations are not absolutely
independent, but are subject to moral restrictions and
ideals in their dealings with one another. Yet a recent
writer on philosophy of religion sees fit to reject this
view as false, because it is a "cosmopolitan Judaism."[20]
A striking instance of the rejection of the ethical ideal
in international relations is afforded by the testimony
of Adolf Hitler, leader of the German Fascist movement, before the Supreme Court in Leipzig in 1930. He
was being asked about the policy of his party, and he
stated that one aim was to do away with the Versailles
Treaty (an aim which ethical internationalism would
on the whole indorse). He was then asked how he proposed to do it, and replied that he would do it first by
negotiations, then by evasion—by legal means, and if
necessary by illegal means. He then made the revealing
remark: "I feel myself obligated in my action to the

[20] Leisegang, RP, 8.

German people alone."[21]   This is no strange doctrine to readers who are familiar with the slogan, "Right or wrong, my country"; yet it comes with ironical force from a leader who avows himself to be an exponent of a lofty idealism as against the materialism of his opponents.

A burning question of the future of civilization is that of whether nations will continue the practice of resort to arms for the settlement of their grievances. That they ought not to do so is plain from the devastating, even annihilating, character of modern warfare. As regards past wars it was in some cases perhaps legitimate to appeal to the Law of the Best Possible and argue that, while war and its consequences would be bad, peace and its consequences, under the conditions, would be still worse. However, the possibility of finding circumstances in the relations of civilized states in which such argumentation will again be applicable is, for the reason stated, so slight as to be negligible. Hans Driesch has recently written: "Practically, war today must always unconditionally be avoided, even that for the defense of 'neutrality.' There are morally praiseworthy means which are much more effective than it, namely, passive resistance and boycott."[22] We may add that preventive measures, based on international understanding and co-operation, are even more important than emergency measures such as Driesch names. It is fatal to surrender to pessimism in spite of the feeble showing of the League of Nations.

The moralist recognizes that the rightness of an ideal is no guarantee of its realization; but he also recognizes that the difficulty of its realization is no argument against it, if it is right.

---

[21] From the *Berliner Illustrierte Nachtausgabe*, Sept. 25, 1930.
[22] Driesch, ST, 117.

SELECTED BIBLIOGRAPHY

The best book on the problem as a whole is Palmer, ALT. Leighton, ISO, is also excellent.

See the treatment of altruism, benevolence, or social ethics in any manual. Note especially Bowne, POE, 231-303; Dewey and Tufts, ETH, 387-389; Drake, PC, Chap. XI; Everett, MV, Chap. VIII; Mecklin, ISE; Parker, HV, 177-198; Paulsen, SOE, 636-663.

CHAPTER XV

11. THE LAW OF THE IDEAL OF PERSONALITY

1. THE LAW OF THE IDEAL OF PERSONALITY AND ITS PLACE IN THE SYSTEM

STATEMENT of the Law of the Ideal of Personality: *All persons ought to judge and guide all of their acts by their ideal conception (in harmony with the other Laws) of what the whole personality ought to become both individually and socially.*

This Law brings the System of Moral Laws to its climax. It prescribes the construction and use of a goal or ideal to guide the direction of moral development. It adds to the Laws of Individualism and of Altruism a definitely concrete unity of purpose, an æsthetic fact which calls on the individual to create out of the materials of his life the plan of a harmonious whole which he aims to realize. It makes the ideal more specific than did the Law of the Most Inclusive End. It presupposes and correlates all of the previous Laws, and, as was shown in connection with the discussion of the place of the Law of Ideal Control in the System (Chapter XII), it is at once the synthesis and the supplementation of the two Laws of ideals with which the Logical Laws and the Axiological Laws culminated, namely, the Law of Autonomy (that self-imposed ideals are imperative) and the Law of Ideal Control (that ideal values should control empirical values). The Personalistic Laws and the whole System now find their ultimate unity and consummation in the obligation to form and to apply a conception of a life purpose, which is not only self-imposed and ideal, but also concrete and unified. The Law might read: "Know your own mind," or: "Have a consistent life plan," or: "Be aware of your highest possibilities." But none of these brief formulas brings out the full force which is found in the formal statement of the Law.

2. Proof of the Law of the Ideal of Personality

If the Law of the Ideal of Personality were not true, the unification of value-experience would not be obligatory, which would violate the Axiological Law; the highest attainable ideal would not be obligatory, which would violate the Law of Ideal Control; and the realization of that ideal in individual and social experience would not be obligatory, which would violate the Laws of Individualism and of Altruism. Hence the Law of the Ideal of Personality is true.

3. Its Basis in Experience and History

The primary empirical basis of the Law of the Ideal of Personality is the experienced fact of a unity of consciousness as the immediate datum of all experience, the implications of which lead us to acknowledge a whole self—a total personality. Experiences of obligation and of rational law, which supply the ground for our belief in a past and a future self lying beyond the immediate present, also point toward the conception of an ideal that ought to be attained. Moreover, the activity that is constantly going on in our experience needs to be directed by a plan of action, an ideal, which should, in the last analysis, be a unity because the self is a unity.

The conception of an ideal of personality is an ancient one. Heroes and gods embodied various ideals. The caste system of India, with all its disadvantages, sufficed to set a certain standard for each caste, as did

Plato in the *Republic;* Confucius pictured the "superior man"; the Greeks had one ideal of the "wise man" and the Hebrews another. It was in Jesus that the ideal of personality had its highest historical illustration. The knight, the crusader, the Cavalier, the Puritan, the saint, the reformer, the soldier, the inventor, the scientist, the poet, the artist, the husband, the wife, the king, the subject, the president, the citizen, the farmer, the laborer, the capitalist—each of these words suggests a historical type of personality which embodies a specific ideal.[1]

But it was in the Eighteenth Century that the ideal of humanity was made a specific theoretical interest and problem.[2] It is conspicuous in such writers as Rousseau, Kant, and Herder. The capacity for reason, for science and art, for morality and law, and for friendship, are some of the marks of their ideal of humanity. Kant, in a very interesting passage, points out that everything in the universe—plants, animals, the structure of the world—embodies *"Ideen"* (ideals), yet that no being conforms to the ideal of the perfection of its kind, not even man, who bears in his soul the ideal of humanity as the pattern for his acts.[3] Elsewhere, Kant remarks that the "faculty of acting purposively is the characteristic of humanity,"[4] a view strikingly similar to William James's contention that the self is a "fighter for ends."[5]

The conception of an ideal of humanity or personality has been prominent in many other thinkers. Schleiermacher presented it in the form of the Ideal

---

[1] See Spranger, LF.

[2] See Kant, GMS (edited by Otto), 199-204. Kinkel, HG, is a valuable German study of the ideal of humanity.

[3] Kant, KdrV (A), 317-318.

[4] Kant, *Metaphysik der Sitten,* in *Werke,* III (PhB), 233.

[5] James, POP, I, 141.

of the Wise Man, in whom moral force and purpose is uninterruptedly and exclusively active.[6] The ideal of personality likewise occupies a prominent place in T. H. Green's *Prolegomena to Ethics* and in Borden P. Bowne's *Principles of Ethics*. Nietzsche's Superman or Beyond-Man (as *Übermensch* is sometimes translated) is an ideal of a personality of great courage, strength, and creativity. One's ideal of personality affects one's whole being; "tell me what kind of man you are," says Fichte in a much-quoted phrase, "and I will tell you what kind of philosophy you hold." Steinthal makes "the moral personality" the "first ideal" of ethical theory.[7] William Stern and Max Scheler and Ottmar Dittrich (the historian of ethics) all call their ethical standpoint personalistic, thus putting personality in the foreground.

Further illustrations of the recognition of the ideal of personality as a fundamental ethical principle could readily be multiplied. That ideal is an established result of the development of ethical science.

4. Personal and Impersonal Ideals

When an ethicist asserts that the Law of the Ideal of Personality is the supreme and culminating ethical principle, he appears to be running counter to one very important achievement of the race, namely, the ability to be impersonal. It is often said that there are three levels of conversation; the lowest deals with personalities, a higher with things, and the highest with ideas. Science is impersonal; it does not consult the preferences or the moral character of individuals, but it seeks for impersonal, objective truth—a truth that is above "the personal equation" and that eliminates or seeks

---

[6] Schleiermacher, *Werke*, I, 151.
[7] Steinthal, AE, 97.

to eliminate all factors due to the personality of the scientist. In his famous essay on genius, Schopenhauer maintains, with well-supported arguments, that genius is objectivity.

Are we then, perhaps, in error when we regard the Law of the Ideal of Personality as the highest unification of moral law? While the thought of Plato is ambiguous, there are many who regard his "Ideas" as impersonal realities, which are the objects of knowledge and the criterion of goodness; and we give unstinted admiration to those who, like Plato, put the cause which they serve above their own personality. In Chapter XIV we found that Schwarz places social values above individual ones; but he also places the impersonal—truth and objective value—above the social, "higher," he says, "than the works of love, courtesy, and mercy."[8]

There is undoubtedly a truth underlying this protest against personalistic ethics. Devotion to right should stand above personal preferences; personalistically stated, if the individual does not prefer right to his fancies and desires, he ought to. But no love of right or truth, no scientific or Platonic objectivity, should conceal from us the fact that disciplined devotion to truth or beauty or goodness is itself a personal achievement, an experience of personal value. We say that a man's fondness for calf's liver is personal, whereas his proof of the first proposition of Euclid is impersonal. Yet this is a very loose use of terms. The act of proving a proposition in geometry is a personal act which is recognized as valid by all persons who think. We use the word "impersonal" in this connection not to mean that the proof has no relation to persons, but that it has a relation to all persons.

It is, however, probably a fact that if one concen-

---

[8] Schwarz, SL, 372.

trates all of one's attention, or the bulk of it, on truths which concern all persons in general and no one person in particular more than another, there is a natural psychological tendency to underestimate the individual and to ignore the requirements of the Law of Specification in human relations.   This is, in some respects, a gain; it frees the person who is thus minded from many of the admittedly annoying obligations of ordinary life. Yet this gain comes only at a great loss to himself. When the impersonal admirer of pure objectivity takes account of what he has contributed to the world, it may turn out that he has lost the quality of humanness and almost of humanity; and in the long run the knowledge of objective truth would be self-defeating and useless if it were possessed by a race of beings like him.

Paul Ernst doubtless expresses this point of view in an extreme form in one of his dialogues, but he is describing a danger that is felt by most responsible men of science, as well as by their poet-critics, when he makes The Poet say to The Scholar: "You will not deny that the scientific methods of today have, it is true, carried the sciences rapidly forward in the way in which you desire, but that among men of science today there are fewer outstanding personalities and more blockheads than there used to be."[9]   The scientific machine age has tended to depersonalize us.   Can that seriously be counted as a gain?   Is not Treitschke nearer right than the advocates of purely impersonal value when he says that "the name of no man endures in history if he was not greater than his deeds"?[10]

As opposed, then, to a mistaken overemphasis on the impersonal, it must be said that there are no strictly impersonal ethical ideals.   There are ethical proposi-

[9] Ernst, EG, 58.
[10] Treitschke, DL, 28.

tions about "What *I* ought to do (or be or think)" and
about "What *we* ought to do (or be or think)," but
none about "What *it* ought to be." There are no impersonal moral causes; all moral causes aim at personal
values—for all persons, for some persons, or for one
person. But if no person is benefited, then there is no
moral value; this follows from the very nature of value-
experience. The legislator or the scientist who has no
particular persons in mind as his beneficiaries, really is
giving values to an entire nation or to all humanity.
The "eternal values" are not values merely because they
are eternal, but, rather, because they satisfy and en-
noble all persons who are loyal to them.

This personalistic aspect of the moral good accounts
for the familiar fact that example is often more effective
than precept. The former is a personal deed, the latter
an impersonal concept. Hence comes the significance of
"heroes and hero worship," hence also the fact that most
great religions have personal founders and personal
gods. The chief advantage of Christianity over Moham-
medanism is the personal superiority of Jesus to Mo-
hammed. Or, to take a very different illustration, one
chief source of the power of corrupt political organizations is the strong personality of the "boss." A trivial,
but illuminating, modern instance of the personal nature of ideals is found in the list of qualifications of the
ideal policeman, drawn up by August Vollmer, professor of police administration in the University of Chicago, as reported in the press. It consists of "The
wisdom of Solomon, the courage of David, the tolerance of Confucius, the patience of Job, the strategy of
Napoleon." Wisdom, courage, tolerance, patience, and
strategy are ideals; but they are mere conceptual abstractions until they are realized as values in the personal experience of Confucius or Patrolman Schmidt.

5. Personality as Empirical and as Ideal

Life as we actually live it is the empirical personality of each one of us, our datum self. This empirical personality with its actual combination of good and bad, of rational and irrational, is what we now are. The moral problem arises from the inconsistency between the empirical personality as a whole and the ideals which it recognizes. This we have learned both from the Law of Autonomy and from the Law of Ideal Control. But it is worth noting that the conflict between empirical values and ideal values takes place within the empirical personality and not merely between it and some external authority. It is an autonomous, and not a heteronomous struggle.

Within the empirical personality there is a tendency to prefer one type of action to another. What we wish to be is in most cases not identical with what we are. Not merely environmental conditions, but our own habits and impulses often interfere with the fulfillment of "the preferred personality" by "the empirical personality."

But the preferred personality is not necessarily our ideal. Most sincere persons who are not perfectly disciplined Socrates-natures are able to detect a difference between what they actually prefer and what they ought to prefer. What we actually prefer is a new organization of our empirical personality; what we ought to prefer is a new organization of our actual preferences themselves and of our choices and conduct. The distinction between what we approve and what we ought to approve is necessary for anyone who exercises his reason; for our actual approvals conflict with each other and only a rational ideal—a self-consistent and coherent one—can satisfy the thinking person. Thus there are three stages in the movement of personality toward the ideal: The empirical personality, the preferred personality, and the ideal personality.

6. The Variety of Ideals

By this time some readers will doubtless have become impatient with so much indefinite talk about the ideal. They will say: "Show us the ideal, and it sufficeth us. Tell us what this ideal of personality is, or say no more about it."

This natural and apparently justified demand is based on a misunderstanding. The Law of the Ideal of Personality does not define any specific ideal; it prescribes only that the ideal shall be in harmony with the other Laws and that each person shall frame an ideal. The particular form that the ideal shall take in the life of any individual or group is, within the limits set by the Moral Laws, a matter of individual creative imagination and æsthetic taste. The number of possible ideals is indefinitely great. Each individual differs in some way from others; and it would be far from ideal if a uniform standard were to be imposed on all in such a way as to erase these differences. Each family, each group, each nation, has a unique contribution to humanity and so a distinctive ideal to fulfill.[11] There are likewise differences in the ideal for man and for woman, although not the burdensome and obnoxious differences which tradition has often imposed.

Thus we may say that the Law of the Ideal of Personality is a law of free creativity and of personal diversification. It introduces a large factor of æsthetic variety into the moral life. It also implies very clearly

---

[11] Note the discussion of the different types of character by Rudolf Utitz, "Charakterologie und Ethik," *Jahrbuch der Charak.*, 4(1927), 100-101. See Royce, RQP, Lecture II, on provincialism.

that the ideal is in process of development.   Ideals could justly become static only when the life of thought and action had become static and the powers of creative imagination had failed.   This would be a stage of senility and approaching death.

7. Consciousness of the Ideal

An important problem in the ethics of ideals takes the form, Ought we to be clearly conscious of our ideals or is it better to leave them undefined?

If we recall the paradox of hedonism, we may be tempted to apply it to ideals.   He who seeks pleasure directly and consciously loses it; the best pleasures are unsought by-products of normal activities.   "Don't pursue culture," said Elbert Hubbard, "you'll scare her to death."   Do the same considerations apply to ideals?

There are some cases in life where they plainly do not apply.   If we wish to build a house, the construction will not occur as an unsought by-product of our doing something else, however noble.   We must have a definite plan for the house.   What applies to architecture applies, in the main, to all of the arts.   A unitary and harmonious work of art can result only from a unitary and harmonious plan.   Does it not follow that a unitary and harmonious personality, which is also a work of art, can result only from a unitary and harmonious plan?   And how can the plan function if it is not consciously present before the mind?

Yet, in spite of these considerations, George Herbert Palmer doubts the desirability of having a definite life ideal.   It is only, he thinks, in small matters that a definite plan of action can be formed in advance.   "But in profounder matters I more wisely set out from the thought of the moment and the patent need of improving it than from the future with its ideal perfection."[12] As a protest against too fixed and detailed a conception of what I hope my future self will become and too exclusive concentration on it, Professor Palmer's words are a timely warning. We cannot predict the course of events or of our own growth, and the ideal must be left plastic. Yet we dare not overlook the value of consciously purposeful living. The man who can see furthest ahead is the man whose life will probably attain the highest value. Moreover, Palmer's reference to "the patent need of improving" the present is meaningless unless the word "improving" has a meaning. Its only rational meaning would be that of "bringing nearer to what is good"; and if we have no clear conception of what is good for us, we shall have no idea of whether we are improving. It is true that there is something very futile in constant thought about ideal purposes, if no attempt is made to use them in the guidance of actual conduct. But it is also true that there is something equally futile in the most active and energetic attempts to improve the individual and society which are unenlightened by any clear idea of the meaning of improvement. Without such an idea the development of personality is likely to be guided by accidental pressure from without instead of by ideal purpose from within. No means are useful without an end.

The conclusion seems to be that, while a proper balance should obviously be maintained between thought about ideals and work on their realization, it is clear that all persons ought to devote some time—and most persons more than they do—to clear and intelligent formulation of their ideal for themselves and for the groups with which they are associated. We should be conscious

[12] Palmer, NOG, 137, and the discussion in Everett, MV, 220-221.

of the ideal without being "self-conscious" or excessively introspective.

8. The Twofold Function of the Ideal

An ideal of personality has a twofold function: On the one hand, it guides the conduct of the person who holds it as his plan of action and goal; on the other hand, it is an instrument of criticism, used to point out both the meaning of and also the defects in the present situation.

The person who is especially interested in the function of guidance is of the practical type, while he who is especially interested in criticism is of the idealistic type. It is a common belief in Europe that Americans are typically practical, while Europeans are typically idealistic. The truth or error in that estimate need not concern us now; but the estimate itself serves to illustrate the large scale on which the twofold function of ideals is recognized.

Impartial thought cannot fail to perceive that guidance and criticism are equally necessary in the good life. This is shown by an examination of the consequences of an exaggeration of either aspect. If the function of ideals as plans of action be made to overshadow their function as principles of criticism, the result is a thoughtless optimism that rushes into hasty action without sufficient reflection. The excessively practical emphasis turns out in the long run to involve wasted effort and disappointed hopes. Not Wall Street and "boom" towns and the fact of overproduction alone are evidences of this; but the constitutional inability of human nature to maintain a pace of incessant, feverish action dooms the attempt in advance to failure.

The difference between the city of Washington and the city of Chicago shows the twofold function of ideals very well. Washington was built from the start in accordance with a plan, which, of course, has experienced modifications, yet was purposively present at the founding of the city. It has become America's loveliest city, and many think it to be the most beautiful capital in the world. Chicago, until recently, has grown planlessly, and, as a whole, is a huge, sprawling mass, although with attractive spots. Now, a Chicago city plan is in process of being carried out, which it is hoped will transform an ugly city into a beautiful one. In the case of Washington a proper balance between action and criticism has prevailed, with admirable results. In the case of Chicago action long prevailed over criticism, and now an extraordinary amount of critical destruction and reconstruction is necessary in order to save the day.

As principles of guidance ideals function to encourage and cheer men, to assure them that there is a way of life, a meaning and value in human endeavor. On the other hand, as principles of criticism they may serve to condemn and even to discourage men. This is the truer, the higher and nobler the ideals are. If the Law of the Best Possible be used as a pretext for bringing the ideal down to the level of inclination, then ideals will not disturb us seriously. But if that same Law be used as it was intended, to spur man on to the highest of which he is capable, then the ideal is a source of humiliation to man as he is. The noblest spirits have said, with Emerson, "Hitch your wagon to a star," and have responded to Nietzsche's call to *Fernstenliebe* (love of the furthest, the most distant ideal) as the loftiest principle of life.

Religion has faced, perhaps more explicitly than any other aspect of man's life, the implications of this discrepancy between the actual and the ideal. Pauline,

Lutheran, and Calvinistic Christianity, in particular, have confronted the situation in which man finds himself—condemned by the law of the ideal which he recognizes, yet unable to conform to the ideal. A conspicuous tendency in contemporary German thought, called, from its founder, the Barthian theology, or the theology of crisis ("crisis" being the Greek word for "judgment"), is based on this same situation. The practical question is whether man can draw from purely ethical sources the strength for his moral endeavor, or whether he should find the needed strength for life from other sources—æsthetic, intellectual, or religious. The race as a whole cannot be said to have made up its mind on this fundamental point. Some of the theoretical problems which underlie this extremely difficult practical question will be discussed in Chapter XVI on "The Autonomy of Moral Laws." Having surveyed the System of Moral Laws, we are forced to ask whether moral laws and moral values are independent, or are in some senses dependent on other types of law and value. To this question we now turn our attention.

SELECTED BIBLIOGRAPHY

Bowne, POE, Chap. III an 116-123; Bradley, ES, Essay VI; Brightman, POI, Chap. V; Everett, MV, 166; Green, PTE, 206-220; Nietzsche, Z; Palmer, NOG, Chap. IV; Royce, RQP, Lecture II; S anger, LF.

CHAPTER XVI

THE AUTONOMY OF MORAL LAW

1. The Problem of the Autonomy of Moral Law

THUS far we have been concerned exclusively with moral experience and moral laws, save for the comparison (in Chapter II) of moral law with civil, religious, natural, and logical law. A System of Moral Laws now stands before us. We cannot, however, regard our investigation as complete until we consider the question whether moral law has independent authority or whether it requires extraneous support. A science which has such independent authority is called autonomous.

Mathematics is an example of an autonomous science. Its principles are unaffected by the results of the other sciences, whether physical, biological, or psychological, and by our metaphysics or our religion. Trigonometry remains true whether we have faith in God or not, and the principles of trigonometry are not in the least supported, undermined, or altered by the presence or absence of such faith. Logic is clearly another autonomous science, if, indeed, it is not to be identified with mathematics, as some hold. There are other branches of knowledge which are plainly not autonomous. Astronomy, for instance, has no unique and independent principles of its own. It consists chiefly of the application of mathematics to a selected realm of physical data. Without mathematics and physics, astronomy would have no laws at all. It is true that all sciences, whether autonomous or not, are dependent on psychological data, since thinking and observing are psychological processes. But neither the autonomous sciences, nor such a "heteronomous" science as astronomy, incorporates psychological laws into its own laws. Astronomy may use psychology, for instance, as an aid in determining the distortion in observations due to the "personal equation"; but astronomical principles are not in the least psychological, so that astronomy, while heteronomous as regards mathematics and physics, is autonomous as regards psychology.

In considering the autonomy of the mathematical and physical sciences, our interest is almost wholly in the realm of pure theory. But when we inquire about ethics, whether it is autonomous or not, our theoretical interest is necessarily complicated by practical considerations. If ethics is autonomous, then a person can be good whether he is religious or artistic or neither. If it is not autonomous, perhaps only a religious person or only an artistic person can be good. Much has been written about the limitations of the ethical standpoint. Nietzsche's book, *Beyond Good and Evil,* exemplifies this point of view, as does Paul Feldkeller's recent statement that "the conscience of norm-creating rightness," that is, the power to create new values and standards, is "supermoral."[1] Now, if supermoral considerations of any kind have the function of suspending or altering ethical principles, then those principles are not autonomous, but their sovereignty is in constant peril of invasion by other powers. We have to inquire into the security of the ethical foundations. Is ethics, then, really autonomous, or is it dependent on extramoral factors of some sort? Our answer to this question will have far-reaching implications.

2. Moral Law and Beauty

The autonomy of moral law is often challenged in

[1] Feldkeller, *Forum Philosophicum,* 1(1930-31), 307.

behalf of the claims of æsthetics. Goodness, it is said, cannot justify itself from within, but must call on the aid of beauty. From this point of view there are no laws of obligation, but only principles, or intuitions, of good taste; the good and the beautiful are identical. The conflict between the primacy of duty and the primacy of beauty in matters of human conduct goes back, as Matthew Arnold has shown,[2] to the contributions of the Hebrews and the Greeks to our civilization, although it must be admitted that the writer of *The Song of Solomon* puts beauty above righteousness, and Plato, in his critique of Homer's Olympian ethics, puts righteousness above beauty. But, on the whole, the Hebrews were ethical and the Greeks æsthetic. Even in Aristotle's *Nicomachean Ethics* there is no strong note of obligation or of benevolence; whereas the Hebrew writers of both the Old and the New Testament, in most cases, refer to natural or artistic beauty only to draw a moral or religious lesson from it. The presence of these two inharmonious streams in modern culture, along with a technical and materialistic tendency that is indifferent or hostile to both streams, creates a fundamental problem for ethics.

When it is said that the Greek and the Hebrew traditions are inharmonious, it is not meant that the good and the beautiful are inharmonious. In fact, the natural tendency is to think of them as related. The truly good character is beautiful, and pure beauty stirs in us a longing for goodness. There is a fundamental kinship between the two fields. Goodness is a principle of harmony among all the choices of our will; beauty is that which produces a unique kind of harmony in our feelings. Both, then, are forms of harmony. More-

---

[2] In his famous essay on "Hellenism and Hebraism" in *Culture and Anarchy*.

over, each is to a certain extent subject matter for the other. On the one hand, ethics includes æsthetics. It is one's duty to obey the Law of Specification and the Law of the Best Possible; and both of those Laws would often deal with æsthetic values. The Law of the Most Inclusive End would explicitly impose the obligation of including the appreciation and creation of beauty in the moral life. The Axiological Law, as applied to this problem, would dictate harmony between moral and æsthetic values. On the other hand, æsthetics includes ethics. The great moral problems and struggles of humanity are the theme of paintings and operas, dramas and novels. Furthermore, each bears on our view of the cosmos as a whole. It is natural for man to seek goodness and beauty in the universe beyond his narrow range; and the experiences of moral and æsthetic value are facts which any cosmology must take into account. Great art and great character have often had their roots in a conviction about the nature of the universe. "Art without any metaphysics," says Tillich, "lacks style. It is either abstract formalism or arbitrary formlessness."[3]   Anyone who has seen much of modern art knows what Tillich means without further explanation.

Yet over against these resemblances stand certain marked contrasts. Ethics, as we have found, has primarily to do with the will and the life of action. Æsthetics deals chiefly with our feelings and intuitions. The task of art is "not to realize ideas but to render the essence of being visible, even the essence of that which, from the ethical standpoint, may be worse than nothing."[4]   What æsthetics admires, ethics may condemn. A further difference is found in the fact that an æsthetic

[3] Tillich, SW, 128.
[4] *Ibid.*, 127,

object or experience is complete in itself; the painting is separated from surrounding space by a frame, the stage by footlights and semidarkness, while the symphony stands in no relation at all to the sounds made by the audience and the outside world before, after, or during its presentation. In contrast with the æsthetic, moral experience is always organically related to all that is going on in the relevant environment. It is itself the very movement of life. Even in cases where beauty is a part of life—as in beauty of face and form—the æsthetic loveliness is complete in itself, whether it expresses and produces a correspondingly beautiful character or not. This proposition will be challenged by those who are so dominated by ethical standards that they are unable to assume the æsthetic point of view; but it is confirmed by many works of art as well as by the immoral or nonmoral standards of many lovers of beauty.

Despite these and other differences that might be mentioned, moral and æsthetic experiences necessarily have some effect on each other. Both exist in the same mind, both deal with the same world, both stir the deepest emotions,[5] and both are social phenomena expressed and furthered by social institutions through every century of the history of civilization. That they could be kept wholly apart from each other, so that neither would affect the other, is unthinkable, save in a very few cases of ethical or æsthetic specialists with abnormally "water-tight" mental compartments. But such exceptions prove the rule. The problem is not merely how to live a life of beauty or how to live a

---

[5] "The enjoyment of noble music, of which I had long been deprived, exalted me into ecstasy and carried me away on the waves of a pure motion. Everything became great and good, the past, as it ought to have been and the future rich and radiant. I felt the springs of my best nature welling up." Bonsels, NV, 47.

life of goodness, but, rather, how to develop both factors in the same personality without needless loss of beauty or of goodness to the person.

If the condition thus named is to be fulfilled, it follows that the æsthetic and the ethical should each respect the autonomy of the other. When the moral critic of art seeks to forbid the representation in art of any theme that does not contribute directly to the encouragement and upbuilding of the moral will, he is infringing on the autonomy of beauty and demanding that all art be didactic. But art that is deliberately moralizing, that omits the evil of life and presents the good with the explicit sole purpose of causing others to be good, has rarely achieved æsthetic greatness. The aim to feel and portray beauty conflicts with the aim to persuade others to be righteous. The mediæval morality plays, which seem to be exceptions to this rule, arise in a culture which still feels the unity of life in religion and hence is aware of no sharp contrast between art and morality, both being religious. Religious art is no exception either, for in its greatest forms it presents the beliefs and the problems of religion objectively, not didactically. The more didactic it is, the less successful. The "Creation" is art, a temperance song is propaganda. On the other hand, the æsthete, who cares only for painting and music and poetry and the development of æsthetic feelings and forms of conduct, has a view of life at once too soft and too unintelligent to render possible the attainment of the highest moral values. In his experience the beautiful fails to have respect for the good, and the result is weak beauty and almost no goodness. Beauty needs goodness as much as goodness needs beauty.

The practical question of just how far the respect of each of these principles for the autonomy of the other

should go is a delicate one that can be solved only by
the maturing experience of the race. Those who wish
to maintain the absolute autonomy of æsthetics, yet to
make a gesture of courtesy to moral law, will quote
authorities to the effect that "to the pure all things are
pure," "evil to him who evil thinks," and "beauty is
truth, truth beauty." But such æsthetic enthusiasts
forget that art is just as much in peril from its perverse and immoral abuse as it is from its didactic abuse.
If it is unæsthetic to use beauty primarily to make
men good, it is at least as unæsthetic to use it primarily
to make men bad. Æsthetic and ethical interests are
alike imperiled by vile and disgusting exhibitions on
the stage or the screen and by literature which deliberately appeals to man's lowest nature; and such abuses
are practically more dangerous to real beauty and real
goodness than is the dullest didactic art, because of the
wild passions to which they appeal. Yet it is not clear
that a wise form of censorship for dealing with this situation has been found. To be fully fair, censorship
should forbid very ugly didactic art as well as the immoral. This could hardly be applied practically.
Moreover, forms of censorship have had the effect of
calling public attention to that which is censored and
thus of defeating their own end. Further, there are
many borderline instances of æsthetic productions
which seem to some to imperil morality and to others
to be perfectly innocent. An evil mind will find evil
in the purest art. The moral value of art, therefore,
must not be judged by extreme cases, but by its social
effect on the whole. If the rule that neither the æsthetic
nor the moral should violate the autonomy of the other,
and that each should respect the other, were to be
followed, we should have theoretically a combination
of the Law of Specification with the Law of the Most

Inclusive End, and practically the basis for a wholesome culture.

But the relation between the æsthetic and the moral ought to be much closer than that between two mutually tolerant sovereign powers. There should be co-operation as well as respect and independence. We have already pointed out that interrelationships are necessary for various reasons. Now we must go further, and assert that in case of conflict, the primacy always belongs to moral law rather than to æsthetics. If one grants autonomy to moral law at all, one must also grant its universal claim to the allegiance of every act of will. If there are moral laws at all, they are binding on all persons at all times. Yet this is not to be taken in the sense of an overriding of the æsthetic by the moral; on the contrary, moral law itself, as we have seen, dictates the fullest possible recognition and realization of æsthetic value. It does, however, mean that the moral standpoint has a right that the æsthetic does not have. The moral law may say to man, "Here your æsthetic interest shall give way to considerations of duty—whether intellectual, humanitarian, or biological." There is, however, no æsthetic law that can justly say, "Here your moral law must give way to considerations of beauty." For all æsthetic activity of man, however much it may be a matter of feeling in itself, is to some extent dependent on his will, and every act of will is subject to moral law. If æsthetic impulses claim the right to allow man to violate moral law, they are claiming the right to do wrong, which is a self-contradiction. The Hebrews taught us the beauty of holiness (even if the phrase is an inspired mistranslation!), while the Greeks have taught us the holiness of beauty. But civilization will render both teachings futile and will ultimately destroy itself unless it holds,

not only to what Kant called the primacy of the pure
practical (that is, the moral) reason over the speculative, but also to the primacy of the moral over the
æsthetic in a life that includes both.

3. Moral Law and Religion

When we investigate the relations between moral law
and religion, we confront a problem analogous to that
of the relations of the moral and the beautiful, in that
two fundamental values of life are being compared.
Yet factors enter into the consideration of religion other
than those which enter into that of art. There is even
more difference of opinion about what is truly religious than about what is truly beautiful. More significant is the fact that the relations between religion
and morality are much closer than those between
beauty and morality. If religion be defined as co-operation between man and his God, expressed both in worship and in the conduct of life,[6] then two important
implications follow at once: First, that God is regarded
as the embodiment of the moral ideal, and, secondly,
that he is viewed as the very source or creator of a
moral order in the universe. If God is the source of
moral law, it might be held either that he is superior
to his handiwork and can violate it or call on man to
violate it; or else that he is bound by it, just as any
autonomous person is bound by a self-imposed ideal.
In any case, the relation between religion and morality
is intimate and constitutes an important problem for
any theory of moral law. It is other than logical reasons which lead some ethicists to omit this problem
from theoretical ethics.

----

[6] For this discussion a simple working definition of religion is
adopted, which may not be acceptable to all, but corresponds to very
wide Hebrew, Christian, Mohammedan, and some Buddhist usage.

In popular thought, ethics is almost identified with religion. People who wish to refer to religion without actually mentioning the word often call it man's ethical life. On the other hand, many religious persons view the moral life as a religious act. The existence of a large amount of moral instruction under church auspices leads some to suspect all ethical principles of being due to a religious prejudice of some sort. Moreover, the degree of goodness which is prescribed by the moral law is half instinctively regarded by many as something supernatural, so that unselfish honesty, high courage, or loyal love are often thought of as partaking of the divine.

In one sense it is clear that the moral law is more fundamental than religion.[7] Religion and morality were so intertwined in their origins that it is impossible for us to determine which was which in primitive times. But for civilized and reflective man religion has the distinctive meaning of the worship of a divine power that is believed to be good. Now, it is impossible to regard any being as good, unless one has some conception of what "good" is; and that conception is one's ethics. Moreover, it is unreasonable to believe in the existence of a good God unless experience offers evidence of goodness; and the evidence of goodness is found largely in moral conduct. A substantial part, then, of the basis for religion lies in ethics. Ethics is, therefore, logically prior to religion; religion cannot be true unless ethics is true, but ethics might be true and religion false.

This basic place of the moral law relative to religious belief is evidenced by the moral critique of religious standards and practices which has repeatedly been carried out both by religious believers and by unbe-

---

[7] In this connection see "The Moral Basis of Religious Values," in Brightman, RV, Chap. II.

lievers. This critique could never have been acknowledged as justifiable unless the priority of moral law were granted. Buddha criticized the caste system of Hinduism; Plato criticized the morals of the Homeric gods; the "law of Moses"[8] criticized the practices of the Canaanitic religion; Jesus and Paul criticized certain standards of the Mosaic legislation; in short, the history of religious progress is a history of the purification of religious faith by appeal to moral law. The moral consciousness has repudiated such religious phenomena as the intolerance, the persecutions, the witch-burnings, and the religious hatreds and wars of the past, and instead has brought to religion the highest ethical ideals.

But these facts do not solve the problem. They serve only to make it more acute. The question is really where the highest ethical ideals themselves come from. Are they to be regarded as a solely human product, or are they in some way the expression or unfolding of a divine purpose and plan in the universe? A complete discussion of the problem thus raised would lead to an entire metaphysics; yet some brief consideration of it is unavoidable in any theoretical treatment of moral law. The problem is summarized in German philosophy by the phrase: Autonomy or theonomy? In this phrase, autonomy (self-law) means (as in the Law of Autonomy) that the validity of obligation is derived from the fact that it is self-imposed; theonomy (God-law) means that it is derived from the fact that God imposes it.

Autonomy is the principle on which the System of Moral Laws has been built up; and theonomy, from that

---

[8] The expression "the law of Moses" is in quotation marks because scholars generally recognize that the legislation in the Pentateuch was the product of a long development after the time of Moses. See Brightman, SH.

point of view, is clearly heteronomous.[9]   It is no more legitimate to appeal to God for the solution of an ethical problem than for the solution of a problem in physics.[10]   The supremacy of moral autonomy is energetically expressed by S. S. Laurie, when he says, "Hence it is that even in the name of science, art, or religion no man can do an unjust act—he cannot even lose his temper without self-contradiction, inner discord, and subversion of the moral order."[11]   The theory of moral autonomy in itself is neither a denial nor an assertion of God's existence.   For Kant, it is true, autonomous morality implied the postulates of God, freedom, and immortality; but he believed in God because he believed in morality and not the reverse.   From the ethical standpoint, the principle of autonomy appears to be final.

Yet, when one considers human civilization as a whole it does not appear that morality is entirely independent of religion.   Although there have been many virtuous persons who have denied the truth of religion, the prevailing tendency has been for religious belief or unbelief to have a profound effect on morals.   Ranke, the historian, once said that "all human activity depends on the religious conception in which one lives."[12]   Obviously this is extreme, but it at least raises a doubt about the absolute sufficiency of moral autonomy.   Within the last few years a large body of literature has been produced, especially in America, occasioned by the increase of religious unbelief.   Walter Lippmann's *A Preface to Morals* is the most distinguished and most representative product of this movement.   Lippmann's book rests

---

[9] This is in agreement with Feldkeller, *Forum Philosophicum*, 1(1930-31), 311, n. 5.

[10] Steinthal, AE, 10.

[11] Laurie, EER, 195.

[12] Cited by Wach, ERS, title-page.

throughout on the thesis that the collapse of a religious
view of the world necessarily occasions either a moral
collapse or a radical moral readjustment.[13]

In some of its forms religion has laid so much stress
on the transcendent superiority of God to everything
human, and consequently on the absolute need and the
absolute authority of a divine revelation, that in this
mood religion has inclined to regard man as a "worm
of the dust" and to estimate his morality as "filthy
rags." The "works" of morality have been disparaged
in the interests of faith. Sören Kierkegaard has a sermon in which he proves that it is religiously edifying
for man always to be wrong in the sight of God.[14] When
religious thought has not gone to such extremes as this,
it has often regarded the moral law as the command of
God, the *lex aeterna* of the scholastics. James Martineau states a typical position of religious ethics when
he declares that "in morals, it is *Self* and *God,* that
stand face to face."[15] For him, morality is theonomy.
Tillich goes so far as to say that it is ungodly to distinguish between duties toward God and other duties,
for "there is only one duty, namely, that toward God,
the direction of life toward the Unconditioned."[16]

How, then, is the problem of autonomy or theonomy
to be solved? It appears that the conflict between the
two has been exaggerated by zealous partisans and that
both principles can be preserved if each be given its
proper place. As far as the moral life itself is concerned, autonomy is the last word. The moral laws are
valid because they are a reasoned account of the nature
and implications of moral experience, not because they

---

[13] See the references to Lippmann in the index of Brightman, PG.

[14] Cited and discussed by Leisegang, RP, 38-39.

[15] Martineau, TET, II, 5. *Cf.* Garvie, CIHS, 137.

[16] Tillich, SW, 144. But he grants (p. 147) that theonomy and
autonomy are equally essential.

are commanded by an eternal lawgiver or communicated on a Mount Sinai. Moral law is autonomous and independent of religion and of the existence of God so far as the obligatory nature of its principles is concerned. But there are at least two respects in which morality is dependent on religion. In the first place, it is dependent on religion for some of its content. Morality does not derive the Law of the Most Inclusive End, for instance, from religious faith, but if that Law be true and if religion be a real value, then it is a part of one's duty to worship God and (in accordance with the Law of the Best Possible) to achieve the highest type of religion of which one is capable. In the second place, if the existence of God be a reality,[17] then it is he who has created us as moral beings, so that in this sense autonomy depends on theonomy. Yet even from this standpoint, the moral law can hardly be a purely arbitrary creation of the *will* of God; rather, it is an expression of the *reason* of God, and the divine reason must be eternal and uncreated. Otherwise, there was a time when God was not reasonable or moral, which is inconsistent with his very nature as God and hence impossible. Here lies the truth in the scholastic view of the moral law as a *lex aeterna*. Moral law embodies the eternal principles of goodness as geometrical law embodies the eternal principles of space relations. This does not imply that any human being has an adequate knowledge of the one or the other; but it does imply that both are principles of reason which may be discovered by autonomous thought. Autonomy is the guide to theonomy.

So much for purely theoretical considerations. There still remain practical aspects of the relation between

---

[17] See Brightman, PG, for discussion of the evidence for God's existence, especially Chap. VI.

ethics and religion that should not be overlooked. The question at issue may be put in this form: Is religious motivation a practical necessity in the moral life? That it is inspiring and helpful in many cases, perhaps in most, is very evident. Belief in cosmic goodness is a genuine support and aid in the humble tasks of terrestrial goodness. But to make religious faith essential to moral living is both unfair and perilous. Unfair, because theory has shown that autonomy is logically prior to theonomy; and perilous, because this view would compel one who lost his religious faith also to lose his allegiance to moral law, which would be a needless calamity in view of the religiously neutral proof of the moral laws.

However, it is hardly to be doubted that the performance of the autonomous duties of the moral law out of a joyous and worshipful love of God, unifies life better, elicits deeper and more varied emotions, and affords a more rational goal for moral action in periods of failure and depression than does an autonomous ethics which, however loyal to ideals it may be, denies the reality of God. If one is intellectually convinced that there is no God, then the only possible course for him is to renounce all religious motives except the "high religion" of Mr. Lippmann, which expects nothing whatever from the universe. But if one finds the being of God intellectually more probable than his nonbeing, it would be folly to fail to draw the practical inferences from that belief.

It is significant that many of the greatest thinkers, Christians and non-Christians alike, have made love to God the highest motive in life. Such was the view of Plato and of Spinoza as well as of Saint Augustine and Saint Thomas. Among recent writers James Ward makes it the climax of his *The Realm of Ends*, while the unorthodox Georg Simmel makes this enlightening comment on it: "With the idea of love to God the idea that we obey him on account of his power is disenthroned. We love him because he possesses the properties which appear to us in ourselves as the noblest and best."[18] This is equivalent to a reconciliation of autonomy and theonomy through love; the love of God is consistent with autonomy because it is recognized as embodying the highest values which autonomy discovers in experience.

But sometimes religious writers go very far in their desire to elevate religious motives above moral ones. Alfred E. Garvie, in his book, *The Christian Ideal for Human Society,* has expressed himself as follows: "Love constrains a large part of human life without any consideration of moral principle, and conformity to it. The mother cares for her babe, not because it is her duty, but it has become her delight. Indeed, so long as morality is still a duty, the character has not been conformed to the ideal; the better a man is, the less will he act from duty, as obedience to law, because his sentiments have become what they ought to be. The legal view is lower than the Christian. . . . Kant . . . was still moving among abstractions. When inclination and principle conflict, then duty must be done because it is duty, however uncongenial it may be. . . . The importance of this modification of a too abstract moralist standpoint cannot be exaggerated."[19]

Garvie's argumentation rests on the assumption that there is something incompatible between duty and love. He is tormented by the old and fallacious idea that duty must be disagreeable. It is true that duty must be thoughtful and that thought is somewhat difficult. But

---

[18] Simmel, MW, I, 176.
[19] Garvie, CIHS, 254.

love must also be thoughtful. A purely impulsive love, that takes no thought of consequences, uses no judgment, makes no plans, but loves blindly and passionately, is equally disastrous whether its object is divine or human. Garvie's plea is in danger of asking for emancipation from intelligence as well as from duty. There is no good reason for and there is no good reason against the presupposition that love and duty are incompatible feelings. It may be added that Garvie perhaps makes a further presupposition which adds to his confusion, namely, that the person who is guided by moral law in his conduct must constantly be thinking of it, and, as it were, mentally reviewing the statement and the proof of each Moral Law whenever he performs a good act. This is, of course, both psychologically and logically unsound. We cannot be giving conscious attention to theory and practice at the same time; yet we can be guided throughout our practice by decisions based on theory. "The dance of life" has its rhythm; and if we lose the rhythm, we lose also the spirit of the dance. The dance and the love, the worship and the joy of life, gain, rather than lose, by intelligent guidance. Moral law is not mere "legalism"; but intelligent guidance, given at the times when such guidance is needed, will preserve and not destroy the values which it is guiding.[20]

4. MORAL LAW AND METAPHYSICS: IS ETHICS DEPENDENT ON METAPHYSICS?

The question of the relation between ethics and metaphysics is closely connected with that of the relation between ethics and religion, which we have just been

---

[20] Note Laurie's remark that "a being who can act only from immediate impulses is neither moral nor immoral. Morality enters with reason." EER, 59. Would Garvie have us do right only when we feel a joyous impulse?

discussing, for religion culminates in the idea of God, which is a metaphysical concept. By metaphysics we mean a rational account of reality as a whole. The sciences are accounts of parts of reality; metaphysics tries to view reality as a connected whole. The idea of God is the idea of a being who either is the whole of reality himself (pantheism) or stands in such a relation to the whole that everything outside himself finds the ultimate ground and purpose of its being in him (deism and theism). But the point of view of religion is that of worship and love, while the point of view of metaphysics is that of rational understanding.

Stating the problem simply, it runs: Does ethics depend on our theory of the nature of reality as a whole? Must it surrender its autonomy to metaphysics?

There are numerous facts which point in the direction of an affirmative answer to this question. Surely, our conception of what ought to be is derived from our conception of what is and what can be. The period of idealistic philosophy in the first third of the Nineteenth Century in Germany was a time when metaphysics was supreme. Hegel and Schopenhauer, the great opponents, agreed in deriving their ethical theory from their metaphysics.[21] When, after the death of Hegel (1831), confidence in metaphysics waned and a scientific, technical, and materialistic world view came in, there was a collapse of moral idealism that seemed to follow on the collapse of metaphysical idealism. The writings of Ernst Troeltsch and Rudolf Eucken abound in references to this twofold collapse; and even so caustic a critic of Hegel as Rudolf Haym could

---

[21] Hegel's treatment of morality in the *Phänomenologie* is called "The Moral World View," while Schopenhauer says explicitly that "the demand that ethics build on metaphysics is irrefutable." See Schopenhauer, *Werke*, III, 659.

write, during the period soon after the fall of Hegelianism: "We are now in the midst of a great and almost universal shipwreck of the spirit and of any faith in the spirit."[22] About the same time, Trendelenburg said that "ethics which does without metaphysics loses depth in the ideal realm."[23] Hartmann was profoundly convinced of the essential connection between metaphysical and ethical thinking. If one is sure that the world is metaphysically meaningless, one will naturally infer that his own life is likewise meaningless. As Hartmann puts it: "The nonsense of subjective arbitrariness is the adequate counterpart to the objective nonsense of existence."[24]

In practical life the relation between metaphysics and ethics is often very close. Puritan ethics was the outcome of the Puritan world view; and Cavalier ethics of the Cavalier world view. The French Revolution and the Russian Revolution were at once the negation of a traditional metaphysic and the consequence of a new metaphysic. Politics in Germany is a strife of *Weltanschauungen;* the Communist is a Marxian materialist, the National Socialist feels himself to be an idealist opposing materialism, while the Centrist represents the Catholic world view.[25]

The facts that we have been considering show that there is an actual relation of some sort between metaphysics and ethics, but they do not reveal clearly the nature of that relation. Now, it may be shown that ethics cannot depend wholly on metaphysics. If ethics were wholly dependent, then we could not have any

[22] Haym, HSZ, 5.
[23] Trendelenburg, HP, 29.
[24] Hartmann, PSB, 767-768.
[25] A. C. Armstrong has shown that the relation between metaphysics and ethics is not always so close as appears. *Cf.* his "Philosophy and Political Theory," in *Jour. Phil.*, 16(1919), 421-428.

moral obligations until we had a metaphysical system; and we could not have the right conception of our obligations until we had the right metaphysics. Moral experience could not, then, exist until after our metaphysical construction was completed. But on the other hand, metaphysics could not be completed until we had moral experience, since metaphysics is the view of reality implied by our experience as a whole. The view that ethics is wholly dependent on metaphysics, then, leads to the conclusion that both ethics and metaphysics are impossible.

Since, however, ethics is the organization and interpretation of the phenomena of moral experience, it, like every other science, is prior to metaphysics, and furnishes metaphysics with subject matter. Now, this is perfectly compatible with the fact that metaphysical theory, like religious faith, has an effect on ethics. Ethics is never a completed science, as moral living is never completed. Metaphysical conceptions modify, accordingly, the ethical conception of what values are worth living for. Metaphysical skepticism, for instance, would make it absurd to devote one's life to the construction of a metaphysical system; and metaphysical materialism would destroy the value of prayer and religious faith. Our picture of the world, then, modifies appreciably our conception of what constitutes "the best possible" and of what elements enter into "the ideal of personality." But it cannot be stated too emphatically that the influence of metaphysics does not affect the principles of the Moral Laws. Those Laws are a rational account of moral experience, whatever the state of the rest of the universe may be. They remain true within their realm, the realm of human living, irrespective of what may lie beyond human experience or beyond the grave; for they claim only to describe the best known type of human experience.

5. MORAL LAW AND METAPHYSICS: FREEDOM

Kant held to three metaphysical postulates of ethics, as we have said, namely, God, freedom, and immortality. As a result of our previous discussion we may say that neither the postulate of God nor the postulate of immortality is necessary to ethical theory, although the acceptance or rejection of these postulates makes a real difference in the concrete values for which the moral person strives. But there is a fundamental distinction between belief in God and immortality on the one hand and belief in freedom on the other. The former beliefs have to do with the content which we attach to the Axiological and Personalistic Laws, although not with the Laws themselves, while the latter concerns the very act of choice and so bears on the Formal Laws. The act of choice is the center of the ethical life.

In Chapter III (to which the student should refer) we discussed freedom from a purely psychological point of view as the experience of choice, postponing until the present chapter a metaphysical consideration of freedom. Two questions confront us: What is the metaphysical truth about freedom? and What, if any, is the relation of this truth to ethics?

Let us, then, seek for the metaphysical truth about freedom. First of all, we should define exactly what our problem means. The metaphysical truth about anything means the truth about its setting in reality as a whole; to approach metaphysical truth we need to think about the relations of the subject matter which we are investigating to all the rest of our knowledge and experience. It is true, for example, that I exercise the power of choice; but this truth is not metaphysical.

It is purely empirical. It does not tell us whether an act of choice is a necessary product of previous conditions or a spontaneous and self-determining act. We can never ascertain which of the two it is by considering it alone. We must take its relations into account; not merely its relations to previous conditions, but its relations to the best view we can get of experience as a whole, and of the universe which experience implies. Hence the assertion and the denial of freedom are both theoretical metaphysical propositions.

Since confusion has often arisen from vagueness, it is desirable to specify the sense in which terms will be used in our treatment. By determinism is meant the theory that any given act of choice is an unequivocally necessary consequence of the situation immediately preceding it. The situation includes all relevant factors, both psychological and environmental. Given that situation, the choice is inevitable. Given any number of precisely similar situations, a precisely similar choice is inevitable. By the theory of free will or freedomism[26] is meant the view that a given act of choice is not unequivocally determined by the immediately preceding situation, but that the person himself determines his choice by a spontaneous, selective act. Freedomism grants that every free act has necessary consequences and that the situation in which the act of choice occurs determines the possibilities from which selection can be made; but it denies that the choice itself is externally determined. Its causation is internal to the act and purely personal, not impersonal or external to it.

Many have said that the issue between determinism and freedomism is a purely psychological one. An act

---

[26] "Freedomism" is an awkward word, but it is less misleading than "indeterminism," and more consistent terminologically than "libertarianism."

of choice is a psychological datum, subject to psychological investigation. But there are reasons for believing that a purely psychological investigation can never solve the problem of freedom one way or the other.

Determinism is the application to psychology of a type of causality that has proved useful and even essential in the development of the physical sciences, namely, the mechanical. Stated in general terms (abstracting from any special reference to physics) this type of causality means uniformity of sequence; given certain antecedents, certain consequents will follow. For our view of the physical world this type of causality, according to Kant, is *a priori* necessary. Certain it is that we assume it to be universally valid; if we have not found the cause of an event, it never occurs to us to suppose either that it has no cause or that causes behave in a random and capricious way so that the same cause might have any one of two or three effects. It is the ideal of a causally connected order that enables us to build up the conception of an objective world as distinguished from our subjective experiences. Now, the problem of freedom is the question whether this type of causation, which has served the physical sciences well, is equally applicable to consciousness. There are at least two traits that a causal law must have in order to be valid. It must rest on empirical observation of fact and it must be so formulated as to be capable of verification.

It is evident that there are great difficulties in proving the universality of mechanical causation in the personal life. Empirical observations do warrant the formulation of certain verifiable mechanistic laws of consciousness, such as those dealing with the relations between peripheral stimulus and conscious sensation, and numerous other generalizations of experimental psychology and perhaps of psychoanalysis. But such laws can be formulated only when specific factors in consciousness or the environment can be isolated, observed, and controlled. They are most satisfactorily proved to be necessary and "mechanistic" when the relation between cause and effect can be formulated mathematically, so that from the quantum of cause that is present the exact effect can be predicted. Now, such laws of human choice do not exist in any known psychology; on the contrary, the unpredictable character of choice has to be reckoned with today as in the Garden of Eden.

Why is it that psychology, which knows many conscious mechanisms, still finds itself unable to give a definite and verifiable account of the mechanism of choice? The determinist will reply that he relies on the universality of the causal law, and that he does not intend to be baffled by difficulties. This, then, is the strength of the deterministic case: its reliance on the causal law, its usefulness in our mastery of the physical world, its success in proving some psychological mechanisms, and its *a priori* universality. The freedomist will meet this by saying that all this is a begging of the question; for precisely the question at issue is whether mechanical causality is *a priori* true of conscious choice. Determinism asserts that it is true of the mental realm because it is true of the physical. But the essential logical reason for predicating it of the physical realm—namely, that it assures an objective order as distinguished from chaotic subjective experience—no longer obtains in the mental realm. Subjective experience is undeniable fact, however it is ordered. The type of causality to be found in it therefore remains an open question.

By its methods, its presuppositions, and its problems

physical science is able to recognize none but mechanical causation (in the sense in which we have defined it). If the universality and exclusive right of such causation were called in question, the whole structure of the physical sciences as it now exists would be imperiled. Today there are signs, even within physics, of just such questioning; laws are being viewed by some as statistical approximations instead of absolute necessities. There is the famous statement of Sir James Jeans that the universe is more like a great thought than like a great machine, and the similar view of Eddington. Some scientists, however, are unwilling to let psychology and ethics profit by the changes in physical conceptions. It is true that a view of the nature of the physical world does not carry with it at once any view of mind. But the breakdown of the idea of the concept of mechanical necessity as the type of causation in the physical world certainly destroys the force of the *a priori* argument for determinism.

Moreover, mechanical cause has two serious defects as an ultimate explanation of any event: it is (as Bowne said) tautologous, and it makes novelty inexplicable. First, it is tautologous because it explains the present combination of existing elements in any state of affairs by the fact that it followed a previous, but different, combination of the same elements, in accordance with law; no matter how far back one goes, one has always the same elements in different combinations—these elements not coinciding with the present table of chemical elements, but with the ultimate units, whatever they may be. To say that the universe is always no more than a recombination of the same elements is tautology. Secondly, it makes novelty inexplicable. There are mechanists who accept what is called "emergent evolution," and who hold that when certain combinations of the elements obtain, then something genuinely new emerges.[27]   But on mechanistic principles this emergence is utterly magical.   It is a sheer miracle.   Therefore a different type of causality is needed for any ultimate explanation of the facts, especially for the facts of mind.[28]

Now, ethical experience furnishes us with the desired type of causation, namely, free, purposive choice.   One-sided advocates of determinism have argued that freedom was not causation, but chance.   From the point of view of mechanism, this interpretation is intelligible; but it fails to appreciate the possibility of another type of causation than the mechanical.   Freedomism does not hold to uncaused events, but to events nonmechanically caused.   Freedom differs from mechanism in the following respects: it deals with a situation which is a genuine living whole instead of being a complex of permanently existing elements;[29] it contains the decisive causal factor within itself in the power of choice instead of being determined by what is external to it;[30] and it grants to man's will the power of choosing to obey (or to disobey) rational and moral ideals whatever the other circumstances may be, instead of holding that

---

[27] Sellars, EN, defends this view.

[28] Bowne, MET, 404-420.

[29] In fact, mind contains no elements which actually exist before or after their presence in consciousness.   The structure of mind is therefore totally different from the supposed structure of physical objects.

[30] There must be something in the universe which originates change.   The mechanistic assumption is that this something is always ultimately external to the present situation; while the freedomist assumption is that in cases of choice it is ultimately internal to the situation.   The determinist often asserts that he holds to psychic causation.   But since every operation of psychic causation is, on his view, determined by previous conditions, his assertion really is equivalent to saying that the psychic is caused by the nonpsychic.   The freedomist, who holds that human will is a divine creation, denies that such creation determines choice.

choice is wholly a function of the circumstances. This type of causation has not hitherto proved useful within the realm of the physical sciences, but it may yet receive more attention even there with the growth of statistical views of law.

Further considerations pointing to the validity of free causation in ethical situations may be briefly mentioned. Freedom, as the self-determination of the will, accounts for the factor of novelty in the development of character as determinism cannot. The choice is a new act, a new contribution, and may determine a new direction in the development of personality for better or for worse. Likewise, it rests on a factor which mechanism cannot deal with, namely, the uniqueness of each moral situation; each act of choice finds the person somewhat different from what he was when he previously made a similar choice. The act is individual, unique, *einmalig* (happening only once). This at least makes any experimental verification of the mechanistic view impossible and opens the way to a theory of freedom.

The strongest argument in favor of the hypothesis of freedom is that without it we are not even free to think, to say nothing of making other moral choices. The power to think means that the individual can impose on himself the ideal of logic or scientific method and hold it through thick and thin. In the presence of illogical thinking, of problems, or of unexplained data, the free thinker can hold himself to the ideal of thought. Freedom makes this intelligible. Determinism, however, must hold that every view which the mind entertains is determined by the sum total of previous conditions rather than by logic alone. Without freedom all opinions are equally necessary and the mind is not free to judge or to will. All other sciences, then, as well as the special science of ethics, must pre-suppose freedom.[31]   The other sciences use freedom in building up ideals of truth and method, observing facts, forming hypotheses and testing them; but ethics not only uses freedom in building its system, but also appeals to freedom in every one of its laws.   The claim that "all persons ought" to do so and so is logically and ethically futile unless all persons can do what they ought to.[32]   Unless freedom is real, there is no reason to believe that they can.   Even determinists act as if they were free.

Hence we have now answered both questions with which we started.   To the query, What is the metaphysical truth about freedom? we have answered that choice is an ultimate fact not determined by circumstances external to it, but selecting from the given possibilities one which will have necessary consequences for the future.   To the question: What is the relation of this metaphysical truth to ethics? we have answered that it is a constituent of every ethical (and therefore of every rational) choice, without which moral law would be meaningless.   Those who do not accept this view behave as though they did, and those who do accept this view recognize that the field of choice and the consequences of choice are determined, and also that free choice is a rare event.

---

[31] This contention of Bowne's has also been urged by Simmel, Spaulding, and Urban, among others.   A related thesis, namely, that science rests on the ethical foundation of the recognition of the personality of other (*Persönlichkeitsannahme*), is defended by Schroedinger, *Voss. Zeit.*, December 25, 1930.   Ulrici well showed the ethical basis of science in his article "Über die ethischen Motive und Zielpunkte der Wissenschaft." *Zeit. f. Ph. u. ph. Kr.*, 51(1867), 204-218.

[32] John Laird has recently put it thus: "I fear, however, that any injunction to 'do the best one can' has (to use modern philosophical slang) a slightly Pickwickian flavor, unless it can properly be enjoined in the libertarian's sense." *Jour. Ph. St.*, 6(1931), 58.

Does this result deny or impair the autonomy of moral law? Does it make ethics dependent on metaphysics? It must be admitted that it impairs to some extent the absolute autonomy of the science. If reality as a whole were such that freedom were impossible, then ethical law would have no validity. Moral science thus stands in inseparable relation with the organic whole of truth. But the postulate of freedom is immanent in every ethical situation, and therefore imperils the autonomy of ethics far less than would the supposition (which we deny) that the validity of ethics depends on whether our metaphysics is theistic or atheistic or whether we accept or reject immortality. Save for the metaphysics of freedom, then, ethics is independent of metaphysics; and the practical fact of freedom is present in every ethical choice, even if the theoretical justification of it must carry us beyond a mere description of the fact.

6. Moral Law and Metaphysics: Is Metaphysics Dependent on Ethics?

We have shown that ethics is at one point dependent on metaphysics, namely, in its postulate of freedom. So far as ethics is concerned, however, all that is implied by this is conveyed by the word "postulate." Ethics simply postulates the metaphysical validity of freedom; but it does not have to wait for the development of an entire metaphysical system before it goes ahead on that basis. Ethics, while dependent on a metaphysical truth, is not dependent on a metaphysical system. There still remains the question whether, in any sense, metaphysics is dependent on ethics.

In one sense metaphysics is clearly an ethical enterprise. It is a free product of the spirit, and can exist only as men choose to deal with its problems. Yet this is a somewhat external relation to ethics. Chemistry stands in a similar relation, but the subject matter of chemistry is in no way affected by the subject matter of ethics. The moral man uses the results of chemistry as instrumental values, but the laws of chemistry are not themselves laws of obligation or value. They are laws of perceived fact and describe what is without prescribing what ought to be.

The question about metaphysics, therefore, is whether its relation to ethics is like that of chemistry or whether the very subject matter of ethics is part of the subject matter of metaphysics. If metaphysics is a complete, rational account of the real, then obviously it must include all that is real. Now, moral experience and moral laws are just as real as sense experience and physical laws. Hence it is logically necessary for an adequate system of metaphysics to take account of ethics. Accordingly, the question is, now, not whether metaphysics must consider ethics, but only to what extent and in what way that consideration shall occur.

Here two fundamentally different world views take radically different attitudes. One, the naturalistic philosophy, recognizes the existence of moral experience but regards that experience as purely subjective in man, and as shedding no light on and having no implications for the structure of the universe beyond man. The naturalistic view of the universe is based on the data of sense perception, and moral experience is regarded by philosophers of this school as adding nothing to those data for our understanding of the world. The other world view may be called the idealistic philosophy. It is necessary to explain that the term "idealistic" is here used not in the strictly technical sense of "mentalistic" or "personalistic," but in the broad sense that implies the recognition of moral ideals and values as forming an essential part of the objective structure of the universe. Idealists hold that moral experience points to an objective moral order in reality, as truly as sense experience points to an objective physical order, and most idealists believe that the objective existence of both orders can be understood rationally only if both are the activity or thought or experience of a supreme mind that generates the whole cosmic process and controls its ongoing.

The conflict between these two world views is one of the eternal battles of thought. In ancient Greece, Democritus the naturalist and Plato the idealist were worthy exponents of each view. In modern Germany, Hegel the idealist was opposed by Feuerbach the naturalist; the naturalistic Haeckel and the idealistic Eucken both taught at Jena. The two views are not usually held today in a form so pure as to retain the sharp outlines of logical opposition. James and Dewey, the great American empiricists, have marked idealistic currents in their thinking; while Bosanquet, the British idealist, writes *The Meeting of Extremes in Contemporary Philosophy*. But the battle is not over. For all the noteworthy concessions a materialist like Sellars makes to idealistic thought, he, like the realistic Perry, stands firmly in opposition to any recognition of moral factors in metaphysics; while idealists and theists of every school incline more and more to accept Lotze's dictum that the true beginning of metaphysics lies in ethics, and to hold that moral law is one of the expressions of the very purpose of the universe.

It is not the duty of ethics to decide between these two philosophies. The Moral Laws are true whichever philosophy we accept. But the Moral Laws and the moral experience from which they are derived, are realities with which every philosophy must reckon. It seems to the present writer that only an idealistic philosophy of some sort can give an adequate and coherent interpretation of the personalistic data and laws of ethics. Yet all human thought is subject to the corrections of further experience and further insight. In its thinking, as in its living, mankind needs to be guided by the Law of the Best Possible and so to continue unweariedly in the search for truth in theory and practice.

SELECTED BIBLIOGRAPHY

On the chapter as a whole: W. A. Heidel, "Metaphysics, Ethics, and Religion," in *Phil. Rev.*, 9(1900), 30-41; Hoffmann, GM (Part B, III; in German); Jones, FE; Lippmann, PM (a challenging analysis); Mackenzie, MOE, 30-31, 431-453; Palmer, FOE (a gem); Seth, SEP, 361-467; Turner, PBMO; Unamuno, TSL.

On morality and religion: Brightman, RV, 32-69; Calkins, GMG, 168-177; Everett, MV, Chap. XIII; Jones, FEL, 85-119; Martineau, RER; Rashdall, TGE, II, 250-301; Royce, PL, 349-398; Ten Broeke, MLR; Urban, FOE, Chap. XIX.

On freedom: Fellin, WF (a remarkably complete bibliography of the whole subject). Since the literature for determinism is very well known and good material on freedomism is less familiar, the following works are chiefly on the freedomist side: Bowne, TTK, 96-102 and 239-244, also PER, 159-216; Hocking, SBF; Hudson, TLB, 195-244; James, POP, II, 569-579, and WB, 145-183; Leighton, MC, 448-457; Palmer, POF; Sellars, PPP, 362-384 (critical); Spaulding, WAI, 35-69 (the best recent essay on freedom).

OUTLINE OF THE HISTORY OF ETHICS

I

GREEK ETHICS (900 B. C.-529 A. D.)

A. Conventional Ethics:

  1. The religious tradition: "Homer" (900 B. C.), and other poets.

  2. The secular tradition: the Seven Sages (about 600 B. C.), and the ethical utterances of early philosophers (Pythagoras, Heraclitus, Democritus, etc.).

B. Relativistic Criticism of Convention: the Sophists (Humanists). Persian Wars (500-449 B. C.).

  1. Popular moralizing on pessimistic foundations:
    Prodicus (465(?)-390(?) B. C.).
      "Hercules at the Crossroads."

  2. Conservative relativism:
    Protagoras (480-410 B. C.).
      "Man is the measure of all things."
      "What is good and useful for one may very well be harmful to another."

  3. Radical relativism:
    Thrasymachus (Ca. 425 B. C.).
    (Callicles, Polus, Euthydemus.)
      Might makes right.

C. Rational Criticism both of Convention and of Relativism:
    Socrates (470-399 B. C.).
      Knowledge is virtue.
      Virtue is happiness.

D. Development of Socratic Ethics into Perfectionism:

  1. Plato (427-347 B. C.).
    Temperance.
    Courage.
    Wisdom.
    Justice.
    The *Republic*.

  2. Aristotle (384-322 B. C.).
    The doctrine of the Mean.
    Nicomachean Ethics and *Politics*.

E. The Dissolution of Socratic Ethics into its Separate
Factors: the Minor Socratic Schools:
1. The Factor of Abstract Thought:
Antisthenes the Cynic (440-370 B. C.). *Extreme Rationalism.*
Cf. Diogenes of Sinope (d. 323 B. C.).
Independence of externals.
"Reason" alone.
2. The Factor of Abstract Pleasure:
Aristippus the Cyrenaic (435-355 B. C.). *Extreme Hedonism.*
Present, physical pleasure.
But "I possess, I am not possessed."

F. Development of Cyrenaicism into Epicureanism (Hedonism):
Epicurus (341-270 B. C.).
Permanent, mental pleasure.
Lucretius (97-55 B. C.).
De rerum natura.

G. Development of Cynicism into Stoicism (Formalism):
Zeno (336-364 B. C.).
Cleanthes (331-250 B. C.).
Chrysippus (280-208 B. C.).
Seneca (3-65 A. D.).
Epictetus (50-120 A. D.).
Marcus Aurelius (121-180 A. D.).
Good will.
Cosmopolitanism.
Religious interest (pantheism).

H. Justinian closes schools of Neoplatonic Philosophy in Athens, 529 A. D.

II

ORIENTAL AND CHRISTIAN ETHICS

A. Altruism in India and China:
Buddha (568-488 B. C.).
Confucius (551-478 B. C.).

B. The Development of Morality among the Hebrews:
1. Ancient, conventional morality.
Social solidarity, religious ceremonialism.

2. Moral criticism of convention by the prophets (760-540 B. C.).

Amos, Hosea, Isaiah, Jeremiah, Second Isaiah.

Individual responsibility, inner life, universal humanitarianism.

3. Development of social and religious institutions by the priests (597 B. C. on).

Ezekiel, Ezra, Nehemiah.

The institutionalization and conventionalization of the prophetic morality; racial consciousness.

4. Contemporaneous growth of personal piety and prudential morality.

The Psalmists.

The Wise Men (Sages).

5. Lack of any such criticism of morality as among the Greeks, combined with a higher valuation of morality.

C. The Rise of Christianity:

1. Founded by Jesus (6 B. C.-29 A. D.) on the Ethics of the Prophets *vs.* Priests and Sages.

Golden Rule.

"Goodness and severity" (*cf.* Rom. 11: 22).

Different in type from Greek Ethics: more altruistic, less cultural.

2. Developed and applied by Paul (1(?)-64 A. D.).

"Love" (1 Cor. 13).

"Interimsethik"?

3. Ascetic and anti-Greek Tendencies in Christian Ethics:

Tertullian (160-222 A. D.).

"Certum est quia impossibile est."

4. Cultural and Greek Tendencies in Christian Ethics.

Clement (150(?)-215(?) A. D.).

5. Independent Christian Synthesis: Voluntarism.

Augustine (354-430 A. D.).

"The City of God."

(Roman Empire in West ends in 476.)

III

MEDIÆVAL AND RENAISSANCE ETHICS

Chronology:

Middle Ages: 529-1453.

Humanistic Renaissance: 1453-1600.

Scientific Renaissance: 1600-1690.

Note: The modern spirit dawns with the scientific Renaissance.

1. The Platonic-Christian Synthesis: imperfectly developed.

   John Scotus Erigena (800-877 A. D.).

   Platonic virtues plus Pauline (faith, hope, love), as Augustine. Ascetic and negative ethics. Union with God the goal of life.

2. The Aristotelian-Christian Synthesis:

   Thomas Aquinas (1225-1274).

   Based on Aristotle and Augustine. God is *summum bonum*. Less mystical than Erigena.

3. Critique of Christian tradition by the "Greek" Renaissance and the Protestant Reformation.

   Revival of study of other Greek moralists than Plato and Aristotle, 1453 on.

   Reformation (Diet at Worms, 1521).

   Calvinism, Puritanism.

IV

MODERN ETHICS (1600-   )

A. Radical Criticism of Theological Ethics during the Scientific Renaissance:

   Spinoza (1632-1677).

   Ethics of self-realization.

   "Amor intellectualis dei."

B. British Ethics: mainly empirical, hedonistic, altruistic.

1. Ethics of political authority:

   Thomas Hobbes (1588-1679).

   "Bellum omnium contra omnes."

   Social contract.

   Leviathan.

2. Ethics of self-interest (egoism):

   Bernhard de Mandeville (1670-1733).

   The Fable of the Bees.

3. Ethics of pleasure (utilitarianism, universal hedonism):

   a. Jeremy Bentham (1748-1832).

   A Fragment on Government.

Principles of Morals and Legislation.
Quantity of pleasure.
Intensity, duration, certainty, propinquity, fecundity, purity, extent.
Four sanctions: physical, moral (popular), religious, political.

  b. John Stuart Mill (1806-1873).
Utilitarianism.
Qualitative differences in pleasures.
Greatest good of the greatest number.
Conscientious feelings of mankind.

  c. Henry Sidgwick (1838-1900).
The Methods of Ethics.
Quantitative differences only.
Axiom of rational benevolence (intuition).
Prudence (intuition).
Justice (intuition).
Rational Hedonism.

4. Evolutionary Hedonism:

  a. Herbert Spencer (1820-1903).
Data of Ethics.
"Synthetic philosophy": evolution.
Pleasure accompanies preservation and enlargement of life: pain, the obstruction of life.
Altruism biologically grounded.
Society an organism.

  b. Sir Leslie Stephen (1832-1904).
Science of Ethics.
Vs. atomistic view of society (Spencer *vs.* Bentham and Mill).
Health rather than happiness the moral end.
They tend to coincide, but not perfectly.

C. German Ethics (and related systems): mainly rationalistic, idealistic, and individualistic.

1. The Ethics of Rational Will (formalism):

  a. Kant (1724-1804).
Metaphysic of Morals.
Critique of Practical Reason.
The categorical imperative.
Value and dignity.

The postulates of pure practical reason (God, freedom, immortality).
Eternal Peace.
b. Johann Gottlieb Fichte (1762-1814).
2. The Ethics of Pity:
Arthur Schopenhauer (1788-1860).
The Basis of Morality.
Pessimism.
One Will.
Pity.
3. The Ethics of Perfection:
a. Georg Wilhelm Friedrich Hegel (1770-1831).
Absolute Idealism.
Dialectic (thesis, antithesis, synthesis).
Self-realization of human spirit.
Thesis: *Das Recht.*
(Property, contract, crime and punishment.)
Antithesis: *Die Moralität.*
(Principle, purpose, good and evil.)
Synthesis: *Die Sittlichkeit.*
(Family, civil society, the state.)
Thesis: subjective spirit; antithesis: objective spirit (as above); synthesis: absolute spirit.
b. Thomas Hill Green (1836-1882).
Prolegomena to Ethics.
Perfectionist.
"Value in, of, and for a person."
Ideal of personality.
c. Friedrich Paulsen (1846-1908).
Modern Aristotelian perfectionism.
d. Borden Parker Bowne (1847-1910).
American perfectionist.
The Good.
Duty.
Virtue.
Influenced by Schleiermacher.
Unites intuitionism and utilitarianism.
4. The Ethics of Power:
Friedrich Nietzsche (1844-1900).
Thus Spake Zarathustra.
The Will to Power.

Superman.
The eternal recurrence.
Vs. democracy, pity, and Christianity.
D. Recent Tendencies.
　1. Theory of value:
　　Kant, Lotze, Meinong, Ehrenfels, Urban, Münsterberg, Everett, Perry, etc.
　2. Idealistic Ethics:
　　a. Josiah Royce (1855-1916).
　　　The Philosophy of Loyalty.
　　b. W. R. Sorley (1855-   ).
　　　The Ethics of Naturalism.
　　　Moral Values and the Idea of God.
　3. Naturalistic Ethics:
　　a. Bertrand Russell (1872-   ).
　　　"Love and knowledge."
　　b. Edward Westermarck (1862-   ).
　　　Origin and Development of Moral Ideas.
　　　Relativism.
　4. Pragmatic Ethics:
　　John Dewey (1859-   ).
　　　Originally a neo-Hegelian.
　　　Perfectionism (Dewey and Tufts).
　　　Biological and economic emphasis.
　　　Social progress.
　　　Instrumental values emphasized more than intrinsic (*cf.* instrumentalism).

BIBLIOGRAPHY

NOTE: This bibliography is also a key to the abbreviations used in the notes. The abbreviation for a given book follows the author's name. Undesignated Roman numerals refer to volumes, Arabic numerals to pages. Chapters are designated by the abbreviation "Chap."

Abbott, Thomas K. (tr.).—KME
Fundamental Principles of the Metaphysic of Ethics by Immanuel Kant. New York: Longmans, Green, 1873 and later edd.

——————— KTE
Kant's Theory of Ethics. London: Longmans, Green, 1898.

Allers, Rudolf.—WSP
Das Werden der sittlichen Person. Freiburg: Herder, 1929.

Aristotle (H. Rackham, tr.).—*Nic. Eth.*
The Nicomachean Ethics. New York: G. P. Putnam's Sons, 1926.

Barrett, Clifford (ed.).—CIA
Contemporary Idealism in America. New York: Macmillan, 1932.

Barth, Heinrich.—PPV
Philosophie der praktischen Vernunft. Tübingen: Mohr, 1927.

Bentham, Jeremy.—DE
Deontology. 2 Vols. Ed. John Bowring. London & Edinburgh: Longmans, Green, 1834.

——————— PML
An Introduction to the Principles of Morals and Legislation. Oxford: Clarendon Press, 1879.

Bergmann, Julius.—UR
Über das Richtige. Berlin: Mittler, 1883.

Blakey, Robert.—HMS
History of Moral Science. 2 Vols. Edinburgh: Duncan, 1836.

Bonsels, Waldemar.—NV
Notizen eines Vagabunden. Berlin: Knaur, 1930.

Bosanquet, Bernard.—SSE
Some Suggestions in Ethics. London: Macmillan, 1919.

Bowne, Borden P.—POE
The Principles of Ethics. New York: American Book Co., 1892.

————— TTK
Theory of Thought and Knowledge. New York: American Book Co., 1897.

————— MET
Metaphysics. New York: American Book Co., 1898.

————— PER
Personalism. Boston: Houghton Mifflin, 1908.

Bradley, F. H.—ES
Ethical Studies. 2nd ed. Oxford: Clarendon, 1927.

Brentano, Franz.—USE
Vom Ursprung sittlicher Erkenntnis. Herausg. v. Oskar Kraus. Leipzig: Meiner, 1922.

Brightman, Edgar S.—SH
The Sources of the Hexateuch. New York: Abingdon, 1918.

————— ITP
An Introduction to Philosophy. New York: Holt, 1925.

————— RV
Religious Values. New York: Abingdon, 1925.

————— (ed.) P6IC
Proceedings of the Sixth International Congress of Philosophy. New York: Longmans, Green, 1927.

————— POI
A Philosophy of Ideals. New York: Holt, 1928.

————— PG
The Problem of God. New York: Abingdon, 1930.

Calkins, Mary W.—GMG
The Good Man and the Good. New York: Macmillan, 1918.

Cleveland, Frederick A. (ed.).—MSK
Modern Scientific Knowledge of Nature, Man, and Society.
New York: Ronald Press, 1929.

Dewey, John, and James H. Tufts.—ETH
Ethics. New York: Holt, 1908.

Dewey, John.—HNC
Human Nature and Conduct. New York: Holt, 1922.

Diamond, Herbert M.—RC
Religion and the Commonweal. New York: Harper, 1928.

Dilthey, Wilhelm.—LS
Leben Schleiermachers. Herausg. v. H. Mulert. Berlin:
Gruyter, 1922.

——————— GW, II
Die Geistige Welt. 2. Bd. Leipzig: Teubner, 1924.

——————— GDG
Studien zur Geschichte des deutschen Geistes. Leipzig:
Teubner, 1927.

Dollinger, Robert.—SK
So Spricht Sören Kierkegaard. Berlin: Furche, n. d.

Drake, Durant.—PC
Problems of Conduct. Boston: Houghton Mifflin, 1921.

Dresser, Horatio W.—ETH
Ethics in Theory and Application. New York: Crowell,
1925.

Driesch, Hans.—MET
Metaphysik. Breslau: Hirt, 1924.

——————— ST
Die sittliche Tat. Leipzig: Reinicke, 1927.

Dunham, James H.—POE
Principles of Ethics. New York: Prentice-Hall, 1929.

Dünnhaupt, Rudolf.—SSRK
Sittlichkeit, Staat und Recht bei Kant. Berlin: Junker
u. Dünnhaupt, 1927.

Eisler, Rudolf.—KL
Kant-Lexikon. Berlin: Mittler, 1930.

Elsenhans, Theodor.—WEG
Das Wesen und Enstehung des Gewissens. Leipzig:
Engelmann, 1894.

Ernst, Paul.—EG
Erdachte Gespräche. München: Müller, 1931.

Everett, Walter G.—MV
Moral Values. New York: Holt, 1918.

Fabricius, Caius.—AG
*Der Atheismus der Gegenwart: seine Ursachen und seine
Überwindung.* Göttingen: Vandenhoeck & Ruprecht, 1922.

Fellin, J.—WF
Die Willensfreiheit. Zur Bibliographie des Problems.
Graz-Wien-Leipzig: Leuschner und Lubensky, 1928.

Feuerbach, Ludwig.—*Werke*
Sämmtliche Werke. X Bde. Neu herausg. v. W. Bolin u.
F. Jodl. Stuttgart: Frommann, 1903-1911.

Fite, Warner.—MP
Moral Philosophy: The Critical View of Life. New York:
Lincoln MacVeagh, 1925.

Freud, Sigmund.—FOI
The Future of an Illusion. London: Woolf, 1928.

Fung, Yu-Lan.—CSLI
Comparative Study of Life Ideals. Shanghai: Commer-
cial Press, 1924.

Galloway, George.—POR
Philosophy of Religion. New York: Scribner, 1914.

Garvie, Alfred E.—CIHS
The Christian Ideal for Human Society. London: Hodder
& Stoughton, n. d. (1930).

Green, Thomas H.—PTE
Prolegomena to Ethics. 5th ed. Oxford: Clarendon, 1906.

Guardini, Romano.—GGS
Das Gute: das Gewissen: Und die Sammlung. Mainz:
Matthias Grünewald, 1929.

Gury, Joannes P.—CTM
Compendium Theologiae Moralis. Ratisbonae: Manz,
1874.

Guyau, J.—ME
La morale d'epicure et ses rapports avec les doctrines contemporaines. Paris: Alcan, 1886.

Hadfield, J. A.—PAM
Psychology and Morals. New York: Robert M. McBride, 1925.

Haines, C. R.—MA
The Communings with Himself of Marcus Aurelius Antoninus, Emperor of Rome; Together with his Speeches and Sayings. London: William Heinemann, 1916. (Loeb.)

Hartmann, Eduard von.—PSB
Phänomenologie des sittlichen Bewusstseins: Prolegomena zu jeder künftigen Ethik. Berlin: Duncker, 1879.

————— GGP
Zur Geschichte und Grundlegung des Pessimismus. Leipzig: Haacke, 1891.

————— ES
Ethische Studien. Leipzig: Haacke, 1898.

Hastings, James.—ERE
Encyclopædia of Religion and Ethics. 12 Vols. and Index. New York: Scribner, 1908.

Haym, Rudolf.—HSZ
Hegel und seine Zeit. 2nd ed. Leipzig: Heims, 1927.

Heermance, Edgar L.—CE
Codes of Ethics: A Handbook. Burlington (Vt.): Free Press Printing Co., 1924.

Herbart, Johann Friedrich.—*Werke*
Sämmtliche Werke. 12 Vols. Herausg. v. G. Hartenstein. Leipzig: Voss, 1850-52.

Herder, Johann G.—GG
Vom Geist der Geschichte. Stuttgart: Frommann, 1923.

Hobhouse, Leonard T.—RG
The Rational Good; A Study in the Logic of Practice. London: Allen & Unwin, 1921.

Hocking, William E.—SBF
The Self: Its Body and Freedom. New Haven: Yale University Press, 1928.

Hoffmann, A.—GM
Die Gültigkeit der Moral. Tübingen: Mohr, 1907.

Horne, Herman H.—FWHR
Free Will and Human Responsibility. New York: Macmillan, 1912.

Hudson, Jay W.—TLB
The Truths We Live By. New York: Appleton, 1921.

Hyde, William D.—FGPL
Five Great Philosophies of Life. New York: Macmillan, 1911.

Jahrbücher der Philosophie.
Berlin: Mittler. 1. Jahrgang, 1913; 2. Jahrgang, 1914; 3. Jahrgang, 1927.

James, William.—POP
Principles of Psychology. 2 Vols. New York: Holt, 1890 and later edd.

——— WB
The Will to Believe and Other Essays. New York: Longmans, Green, 1905.

Jones, Sir Henry.—FE
A Faith that Enquires. New York: Macmillan, 1922.

Jones, Rufus M.—FEL
Fundamental Ends of Life. New York: Macmillan, 1924.

Kant, Immanuel.—*Werke* (PhB)
Sämmtliche Werke. Leipzig: Meiner, various dates. (In the Philosophische Bibliothek.)

——— KdrV (A) or (B)
Kritik der reinen Vernunft. The *Critique of Pure Reason* appears in many editions, and the simplest way of referring to all good editions is to use the paging of Kant's own original text. A refers to his first edition (1781) and B to his second (1787). The best English translation is that of N. K. Smith.

——— GMS
Grundlegung zur Metaphysik der Sitten. Edited by R. Otto. Gotha: Klotz, 1930.

———— KdpV (Reclam S)
Kritik der praktischen Vernunft. Herausg. v. Raymund Schmidt. Leipzig: Reclam, n. d.

King, William P. (ed.).—BBL
Behaviorism: a Battle Line. Nashville: Cokesbury Press, 1930.

Kinkel, Walter.—HG
Der Humanitätsgedanke. 1. Aufl. Leipzig: Eckardt, 1908. 2. Aufl. Osterwieck: Zickfeldt, 1925.

Kleinsorgen, Wilhelm.—CE
Cellular-Ethik als moderne Nachfolge Christi. Grundlinien eines neuen Lebensinhaltes. Leipzig: Kröner, 1912.

Knudson, Albert C.—DG
The Doctrine of God. New York: Abingdon, 1930.

Koehler, Wolfgang.—GP
Gestalt Psychology. New York: Liveright, 1929.

Laing, B. M.—SMP
A Study in Moral Problems. London: Allen & Unwin, 1922.

Laurie, Simon S.—EER
Ethica or the Ethics of Reason. London: Williams & Norgate, 1885.

Leighton, Joseph A.—MC
Man and the Cosmos. New York: Appleton, 1922.

———— ISO
The Individual and the Social Order. New York: Appleton, 1926.

Leisegang, Hans.—RP
Religionsphilosophie der Gegenwart. Berlin: Junker u. Dünnhaupt, 1930.

Lessing, Theodor.—SWA
Studien zur Wertaxiomatik: Untersuchungen über reine Ethik und reines Recht. 2. erweiterte Ausgabe. Leipzig: Meiner, 1914.

Lévy-Bruhl, L.—MSM
La morale et la science des moeurs. Paris: Alcan, 1927.

Liebert, Arthur.—KE
Kants Ethik. Berlin: Pan-Verlagsgesellschaft, 1931.

Lipmann, Otto und Paul Plaut.—LU
Die Lüge. Leipzig: Barth, 1927.

Lippmann, Walter.—PM
A Preface to Morals. New York: Macmillan, 1929.

Lipps, Theodor.—EGF
Die ethischen Grundfragen. Leipzig: Voss, 1922.

Lodge, Rupert C.—PTE
Plato's Theory of Ethics. New York: Harcourt, Brace, 1928.

Mackenzie, J. S.—MOE
Manual of Ethics. New York: Noble & Noble, 1925.

Martineau, James.—RER
The Relation between Ethics and Religion. London: Williams & Norgate, 1881.

————— TET
Types of Ethical Theory. 2 Vols. Oxford: Clarendon, 1885.

Mecklin, John E.—ISE
An Introduction to Social Ethics. New York: Harcourt, Brace, 1920.

Messer, August.—WP
Wertphilosophie der Gegenwart. Berlin: Junker u. Dünnhaupt, 1930.

Mezes, S. E.—EDE
Ethics: Descriptive and Explanatory. New York: Macmillan, 1901.

Nietzsche, Friedrich.—TSZ
Thus Spake Zarathustra. New York: Modern Library, n. d.

Otto, M. C.—TAI
Things and Ideals. New York: Holt, 1924.

Palmer, George H.—FOE
The Field of Ethics. Boston: Houghton Mifflin, 1901.

—————— NOG
The Nature of Goodness. Boston: Houghton Mifflin, 1903.

—————— POF
The Problem of Freedom. Boston: Houghton Mifflin, 1911.

—————ALT
Altruism: Its Nature and Varieties. New York: Scribner, 1919.

Parker, Dewitt H.—HV
Human Values. New York: Harper, 1931.

Paton, H. J.—GW
The Good Will. London: Allen & Unwin, 1927.

Paulsen, Friedrich.—SOE
A System of Ethics. Tr. Frank Thilly. New York: Scribner, 1899 and later edd.

Perry, Ralph B.—ME
The Moral Economy. New York: Scribner, 1909.

—————GTV
General Theory of Value. New York: Longmans, Green, 1926.

Pound, Roscoe.—LAM
Law and Morals. Chapel Hill: University of North Carolina Press, 1924.

Rand, Benjamin.—CM
The Classical Moralists. Boston: Houghton Mifflin, 1909 and later edd.

Rashdall, Hastings.—TGE
The Theory of Good and Evil. 2 Vols. London: Oxford University Press, 1907, 2nd ed., 1924.

Rée, Paul.—UME
Der Ursprung der moralischen Empfindungen. Chemnitz: Schmeitzner, 1877.

Rickert, Heinrich.—PL
Die Philosophie des Lebens. Tübingen: Mohr, 1920.

Roback, Abraham A.—BAP
Behaviorism and Psychology. Cambridge: University Bookstore, Inc., 1923.

——————— PC
The Psychology of Character. New York: Harcourt, Brace, 1927.

Royce, Josiah.—PL
The Philosophy of Loyalty. New York: Macmillan, 1908.

——————RQP
Race Questions, Provincialism, and Other American Problems. New York: Macmillan, 1908.

Runze, Georg.—EPE
Ethik. I. Praktische Ethik. Berlin: Duncker, 1891.

Ryle, Gilbert (ed.).—P7IC
Proceedings of the Seventh International Congress of Philosophy. Oxford: University Press, 1931.

Schelling, F. W. J.—*Werke*
Schellings Werke. 6 Bde. Herausg. v. Manfred Schröter. München: Beck u. Oldenbourg, 1927-28.

Schleiermacher, Fr. D. E.—*Werke*
Werke. Auswahl in vier Bänden. Leipzig: Eckardt, 1910-13.

Schlick, Moritz.—FE
Fragen der Ethik. Wien: Springer, 1930.

Schopenhauer, Arthur.—*Werke*
Sämmtliche Werke. 6 Bde. Leipzig: Insel, n. d.

Schuppe, Wilhelm.—ERP
Ethik und Rechtsphilosophie. Breslau: Koebner, 1881.

Schwarz, Hermann.—SL
Das sittliche Leben. Berlin: Reuther u. Reichard, 1901.

——————— ETH
Ethik. Breslau: Hirt, 1923.

Sellars, Roy Wood.—EN
Evolutionary Naturalism. Chicago: Open Court, 1922.

——————PPP
The Principles and Problems of Philosophy. New York: Macmillan, 1926.

Seth, Andrew.—HP
Hegelianism and Personality. Edinburgh: Blackwood, 1887.

——————SEP
A Study of Ethical Principles. 12th ed. New York: Scribner, 1911.

Shafer, Robert.—CAN
Christianity and Naturalism. New Haven: Yale University Press, 1926.

Sharp, Frank C.—ETH
Ethics. New York: Century, 1928.

Sherman, Charles L.—MS
The Moral Self. Boston: Ginn, 1927.

Sidgwick, Henry.—ME
The Methods of Ethics. New York: Macmillan, 1907.

Simmel, Georg.—MW
Einleitung in die Moralwissenschaft. 2. Bde. Berlin: Hertz, 1892-93.

—————— LA
Lebensanschauung. München u. Leipzig: Duncker u. Humblot, 1918.

Sorley, W. R.—MVIG
Moral Values and the Idea of God. Cambridge: University Press, 1918 and later edd.

Spaulding, Edward G.—WAI
What Am I? New York: Scribner, 1928.

Spranger, Eduard.—LF
Lebensformen. 3. Aufl. Halle: Niemeyer, 1922.

Stapledon, W. Olaf.—MTE
A Modern Theory of Ethics. New York: Dutton, 1929.

Steinthal, H.—AE
Allgemeine Ethik. Berlin: Reimer, 1885.

Stern, William.—KGE
Kritische Grundlegung der Ethik als positive Wissenschaft. Berlin: Dümler, 1897.

Stoops, John D.—IC
Ideals of Conduct. New York: Macmillan, 1926.

Sutherland, A.—OGMI
The Origin and Growth of the Moral Instinct. New York: Longmans, Green, 1898.

Taeusch, Carl F.—PBE
Professional and Business Ethics. New York: Holt, 1926.

Ten Broeke, James.—MLR
The Moral Life and Religion. New York: Macmillan, 1923.

Thomson, J. Arthur.—WM
What Is Man? New York: Putnam, 1924.

Tillich, Paul.—SW
Das System der Wissenschaften nach Gegenständen und Methoden. Göttingen: Vandenhoeck & Ruprecht, 1923.

Treitschke, Heinrich V.—DL
Deutsche Lebensbilder. Leipzig: Fikent, n. d.

Trendelenburg, Adolf.—HP
Herbarts praktische Philosophie und die Ethik der Alten. Berlin: Akademie, 1856.

Troeltsch, Ernst.—RLRE
Zur religiösen Lage, Religionsphilosophie und Ethik. Tübingen: Mohr, 1913.

Turner, J. E.—PBMO
The Philosophic Basis of Moral Obligation. London: Macmillan, 1924.

Unamuno, M. de.—TSL
The Tragic Sense of Life. London: Macmillan, 1921.

Urban, Wilbur M.—IW
The Intelligible World. New York: Macmillan, 1929.

————— FOE
Fundamentals of Ethics. New York: Holt, 1930.

Utitz, Rudolf.—CH
Charakterologie. Charlottenburg: Pan-Verlag, 1925.

Wach, Joachim.—ERS
Einführung in die Religionssoziologie. Tübingen: Mohr, 1931.

Westermarck, Edward.—ODMI
  Origin and Development of the Moral Ideas. 2 Vols.
  London: Macmillan, 1906.

Wundt, Wilhelm.—ETG
  *Ethik: Eine Untersuchung der Tatsachen und Gesetze des
  sittlichen Lebens.* 3. Bde. 4. Aufl. Stuttgart: F. Enke,
  1912.

INDEX

DATE DUE

FEB 1			

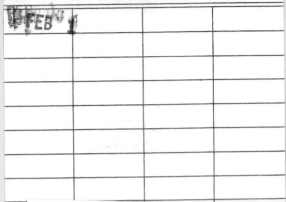

BJ   21953
1011
B855 Brightman
1933   Moral laws

DATE   ISSUED TO

BJ   21953
1011
B855 Brightman
1933   Moral laws

DEMCO